WRITING WEST VIRGINIA

WRITING WEST VIRGINIA

Place, People, and Poverty in Contemporary Literature from the Mountain State

Boyd Creasman

The University of Tennessee Press / Knoxville

Chapter 5 was previously published in *Appalachian Journal*, volume 39,
numbers 1–2, Fall 2011/Winter 2012. © 2012 Appalachian State University.
All rights reserved. Reprinted with permission.

Chapter 7 was previously published in the *Journal of Appalachian Studies*,
volume 16, numbers 1 & 2, Spring and Fall 2010 by Boyd Creasman. © 2010
Appalachian Studies Association. All rights reserved. Reprinted with permission.

Library of Congress Cataloging-in-Publication Data

Writing West Virginia : place, people, and poverty in contemporary literature
from the Mountain State / Boyd Creasman. — First edition.
    pages cm
Includes bibliographical references and index.
ISBN 978-1-62190-184-6 (hardcover)
1. American literature—West Virginia—History and criticism.
2. American literature—Women authors—History and criticism.
3. Women and literature—West Virginia.
4. Social role in literature.
5. Working class in literature.
6. Social values in literature.
7. Appalachian Region—In literature.
8. West Virginia—In literature.
I. Creasman, Boyd

PS266.W4W75 2015
810.9'358754—dc23   2014047477

CONTENTS

ACKNOWLEDGMENTS

I would like to thank the following individuals who helped make this book possible: Irene McKinney, who read this book in manuscript form, offered helpful suggestions and generous encouragement, and spoke freely with me about her work and that of the other authors in this book. Mark DeFoe, who first asked me to teach Appalachian literature and for his many kindnesses over the years. John Saunders and Eric Waggoner, great colleagues who read and offered many fine suggestions for the introduction of this book. All my friends at West Virginia Wesleyan College, which granted me two sabbaticals that allowed me the precious time I needed to work on this project. Pam Balch, the president of Wesleyan, who allowed me some time off to work on the book and who encouraged me in my efforts. My wonderful co-workers Robyn Curry and Melody Meadows, who picked up the slack whenever I was out of the office completing this project. The library staff at Wesleyan, who tracked down many secondary sources for me. Pinckney Benedict, the master conversationalist, who allowed me to interview him. Roxy Todd, who edited an early draft of this book. Brett Miller, who helped me format an early draft of this book. Fred Standley, my mentor for thirty years. And, finally, the two Appalachian women I admire most: my mother, Lora Creasman, and my wife, Alice Creasman.

INTRODUCTION

Three Themes and Three Types of Transcendence

Over the past sixty years, West Virginia writers have created enduring fiction and poetry that depict a proud people in a land of natural beauty and economic hardship. The state's best writing comprises the work of the brief, but brilliant, career of Breece D'J Pancake, whose debut Joyce Carol Oates compared to Hemingway's,[1] as well as the fiction writer Pinckney Benedict, whom Eudora Welty praised as "a strong talent."[2] It is a literature of iconic images, from Preacher's love and hate tattoos in Davis Grubb's *The Night of the Hunter* to descriptions of mountaintop removal's destruction of natural beauty and family homes in Ann Pancake's *Strange as This Weather Has Been*. West Virginia literature presents the often tense relationship between citizens and coal companies in many literary works, most notably in Denise Giardina's *Storming Heaven*, which depicts events that culminate in the Battle of Blair Mountain. The fiction includes the work of National Book Award winner Mary Lee Settle, whose *Beulah Quintet* chronicles the history of the state. West Virginia literature also features as strong an array of independent women found in any literature—fictional characters such as Rachel Cooper and Carrie Bishop, as well as the personae of Irene McKinney's poetry. It is a literature that includes Jayne Anne Phillips's lyrical novel *Lark and Termite*, in which two siblings establish supernatural interconnectedness with each other and with family members, some of whom are no longer living.

These writers capture the culture and history of the Mountain State, in which individuals have continually confronted social and economic marginalization in the attitudes of outsiders and physical challenges in their interactions with the land. While developing themes prevalent in much of

Appalachian literature, West Virginia's writers have made the particular universal, validating Flannery O'Connor's famous assertion that "the best American fiction has always been regional."[3] (However, it is interesting to note that the "Since 1945" section of the most recent edition of the *Norton Anthology of American Literature* includes no West Virginia writers—and no Appalachian writers, for that matter.) Creating characters and personae striving for fulfillment in the face of formidable challenges, West Virginia authors have created a body of work that is worthy of study—and celebration. While some of the state's most recent literature presents unconventional ways of transcending limitations, the work of West Virginia writers has traditionally focused on three themes: place, socio-economic class, and gender.

The first theme, the theme of place, encompasses characters' attitudes toward the land, as well as outsiders' perceptions of the state. The moral quality of characters can often be found in their connection to the land, as seen in Rachel Cooper in Grubb's *The Night of the Hunter*, who knows how to work the land and produce food for the runaway children she raises. It appears in Mogey, a character in Ann Pancake's *Strange as This Weather Has Been*. Although a traditional Christian, he feels a spiritual connection to nature that is more intense than any religious feelings he has experienced at his church. The disappointment of Colly, the narrator of Breece Pancake's story "Trilobites," at failing to keep the family farm operating successfully becomes magnified because of his fascination with the geology of the land. These connections to the land reveal the better sides of their natures.

The theme of place in West Virginia literature is apparent in the often conflicted ways in which residents and outsiders perceive the state. West Virginia characters like Rachel Cooper and Mogey, with their strong sense of connection with the land, would never consider leaving the state. However, many characters in West Virginia literature long for opportunities that would take them outside the state in search of a better fate. Many of the characters in Breece Pancake's stories—for example, Colly in "Trilobites," Bo in "Fox Hunters," and the narrator in "The Salvation of Me"—believe that leaving West Virginia is essential to their survival. In *Strange as This Weather Has Been*, the marriage of Jimmy Make and Lace ends in part because Jimmy Make is convinced that he cannot find a meaningful, high-paying job in West Virginia and Lace decides to stay in the state and fight against mountaintop removal. In Mary Lee Settle's *The Killing Ground*, Hannah McKarkle believes that the only way she can avoid becoming trapped in a traditional gender role and find the freedom to pursue her dream of becoming a writer is to leave West Virginia and go to New York City. The dilemma of staying home and not reaching one's potential versus pursuing opportunity outside the state and losing connection to one's family and traditions represents a major theme in West Virginia literature.

Perceptions of the citizens of the Mountain State often manifest themselves in a second theme, socio-economic class. Like the rest of Appalachia, West Virginians often find themselves cast in the role of "the Other," outside of mainstream American culture, and the targets of negative stereotypes. The importance of socio-economic class in the perceptions of Appalachian men and women cannot be overstated. The countless jokes about people from the region perpetuate the image of Appalachians as uneducated, unsophisticated, unhealthy, unclean, and unmotivated. It is no longer politically correct to denigrate Americans on the basis of gender, sexual orientation, race or ethnicity, yet Appalachians still find themselves the butt of crass jokes. In many ways, West Virginians face a steadier barrage of negativity than do residents from the other states in the region.

While the entire Appalachian region must endure negative stereotypes, West Virginia is unique among the states in the region in that the federal government classifies every one of its fifty-five counties as Appalachian. The state's largest city is Charleston, with slightly over 50,000 residents. All of the other states in the region have counties that are not classified as Appalachian and cities that have populations at least eight times larger than Charleston. This means that of all the states in Appalachia, West Virginia is the most rural—and the most uniformly Appalachian. These factors could help to explain why the Mountain State, more than other Appalachian states, is portrayed negatively in the popular culture and mainstream media.

Much of the stereotypes directed toward West Virginia centers around poverty. At times, the state has been heavily impacted by economic downturns. Poverty has been, and continues to be, an issue in the Mountain State. At one point in 1983, West Virginia's unemployment rate reached 20 percent, roughly twice as high as the national average. Today, the state's unemployment rate is more in line with that of national average, but West Virginia still faces economic challenges. According to the Appalachian Regional Commission, over 20 percent of the citizens in fifteen of the state's fifty-five counties live below the poverty line, with six counties listed as "distressed" and seventeen others listed as economically "at risk."[4] A recent report on child poverty in West Virginia revealed that in 2011, 25.8 percent of the state's children lived below the poverty line and that "1 in 2 West Virginia children with single mothers lives in poverty." Furthermore, the report points out that between 2007 and 2011, "only nine counties in West Virginia had child poverty rates lower than the national average."[5] Given the toll taken by the state's continual economic challenges, it is clear that poverty has threatened the welfare and well-being of West Virginians for decades.

In addition to the economic difficulties, West Virginians face a steady bombardment of negativity from popular culture and the media. From television shows and movies where West Virginia becomes code for backwoods or backward to condescending attitudes in mainstream media, including those found in national news stories, the Mountain State endures more than its share of negative reporting. This reporting, in some instances, is presented objectively and fairly. For example, the state has well-chronicled issues with health, and Gallup, the polling company, has several times named West Virginia one of the states with the highest obesity rates (in 2014, it was tied with Mississippi). In 2014 Gallup announced that West Virginia has been what the media call "the most miserable state" for five consecutive years.[6] These dubious distinctions result from scientific surveys, with significant sample sizes. However, some of the mainstream society's treatment of the state seems unfair and even mean-spirited. In 2004 Abercrombie and Fitch marketed a t-shirt with an incest joke, stating, "It's all relative in West Virginia." Then-Governor Bob Wise asked the company to pull the shirts from its shelves: "'By selling and marketing this offensive item, your company is perpetuating an inaccurate portrayal of the people of this great state,' Mr. Wise wrote. 'Indeed, such a depiction of West Virginians undermines our collective efforts to communicate a positive representation of the spirit and values of our citizens.'"[7] During the water crisis of 2014, in which 300,000 West Virginians in and around Charleston had their drinking water contaminated after a chemical spill in the Elk River, Zlati Meyer, a *Detroit Free Press* journalist tweeted, "West Virginia has its tainted water problem under ctrl. Now, it can work on incest."[8] The outcry was swift and heated. While no one wants to appear humorless, many West Virginians expressed outrage over such a crude joke during a time of catastrophe.

The negative cultural depictions of West Virginia sometimes give its writers a sense of defiance and indignation. Irene McKinney, the poet laureate of the state from 1994 until her passing in 2012, did not always relish the idea of serving as spokesperson for the state, but in her poem "Monkey Heart," she decries the condescension she encountered from a woman in Virginia:

> A woman in Charlottesville told me a joke
> about West Virginians, involving mobile
> homes and incest. When I didn't laugh she said
> she meant no harm, that some of her best
> friends were hillbillies. I didn't tell her
> to stop monkeying around or that she
> reminded me of an ocelot, albeit one
> who had gone to Sweetbriar.[9]

The incident McKinney portrays in the poem shows that other Appalachians also perpetuate the negative stereotypes about West Virginians.

In an interview, McKinney elaborated on the idea that West Virginians believe that other Appalachians discriminate against them, citing as an example the brief life of Breece Pancake. In discussing the challenges faced by West Virginia writers, McKinney expressed her belief that Pancake felt inferior to some of his fellow students while attending graduate school at the University of Virginia and that he struggled not to feel alienated from both his own culture and the graduate school culture. McKinney stated, "The generation ahead of me had a real battle within themselves about 'how much am I going to give up of my culture to fit in?' My generation was the one that was emerging. Like Breece Pancake, who went to the University of Virginia. He was struggling with that same question. He tried very hard to get the two cultures to pull together. He was always asking colleagues to go hunting with him or to go hang out in some bar or go fishing or take drives up in the mountains. It's clear to me that what he was trying to do, what he valued in mainstream culture, he was trying to make some kind of connection with his own culture."[10] This perception of Breece Pancake is borne out in Thomas Douglass's biography of the writer. Douglass asserts that "the old historical perceptions of class distinction and condescension that have existed between Virginia and West Virginia, between landed gentry and backwoods hillbilly, aroused feelings of inferiority and resentment in Pancake . . . ."[11]

Ann Pancake addresses the issue of negative portrayals of the state in the opening pages of *Strange as This Weather Has Been* through the point of view of one of her main characters. Growing up in southern West Virginia, Lace first notices the cultural biases in America while watching television:

"Growing up here, you get the message very early on that your place is more backward than anywhere in America and anybody worth much will get out as soon as they can, and that doesn't come only from the outside."[12] The idea that some West Virginians can be influenced by, and even perpetuate, the negative stereotypes about the state is a recurring theme in West Virginia literature.

The negative stereotypes about the state may explain why many West Virginia writers grapple with questions of belonging and why their relationship with place is so often conflicted. For example, Jayne Anne Phillips has spoken many times about the limitations of the label "regional writer." She once stated that she finds the terms "West Virginia writer" or "regional writer" are "too restrictive to describe what she wants to do" and that leaving the region "provided the physical and psychological distance she needed to write about it objectively."[13] In *Backcountry* Irene McKinney described the difficulty of being perceived as a regional writer, of being defined by place: "For many writers . . . , this struggle with place is a lifelong one, a constant vacillation between wanting to leave and search for the approval of mainstream culture, and wanting to return to one's roots."[14] Many of the state's writers seem to feel, as Phillips does, that the label of regional writer comes with inherent stereotypes and these stereotypes provide an extra difficulty in creating characters who wrestle with poverty or a lack of education. The last thing the writers want to do is perpetuate stereotypes. As Phillips points out, writers from other areas of the nation do not face the same kinds of regional pigeonholing. She said in an interview, "I take issue with the term 'regional writer.' People who write about New York City are also regional writers. They're writing about their particular area of New York. It's kind of a pejorative term in a way." Of course, what Phillips does not say is that writers from New York City are usually considered mainstream writers or American writers, not regional writers.

In addition to the negative stereotypes from inside and outside the region, some West Virginians resent the overly romanticized views of rural poverty that some in mainstream culture perpetuate. In the same interview, McKinney spoke about the ways in which outsiders either engage in negative stereotypes about West Virginia or imagine that the area is full of quaint, unsophisticated, banjo-picking, quilt-making mountain people still clinging to their traditions. "One of the problems that not just West Virginia artists but all citizens of West Virginia have to contend with is that overly romantic view of what it's like to live out in the mountains. People from outside the region really romanticize that, but they don't want to know about the grittiness, especially the politically loaded aspects of Appalachia."[15] McKinney believes that too many outsiders overlook the hardships of poverty in their views of the state:

> I remember what it was like to grow up in West Virginia. It was really a struggle. You know, we were freezing to death all the time in the winter. We had no insulation, no running water. It was a struggle to bathe, to keep clean, to do the laundry. You had to hang it inside in the wintertime, with lines hanging in the kitchen and the living room. It was not romantic. And I tried to pull away from all of that for a time. But then gradually, after I started living in other regions, I was able to allow myself to see what was really valuable to me about the [Appalachian] people.[16]

The romanticizing of poverty oddly can create a hobbling stereotype of its own, particularly to writers working to depict the realities of West Virginia life accurately. These writers can find themselves in a creative catch-22. If they depict harsh socio-economic reality, they run the risk of being perceived as perpetuating negative stereotypes about the state. If they present a character who rises above the limitations of poverty, they run the risk of being seen as romanticizing poverty and discounting the difficulties faced by the poor.

The third dominant theme of West Virginia literature is gender. The state's literary works frequently feature men who attempt to compensate for weaknesses by trying to appear strong and women who break free of traditional female roles to project a sense of strength and accomplishment. The men strive to project financial viability and exhibit sexual power. The male characters in West Virginia fiction who feel inadequate due to economic difficulties include Ben Harper in *The Night of the Hunter*, Clabe Lloyd in *Storming Heaven*, and Jimmy Make Turrell in *Strange as This Weather Has Been*. The masculine desire to portray an image of success is found in the work of almost every one of these writers. As with financial viability, sexuality offers males a way to assert their masculinity. Sexual conquests can validate a man in the eyes of his peers, but, given how the characters often lack other traditional ways of demonstrating their masculinity, sexual rejection can be devastating. In Breece Pancake's story "Hollow," Fuller humiliates Buddy not through fighting but by running away with Buddy's girlfriend, Sally. Buddy sees the rejection in economic terms: He thinks that if he had only been a better provider for

Sally, she would have stayed with him. Furthermore, an appearance of sexual inexperience can be embarrassing to a young man, as seen in Pancake's story "Fox Hunters," in which Bo fabricates a story about a sexual conquest to impress the other men. On the other hand, sexually experienced characters like Rondal Lloyd in Giardina's *Storming Heaven* and Johnny McKarkle in Settle's *The Killing Ground* become so accustomed to thinking of sexuality as only fulfilling a basic human need that they seem incapable of emotional intimacy.

In addition to these familiar masculine gender roles and male attitudes toward sexuality, West Virginia literature also reveals a complex array of female roles. Some women try to define themselves in ways that overcome limitations and counter stereotypes. Traditionally, of course, females in a patriarchal American culture were socialized to be caregivers and housekeepers. As traditional gender roles have evolved, Appalachian female characters appear as variants of four different types: patriarchal, deferential, emergent, or independent.[17] Patriarchal women accept the male-dominated culture as natural and right, as does Icey Spoon in Davis Grubb's *The Night of the Hunter*. Similar to the women in the first category are deferential women, who may be superior in some way to the men in their lives, but who downplay this superiority in order to privilege the male. Less traditional than a patriarchal woman is the one who has begun to question the patriarchy and free herself from its repressiveness and becomes, in a phrase coined by Mary Helen Washington, an emergent woman. Aware of discrimination and making choices that she hopes will free her from patriarchy is the emergent woman's role. In some of Irene McKinney's poetry—most notably, "At 24"—women struggle against traditional roles and try to live life on their own terms. Lastly, independent women assert their lack of dependence upon men financially, emotionally, and professionally. Rachel Cooper in *The Night of the Hunter* and Carrie Bishop in Denise Giardina's *Storming Heaven* become self-reliant and generally free from patriarchal restriction. As we will see, the frequency of independent women in the region's fiction and poetry suggests that Appalachian women possess exemplary self-reliance. However, this striving for independence can come with a price. Nancy Carol Joyner observes how stereotypes about Appalachia and traditional gender roles have presented the women of the region with two issues. "Appalachian women, then, are the Other, both in relationship to the primary culture and to men. Both region and gender are factors in marginalization."[18] During times of economic hardship, women have taken on what were once considered masculine roles, thus facing social criticism while reshaping our conceptions of gender. Therefore, West Virginia literature captures three challenges faced by Appalachian women. Female characters in these works are (1) enduring criticism from outside the region, (2) taking on masculine roles, thereby risking possible friction in their homes and communities, and (3) thus reshaping the dynamics of gender, labor, and economics.

To read widely in West Virginia literature is to discover that the state's writers present their characters as having had to face more than their share of tribulation—often connecting to the themes of place, class, and gender—and that their distress is usually resolved through either tragedy or transcendence. As we have seen, several characters make choices that prove to be self-defeating and even tragic. Ben and Willa Harper in *The Night of the Hunter* lose their lives because of their unwise choices and leave their children to take to the countryside to avoid the villainous Preacher. Jimmy Make Turrell in *Strange as This Weather Has Been* breaks up his family in pursuit of a better job. In Mary Lee Settle's *Know Nothing*, Johnny Catlett unwisely adheres to his affluent family's socio-economic code, refusing to follow his heart and marry the less affluent Melinda Lacey and perpetuating slavery in the way he chooses to operate the family business. These and other examples show how greed, pride, or a lack of self-knowledge can lead to tragedy and defeat.

While some fall victim to tragedy, others characters in West Virginia literature are able to transcend their limitations. This transcendence usually takes one or more of the following forms. First of all, characters may sense a preternatural interconnectedness with another human being. Secondly, characters may suddenly find their everyday experience imbued with magical qualities, as characters find new meaning in their daily lives. This discovery of the new possibilities in the everyday is sometimes linked with a strong connection to place, sometimes with the recognition of natural beauty as something greater and more permanent than the individual. Thirdly, characters may discover a sense of immortality. Contemporary West Virginia literature often appropriates the language of traditional religion to express a more subjective or personal spirituality. In literary works with a greater spiritual focus, authors like Jayne Anne Phillips and Pinckney Benedict sometimes depict supernatural occurrences as way of intensifying a moment of transcendence over a limiting set of circumstances. In a state that has faced many seemingly constant socio-economic challenges, it makes sense that transcendence would become an important theme.

Although the distinction might at first seem arbitrary, there are major differences in how the theme of transcendence is treated from mid- to late-twentieth and twenty-first century West Virginia literature. It is interesting to note that supernatural experiences of a spiritual nature figure prominently in the twenty-first century work of Phillips, Benedict, and Ann Pancake. While this idea will be further developed in subsequent chapters, a quick comparison between two characters, one from 1953 and one from 2009, will illustrate two ways—one more traditional, the other more experimental—in which the theme is incorporated into the literary works. Rachel Cooper, from Davis Grubb's *The Night of the Hunter*, develops a strong sense of interconnectedness with the refugee children she takes into her home during the Depression. She clothes, shelters, and feeds them, but also attempts to instill moral values and responsibility in them by teaching them the Bible and assigning them chores. She also comes to see her everyday life as full of meaning, after she is made to feel inferior after a visit to her upwardly mobile son, Ralph, and his wife. On the way home, she chides herself for having tried to put on airs during the visit: "Why, shoot! It don't matter. I got a new harvest coming on. A new crop. I'm good for something in this old world and I know it, too."[19] Finally, Rachel Cooper's traditional Christian faith makes her feel secure that there is a reason for everything and that she will enjoy eternal life. These three facets of her character give her life meaning and allow her to transcend the challenges she faces.

Lark, from Phillips's *Lark and Termite*, achieves a less traditional, more preternatural kind of transcendence than does Rachel. Lark's sense of interconnectedness is found most obviously in her relationship with her brother, Termite. Lark unselfishly accepts the role of caregiver for her developmentally challenged sibling and reaches a high level of communication with him, seemingly to know what he's thinking most of the time. Lark never resents taking care of her brother and sees the role as giving her everyday life meaning. Furthermore, Lark perceives her world as magical after she and her hometown are transformed after a flood. Finally, as we see in Chapter 9, Lark and Termite both experience a supernatural connection with their parents, which is portrayed as more of a spiritual experience than a traditionally religious experience.

This book will explore the themes of gender, place, and socio-economic class, and how characters can transcend limitations related to these themes through three types of transcendence. The book will focus on the different ways in which West Virginians face adversity in the works of eight of the Mountain State's finest writers: Davis Grubb, Mary Lee Settle, Breece Pancake, Denise Giardina, Irene McKinney, Ann Pancake, Jayne Anne Phillips, and Pinckney Benedict.

Davis Grubb's *The Night of the Hunter* (1953) resonates in the nation's popular cultural consciousness, and it also depends greatly on the themes of class and gender that are prevalent in West Virginia literature. The popular film adaptation, starring Robert Mitchum, immortalized the iconic love and hate tattoos on the knuckles of Preacher's hands, but the novel, for many reasons, also marks an appropriate starting point for analyzing the kinds of challenges subsequent characters face in West Virginia literature. Interestingly, the narrator justifies Ben Harper's crimes of armed robbery and murder as understandable, perhaps forgivable, given the hard times of the Depression. Even the hangman seems to feel that he is executing a good man. Ben feels the pressure to provide for his family, and his actions constitute a misguided masculine attempt at validation. His widow, Willa, moves from the loving relationship she had with Ben to the sexual repression and excessive religiosity of her second marriage to Preacher. While Willa increasingly becomes victimized by Preacher, the last half of the novel introduces the quintessential independent Appalachian woman, Rachel Cooper. Rachel takes in abandoned and runaway children, manages a farm by herself, and ultimately defeats the villainous Preacher. A woman who embodies Christian charity and humility, she stands out among the self-righteous and the hypocritical characters. She is able to experience moments of transcendence through a combination of religious faith and pleasure in everyday tasks. Thus, in *The Night of the Hunter*, Grubb has introduced a number of prototypical Appalachian characters: an impoverished man who resorts to violence to compensate for feelings of inadequacy, a woman who becomes conditioned to think that sexual pleasure runs counter to feminine virtue, and a heroine who embodies feminine independence and self-reliance.

Spanning four centuries, Mary Lee Settle's *Beulah Quintet* traces the development of West Virginia from the awakening of the desire for individual liberty in seventeenth-century England through the settling of then-western Virginia to the conflicts over slavery to the rise of the coal industry and the resulting creation of a wealthy, industrial class. Settle explores the tensions between the powerful and powerless and how sacrifice is the true "price of freedom," a price paid by Johnny Church in *Prisons* and Johnny Catlett in

Know Nothing. Johnny Catlett succumbs to the expectations of his father and seeks to save the family estate and thus perpetuate slavery as part of the responsibilities placed upon him as a male heir. Settle also explores important issues of femininity, in which upper-class women are expected to uphold standards of behavior befitting their social position. In fact, unlike much of the state's literature, which depicts the challenges of characters facing economic hardship, Settle's work also focuses on upper-class society, including antebellum culture and the elite class of Canona, West Virginia that has become wealthy from coal production. (The fictional city of Canona is Settle's version of Charleston.) However, the twentieth century heroines in the final two novels of the *Quintet* rebel against the limitations of upper-class propriety and traditional gender roles. Both Lily Lacey in *The Scapegoat* and Hannah McKarkle in *The Killing Ground* choose to become independent women and reject the gender expectations of their parents' generations, though they learn that they must ultimately leave the region in order to reach their potential. Through their struggles, as well as those of other characters in the *Beulah Quintet*, Settle demonstrates how class and gender shape one's identity.

No Appalachian writer conveys the gritty realism of poverty and the toll it takes on masculinity more vividly than Breece Pancake. In Pancake's short fiction, the men struggle to prove their masculinity in an environment where good money and good jobs cannot be found. Pancake wrote at a time when the unemployment rate in West Virginia hovered around 20 percent, and in many of his stories there is a sense that the region holds little opportunity for the main characters to succeed at their jobs or in their personal lives. In "Trilobites" Colly realizes that his inability to match his father's agricultural success is partially to blame for his mother wanting to sell the family farm. He is reeling from his father's death and from the perceived abandonment of his girlfriend, who has moved to Florida. Colly feels a profound connection to the land, but at the same time he realizes that soon he will have to leave it behind. In the story "Hollow" Buddy embodies one of the recurring themes in Pancake's work: the self-defeating impulses of the Appalachian male. He argues with and strikes his girlfriend, driving her into the arms of his sworn enemy, Fuller. In an attempt to salvage some male ego, he gets into a senseless bar fight. Finally, he considers calling a strike and putting himself and his friends out of work. The theme of senseless violence is also found in "The Scrapper," in which men from two rival towns constantly brawl with each other. The main character, Skeevy, feels great remorse for beating up his best friend and knows he should give up fighting, but he is drawn into one last skirmish as a surrogate paid to box Jim Gibson. Knocked nearly unconscious at the end of the story, he gets back up to take some more punishment. In "Fox Hunters" Pancake explores the dark theme of sexual assault and the attempt of the main character Bo to avoid corruption and escape the area. Bo tries to gain acceptance from a woman that the men call a whore and then approval from the story's immoral older men. Throughout Pancake's stories, we see men who face economic difficulty try to gain a measure of respect by engaging in some form of violence or an often misguided assertion of masculinity.

Denise Giardina's 1987 novel *Storming Heaven* tells the story of ruggedly independent West Virginians battling exploitative coal companies during the early twentieth century. Breathtaking in its portrayal of the brutality and the determination of the workers who fight in mining wars, the novel depicts the lengths to which the companies would go to steal the property of the citizens, oppress the miners who worked for them, and quash any attempts to organize on behalf of the unions. Giardina's prose brings historical events like the Battle of Blair Mountain to life. Though the novel focuses on issues of socio-economic class, it also tells the love story of Rondal Lloyd and Carrie Bishop. This relationship dramatizes many important gender issues. The independent Carrie is a prototypical professional woman, a nurse who sympathizes with the overmatched miners. To the chagrin of her brother who has an office job with a coal company, she moves from emergent woman to independent woman as she becomes more involved with the labor movement. Carrie continually eschews traditional female roles through actions like firing a machine gun in defense of women who are taking provisions from a store and by wearing the clothes of the male miners when she marches with them toward Blair Mountain. The embodiment of traditional masculine behavior, Rondal is a banjo-playing union organizer who risks his life on the job and thinks his work precludes him from serious relationships. Through Carrie and Rondal, Giardina's novel dramatizes many important connections between class and gender in West Virginia literature.

The poetry of Irene McKinney dramatizes the struggles and strengths of impoverished Appalachians, defends the state from the derision of outsiders to the region, delights in a connection with the spiritual side of nature, and develops the most prevalent theme in her work: the right of a woman to define herself as she chooses. McKinney's work depicts the struggle against traditional gender roles from childhood and adolescence through marriage and independence. The longtime West Virginia poet laureate's 2004 book *Vivid Companion* features several of her most accomplished poems. McKinney writes eloquently about the awkwardness of adolescence ("Covering Up"), the tedium of marriage and motherhood ("At 24"), and the wisdom of maturation ("Face"). *Vivid Companion* also chronicles her struggles with cancer, and she addresses the difficulties of fighting disease with candor. However, the tone is never sentimental or self-pitying, and at times it is defiant and transcendent. While gender is the book's focus, her poems also explore how gender is related to class. In many of McKinney's finest poems, we see how the inequities of socio-economic class exacerbate women's struggle against the restrictions of traditional gender roles.

Ann Pancake's 2007 novel *Strange as This Weather Has Been* explores many of the same themes as *Storming Heaven*. Both novels address corruption in the coal industry, but Pancake focuses on the effects on local communities of mountaintop removal. *Strange as This Weather Has Been* chronicles the coming of age of Lace See, as well as her transformation from emergent woman to independent woman. As in *Storming Heaven*, the main female character educates herself about the exploitation of local landowners and devotes her energy to effecting change. Like Giardina, Ann Pancake depicts historical incidents—in this work, the Buffalo Creek disaster is vividly recounted—but shows, through the courage of her main character, that the personal is political. Lace's spiritual connection to the land stokes her resentment of coal company efforts to exploit it for profit. One of Pancake's themes is that spirituality is linked with communion with nature, and some of the most admirable characters in the novel feel the connection to the land that allows them to transcend what they perceive as the limitations of traditional religion and the exploitation of the land for profit. Others see only the economics of the situation, like Lace's husband, Jimmy Make, who refuses to take a job at a pizza parlor and resents the fact that his wife has to work at a Dairy Queen since no traditional mining jobs are available to him. He clearly wishes he had married a woman of less independence, and that he could provide for his family as he once did. Once again, we see the interrelatedness of class and gender as a focus of West Virginia literature.

Unlike any other Appalachian novel, Jayne Anne Phillips's *Lark and Termite* explores the theme of transcendence in ways that reveal the possibilities of the genre of fiction, influenced by Faulkner and Garcia Marquez, but basking in the radiance of its own originality. No writer excels at depicting the awkwardness and beauty of coming of age more than Phillips, and Lark is another in a series of artfully rendered adolescents. Bolstered by the guardianship of her aunt Nonie, but haunted by the absence of her parents, Lark cheerfully takes care of her half-brother, Termite. As Lark works to stay in control of her own destiny and find a connection to her departed parents, she navigates the treacherous tides of self-discovery. The novel explores the ways in which we connect with others, those from different cultures and different times, even those who are no longer living. Phillips reaches the pinnacle of her career with this novel, its lyrical prose exploring the interconnectedness of every human being in the narrative and presenting an Appalachia that is not defeated by limitations, but invigorated by possibilities.

Sharing Phillips's interest in characters transcending limitations, Pinckney Benedict masterfully blends genre fiction and mythology with realist fiction in *Miracle Boy and Other Stories*. In particular, Benedict employs elements of horror, science fiction, and fantasy literature to heighten the suspense in his stories, while creating characters who sometimes rise above their limitations through dreams and visions. For example, the title character of "Pig Helmet & the Wall of Life" experiences all three types of transcendence: a preternatural connection with another person, everyday experience imbued with magical qualities, and the discovery of the possibility of immortality. Benedict sometimes blurs the line between reality and dream in order to heighten the focus on his characters' psychologically fascinating fears and hopes. The author's early work revealed his potential and the influence of Breece Pancake, but nothing could have adequately prepared readers for the exploration of the possibilities of the genre of fiction that is found in *Miracle Boy and Other Stories*. With a fusion of dreamscape and landscape, Benedict imagines new possibilities for Appalachian literature.

The works of these eight writers—Davis Grubb, Mary Lee Settle, Breece D'J Pancake, Denise Giardina, Irene McKinney, Ann Pancake, Jayne Anne Phillips, and Pinckney Benedict—reflect the high quality of West Virginia literature, literature that has not received due recognition, especially outside the state. These authors' work treats quintessential Appalachian concerns: the role of tradition, connection to the land, and leaving the region in hopes of better economic opportunity. The important themes of socio-economic class and its effect on gender roles drive many of the plots of these works, as characters struggle to transcend dire situations and limited opportunities. In their intense focus on possibilities for transcendence, the state's writers increasingly break with traditional literary forms and explore new possibilities for Appalachian literature. With this great literary heritage, it is surprising that there are only four book-length critical studies of the writers treated in this work—two critical studies on Settle and one on Phillips, as well as Thomas Douglass's biography of Breece Pancake. This book seeks to add to that scholarship by celebrating important works of eight of West Virginia's most accomplished writers.

CHAPTER 1

Davis Grubb's
The Night of the Hunter

The success of the film adaptation of Davis Grubb's *The Night of the Hunter* (1953) threatens to overshadow the artistry of one of the finest Appalachian novels. Film critic Roger Ebert has called Charles Laughton's adaptation of Grubb's most famous literary work "one of the greatest of all American films" and stated that "everybody knows the Mitchum character, the sinister 'Reverend' Harry Powell. Even those who haven't seen the movie have heard about the knuckles of his two hands, and how one has the letters H-A-T-E tattooed on them, and the other the letters L-O-V-E."[1] Though increasingly overlooked, the novel is also an accomplished work. It was well received, with most critics focusing on Grubb's masterful handling of plot and suspense. It has continued to resonate with a different generation of readers. Gene Baro, writing in *The New York Herald Tribune* wrote, "Mr. Grubb has written with eloquent power, and also with often singular beauty . . . . This is a remarkable first novel, conveying the strength of a rich talent."[2] As Thomas E. Douglass has pointed out, "To this day, Stephen King heralds the work of Grubb and acknowledges Grubb's influence on his own work."[3] King has said of Grubb's writing style, "His language throws off sparks." Many critics have focused on Grubb's masterful creation of suspense, but what they typically overlook is the importance of class and gender to an understanding of *The Night of the Hunter*, for it is both a suspense novel and a work of social criticism, a page-turner and a critique of the capitalist ideology. It reveals the constraints of sexual repression and the fulfillment of sexual expression. Furthermore, it examines gender roles and depicts both a memorable patriarchal wife and the quintessential independent Appalachian woman. We see characters attempting to rise above their limiting situations, some attempts ending in tragedy and others in transcendence.

Davis Grubb's childhood shaped many of the themes that appear in *The Night of the Hunter*. Born in 1919 in Moundsville, Grubb became attuned with life in the small towns along the Ohio River during the Depression era. His father was an architect with business ventures that failed, and his mother worked for the West Virginia Department of Public Assistance. No doubt Grubb's parents' experiences made him aware of the economic struggles of the time, but he clearly also understood the subculture of the riverboat characters that informs *The Night of the Hunter*. He once said, "I'm not a hillbilly. I'm a river rat."[4] As Edwin T. Arnold has shown, the Ohio River culture in the Moundsville area exposed the young Grubb to a cast of colorful characters. Grubb described the milieu: "In those years I remember it as a place of daily astonishment, entertainments, mysteries, myths, brags, facts and holy awe. Even the commonplaces of those times were days different as bright, colored beads, strung in endless novelty upon the cord of myth, hearthside hearsay and outrageous history. That cord of course was the great Ohio River. . . . ."[5] One of the formative experiences in Grubb's life took place during the Depression. "In the mid-thirties, the Grubbs experienced one of those dreadful days when a man with an eviction notice came to their beautiful house on Seventh Street and ordered them out immediately."[6] Grubb's father died of a heart attack not long after the eviction. According to Jack Welch, Grubb believed that ". . . the pressures of the times and his father's inability to provide adequately for his family caused the decline in health."[7]

Grubb's time in Moundsville and later in Clarksburg provided the source material for the novel. The inspiration for *The Night of the Hunter* came from the conviction of a man in Clarksburg named Harry Powers. (Interestingly, the incident would also form the basis of Jayne Anne Phillips' 2013 novel *Quiet Dell*.) Powers was hanged for "the murder of two widows and three children."[8] In a Clarksburg bar years later, Grubb saw a man in a bar with the L-O-V-E and H-A-T-E tattooed on his knuckles. He would give those tattoos to Harry Powell in the novel. After that short stint in Clarksburg, Grubb relocated to New York City, where he attended art school and worked as a page at NBC before devoting himself to writing. His first success involved the publication of short stories in magazines of large circulation, most notably *Good Housekeeping* and *Collier's*. In the early 1950s, he began work on *The Night of the Hunter*. According to Welch, Grubb wrote a draft of the novel in six weeks and a second draft in another six weeks. He was paid $20,000 by Harper & Brothers for the book, and "Charles Laughton bought the film rights for $80,000 . . . ."

Although this critique focuses on the novel's social commentary as it relates to class and gender, its popularity is largely due to the fact that *The Night of the Hunter* is a classic suspense novel that effectively employs most of the key features of a horror narrative. It has a compelling villain with a great capacity for evil. It also employs two qualities that Douglas Fowler has highlighted as essential to "create pleasurable terror"—"physical confinement" and "the creation and enlargement within the reader or viewer of . . . the Cassandra Situation: to know and be powerless to alter." In Greek mythology, Cassandra had the ability to foretell the future, but no one would heed her warnings. Fowler adds, "Furthermore, successful terror narrative frequently (though not always) makes use of our oldest fairytales and magic stories: the Bible, the brothers Grimm, the archetypal tales from mythology. And it frequently heightens the effect of terror by the use of an extreme contrast between a surface appearance of innocence set off in contrast with a core of evil."[9] Grubb's readers continue to respond to his masterful creation of suspense.

After the publication of *The Night of the Hunter* in 1953, Grubb seemed destined for immortality, meeting and striking up friendships with some of the most famous writers and performers of the time. Oddly, though, he never seemed able to build on his early success. His subsequent work was judged uneven and contrived. Edwin T. Arnold summarizes: "The fact is that many of Grubb's books do tell the same story, and all are hurt, to varying degrees, by his tendencies toward stereotypes and plot manipulation. But Grubb can be an eloquent writer, and his best works transcend the sometimes formulaic stories he imposes on them." Perhaps Grubb's work suffered from a prejudice against genre fiction, works of suspense and mystery. Or perhaps the author indulged in his own excesses of trying too hard to be lyrical and poignant. Arnold's judgments are probably accurate. Grubb created "a large, often uneven, body of work, which is nevertheless impressive in its scope, aspirations, and ultimate achievements."[10] However, if *The Night of the Hunter* is the novel on which his reputation rests, then Davis Grubb deserves a place in Appalachian literary history.

Like many of Grubb's works, *The Night of the Hunter* is set during the Depression, so not surprisingly socio-economic class is a major theme of the novel. As we have seen, Grubb's childhood experiences provided him with the material to shape into an imaginative literary work. Socio-economic class is a focus of the novel from its first pages, as Ben Harper awaits execution after robbing a bank and killing two employees. Interestingly, Grubb and the novel's characters display a willingness to excuse the crime by attributing it to the pressures of poverty. Early in *The Night of the Hunter,* Ben explains his motive to Preacher:

> Because I was just plumb tired of being poor. That's the large and small of it, Preacher. Just sick to death of drawing that little pay envelope at the hardware store in Moundsville every Friday and then when I'd go over to Mister Smiley's bank on payday he'd open that little drawer with all the green tens and fifties and hundreds in it and every time I'd look at it there I'd just fairly choke to think of the things it would buy Willa and them kids of mine.[11]

Perhaps some of the other characters are so willing to forgive the crime because they are so obsessed with where Ben hid the money. Both Preacher and Willa ask him about the money many times, and greed becomes the common denominator among a number of the characters. Still, it is important to note how so many people understand how the economic trials of the time could force a good person to commit a desperate act, especially a husband and father who takes seriously his role as a provider.

Ben Harper clearly possesses two desires of Appalachian men who see themselves as providers: the desire for an appearance of success and a sense of daring. At one point his son John recalls that Ben "never come home of a Friday once without bringing us a present from the five-and-ten."[12] And it takes a highly pronounced sense of daring to for him to believe that he could get away with armed robbery. His unwillingness to divulge the location of the stolen money and especially the enlisting of his children to hide it from the authorities offer more evidence that Ben dares to defy even death in a misguided attempt to provide for his family. As Jessie Bernard has shown, "There were both costs and rewards for those men attached to the good-provider role. The most serious cost was perhaps the identification of maleness not only with the work site but especially with success in the role. . . . Men were judged by the level of living they provided. . . . Families became display cases for the success of the good provider." Bernard adds, "A man who was successful in the good-provider role might be freed from other obligations to the family. But the flip side of this dispensation was that he could not make up for poor performance by excellence in other family roles. Since everything depended on his success as provider, everything was at stake. The good provider played an all-or-nothing game."[13] Ben's "all-or-nothing" actions destroy his son's peace of mind, placing a burden on him that very nearly causes him to lose his mind near the end of the novel. The robbery is clearly a misguided act of male bravado.

Still, the characters in the novel all seem to accept that Ben was motivated by compassion for his family rather than malice toward others. Many of the characters reveal the kind of generosity of spirit that many people extended to the poor during tough economic times. After Ben is hanged, Walt Spoon gives Willa a waitress job at his ice cream parlor even though he really does not need her. "It was a kindness."[14] And as we will see later, Rachel Cooper is the novel's true hero not just for her ability to discern Preacher's evil intentions and defeat him in the novel's climactic scenes, but mostly for her adoption of and care for displaced children, abandoned or orphaned during the lean years of the Depression. Rachel, a self-reliant woman in her sixties, is described as "a strong tree with branches for many birds."[15] Grubb clearly wants to establish the heroism and compassion of the West Virginia people as the novel progresses. However, while the goodness of some of the characters eventually shines through, Grubb depicts in the novel's first few pages how greed can consume and corrupt a person. This is especially true in the scenes with Ben behind bars awaiting execution.

Grubb uses the prison scenes to establish the character of the novel's villain, Preacher, whose greed and obsession with the missing money reveal him right away to be a hypocrite, not the virtuous man of God he pretends to be. After all, Preacher is serving time for car theft. As Ben's cellmate, he utilizes every opportunity to try to persuade Ben to reveal the money's whereabouts, including a proposal to use the money to do God's work. "I could build a tabernacle, Ben, he whimpers. To beat that Wheeling Island tabernacle to hell and gone! Think of it, Ben. A tabernacle built with that ten thousand dollars of cursed, bloodied gold. But wait, Ben! Now it's God's gold. Thousands of sinners and whore and drunkards flocking to hear His word and all because you give that money to build a temple in His name."[16] Preacher's absurd notion of using stolen money to build a church that he would name after a convicted murderer makes his delusions of grandeur (God's special messenger battling the sins of others) obvious to Ben and the reader as well.

Grubb reveals Preacher's loathing of anything sexual and how he has, in the name of doing God's work, punished and murdered a number of widows who have displayed any hint of sexual desire. Strangely, though, Preacher has continually sought encounters with exotic dancers and prostitutes so he can fulfill his twisted misogynistic mission. He later explains to Willa that he went to the burlesque houses "just so's I could witness with my own eyes the degradation and stink to which mortal men and women can fall!"[17] The following passage illustrates his violent tendencies brought about by frustration and outrage with all things sexual:

> He would pay his money and go into a burlesque show and sit in the front row watching it all and rub the knife in his pocket with sweating fingers; seething in a quiet convulsion of outrage and nausea at all that ocean of undulating womanhood beyond the lights; his nose growing full of it: the choking miasma of girl smell and cheap perfume and stogie smoke and man smell and the breath of ten-cent mountain corn liquor souring in the steamy air; and he would stumble out at last into the enchanted night, into the glitter and the razzle-dazzle of the midnight April street, his whole spirit luminous with an enraptured and blessed fury at the world these whores had made.[18]

At one point in Clarksburg, Preacher had paid to be with a prostitute, and the girl had screamed when he pulled out his knife. Preacher was then beaten up by a black handyman. Another time in Cincinnati he had taken "a young mountain whore" to his room. She had been so intoxicated she "passed out naked on the bed." Preacher took out his knife and "delicately scratched a cross in the girl's belly beneath the navel."[19] In the early scenes, Grubb reveals Preacher's violent, misogynistic tendencies to the reader, creating dramatic irony and tension because most of the characters assume that he is a true man of God.

One character who is completely fooled by the Preacher's deceptions is the cleverly named Icey Spoon, who runs the ice cream shop with her husband Walt. She represents a true patriarchal woman of her time, accepting that men should be privileged in society and the women should defer to them. She serves as Willa's confidant while Preacher courts her, and Icey continually urges the pretty young widow to accept the hand of the alleged man of God. In the course of the two women's conversations, Icey makes several statements that define her as a patriarchal woman. In fact, at times she expresses a belief that patriarchy is God's will, denying the possibility of a single mother raising children, telling Willa, "No woman is good enough to raise growin' youngsters on her own. The Lord meant that job for two."[20] Icey's traditional beliefs lead her to misjudge Preacher, as Willa correctly suspects that Preacher might be just interested in the money, but Icey keeps arguing the opposite. "How would I know, said Willa presently, if Preacher was to ask me to marry him—that he wasn't just after the money? Maybe he thinks I've got it hid somewhere. He's a man of God, said Icey, gravely. It's plain enough to me."[21] Icey's blind acceptance of the rightness of a man in a position of authority clearly denotes her as a patriarchal woman. Throughout the novel, the narrator questions Icey's judgment and her unquestioning belief in patriarchy, such as in the following, "Her ideas of the world and of its people were as simple and even and unchanging as the little pastry hearts her cookie cutter made."[22]

Like Preacher, Icey exhibits sexual repression and thinks of herself as morally superior to others. Her thoughts about Willa's potential marriage to Preacher are simple:, "Any woman should be proud to marry a man of God. The ideal aspect to this was that it had none of the sex—none of the nastiness—with which, for her, marriage had always been tainted."[23] In a conversation with Preacher, she criticizes Ben for being "lusty and ornery."[24] Indeed, there are multiple indications that the Harper marriage enjoyed a healthy sex life. For example, when Willa explains that she is not physically attracted to Preacher like she was to Ben, Icey discounts the importance of sexuality to a marriage: "Fiddlesticks! That wasn't love, honey. That was just hot britches. There's more to marriage than four bare legs in a bed. When you're married forty years you'll know that all that don't matter a hill of beans. I been married that long to my Walt now and I'll swear in all that time whenever he took me I'd just lie there thinking about my canning or how I'd manage to git one of the boys new shoes for school. . . ."[25] Icey urges Willa not to worry about not knowing Preacher well: "A husband, grunted Icey, is one piece of store goods you never know till you take it home and get the paper off."[26] In many ways, Icey and Preacher are linked with a pronounced sense of piety stemming from disdain for sexuality. After Willa's murder, Preacher convinces Icey that Willa has run off in pursuit of lust: "She still longed for the old life, said Preacher softly. Carousin' of a night and beer drinkin'—and that other, I reckon. I couldn't give her that kind of life. I wouldn't if I could, dear hearts."[27] Grubb makes Preacher's repressed sexual attitudes an important feature of his character, and of his ability to fool the patriarchal woman Icey Spoon.

After Willa marries Preacher, she accepts his worldview, including the belief that sexual desire is sinful. She defers to Preacher's authority in the marriage on their sexless wedding night; however, she is clearly surprised at her new husband's lack of desire for her and had assumed that they would have sexual relations. At the hotel, she thinks, "He is not Ben but I will learn to love him even more because he is a man of God." Clearly, Willa had thought of sexuality as a healthy part of her first marriage and of her own fulfillment, "Because I have one nice thing that I gave to Ben and I will give it to him, too—the only nice thing that I ever owned: my body."[28] However, Preacher reacts to any thoughts of sex with anger. He chastises her by saying, "You thought, Willa, that the minute you walked in that door I'd start to pawing and feeling you in the disgusting, abominable way men are supposed to do on their wedding nights! Eh? Ain't that right, now?"[29] He then makes her get out of bed and take off her nightdress and stand naked in front of him. Preacher says, ". . . that body was meant for begetting children! It was not meant for the whoring lust of whoring men! That's filthiness!"[30] Deferential to her new husband, Willa quickly accepts that her marriage with Preacher will be celibate, but then she thinks the following, "He is right but just the same it is queer that he would know he is right because he has never had a woman ever in all his life."[31] She realizes that he has sexual issues, but she does not see them as linked with his sense of his own righteousness.

Grubb depicts Willa's second marriage as unhealthy and unloving. John notices the change in Willa after her marriage to Preacher. "Her eyes bore dark shadows and her mouth was thinner—paler—and her flesh itself seemed to have capitulated to the urgent moral protocols of her marriage until the very roundness of her sweet figure had turned epicene and sour in that lean season."[32] However, Willa enjoys her newfound devotion to God, becoming a main attraction at Preacher's tent revival meetings. Grubb mocks her newfound religious fervor by stating, "Willa had discovered sin."[33] She begins to criticize the sexuality of her first marriage, giving a dramatic testimony at Preacher's tent revival meetings:

> . . . I drove a good man to lust and murder and robbery because I kept a-hounding him and a-pestering him night and day for pretty clothes and per-fumes and face paint and do you know why I wanted them things? I wanted them so's he would lust after my body more and more and more!—instead of thinkin' about the salvation of them two little kids down yonder! And finally he couldn't stand it no more and he went out and took a gun and *slew!*—yes, slew two human beings and stole their money and come home with it to give

it to me and say: Here! Here! *Here,* Whore of Babylon! Take this money that is tainted with the blood of Abel and go to the store and buy your pretty dresses and per-fumes and paint! But, brethren!—ah, that's where the Lord stepped in! That's where Je-e-esus stepped in![34]

Of course, Willa obviously distorts the facts for the sake of a compelling testimonial, further suggesting that she has fallen under Preacher's spell rather than having made a choice of her own free will.

She continues to try to tell herself that all is well in her life and in her relationship with Preacher. In spite of her belief that she is now serving God by living in a sexless marriage, a dream Willa has one night suggests that unconsciously she still desires the physicality of her relationship with her first husband. Willa dreams of the gratification she felt on her wedding night with Ben. ". . . and he had stared at her with his gentle, burning eyes and said how beautiful her breasts were. It was the first time he had seen her naked. Why, sure they are! She laughed, blushing, eyes flashing, running to him, still giddy from the whiskey they had drunk. Why, sure! It's the only pretty thing I own—my pretty figure."[35] Willa wakes up and remembers that Preacher had taught her sexuality is "the Devil's way," reverting to her second husband's belief system and to her own expanding sense of righteousness. "Praise the Lord! She whispered fiercely. Praise the Lord!"[36] She continues in this vein until the tragic end of her marriage. At one point, she tells Icey about how she tries to manage the ill will between John and Preacher. "I'm needed she said. To keep peace and harmony between them. It's my burden and I'm proud of it, Icey!"[37] Willa increasingly mistakes self-righteousness for moral superiority.

By following Icey's wrong-headed advice instead of her own instincts, Willa becomes a patriarchal woman and meets a tragic end. After Preacher continually badgers the children about where the stolen money is hidden and denies ever having done so, Willa finally learns the truth about her second husband. Preacher resorts to violence after Willa questions whether the money is somewhere near, not at the bottom of the river like Preacher had claimed. "Then she thought: Why is my lip bleeding. Why can I taste the blood running back into my teeth and tongue? And then she remembered that he had struck her with the dry, shiny flat of his hand and it had happened only a second before though it seemed like a long time."[38] When he comes after her with the switchblade, her dying thought is "It is some kind of razor he shaves with. I knowed what it was the first night."[39] Willa's violent death comes fast upon her subservience to an evil man and her betrayal of her son, John.

The story of Ben and Willa Harper is, in some ways, a prototypical Appalachian narrative. A man who feels demeaned by economic difficulties commits a self-defeating act. In this case, Ben's robbery and murder, along with his ensuing execution, leave Willa at the mercy of a predator. Willa chooses to adopt Preacher's worldview and fails to read the many signs that the so-called man of God preys upon those who trust in him. Ben's and Willa's actions end in the ultimate tragedy—the loss of their lives. However, they very nearly cost their children their lives, by forcing them to flee the Preacher and risk their lives on the run. Their misguided actions force others to serve as surrogate parents for John and Pearl because the children find themselves in harm's way.

In fact, one of the most predominant themes in Grubb's work is society's treatment of children. As Douglass has shown, children are the major focus in Grubb's *The Voices of Glory* (1962), a collection of first-person narratives that center on the author's concerns about society's treatment of the poor. "Throughout *The Voices of Glory*, sympathy and justice for children resound."[40] In *The Night of the Hunter*, John barely withstands the pressure of knowing where the money is and battling the villainous Preacher's attempts to discover it. Preacher is often emotionally abusive to John, and if not for his surrogate father, Uncle Birdie, an alcoholic river dweller, the young boy might have broken down before he ever had a chance to meet his protector Rachel Cooper. Uncle Birdie is a victim of classism, as seen in Willa's condescending attitude toward him: "At the wharf John spied the face of Uncle Birdie, and Willa stiffened when the old man waved courteously and she told John he should not speak to that dirty old man"[41] Still, it is clear that John admires Uncle Birdie, who, by fulfilling his promise to repair a skiff, provides the boy with the means of fleeing Preacher by rowing out into the currents of the Ohio River.

When John and Pearl reach the home of Rachel Cooper, the reader is introduced to a protector of children, the most impressive character in the novel and one of the most independent women in all of Appalachian literature. Grubb captures the essence of her character in an introductory paragraph:

> She was old and yet she was ageless—in the manner of such staunch country widows. Gaunt, plain-spoken and hard of arm; she could stand up to three

of the shrewdest cattle dealers in Pleasants County and get every penny she thought her hog was worth. Or if pork was off that year she would butcher and can her own sausage and smoke her own hams and have enough left over to present the preacher's family with a nice meal of spareribs. In the summer she sent the children into the woodlands and brush filth with buckets for berries, and it was her old, wise hands that taught the children how to pick them and schooled their eyes in the ways of berry-finding. She had a cow and she churned her own butter and sold it at New Economy wrapped in cool, damp swaths of immaculate muslin. She had chickens and their eggs went to market, too, in a bright yellow basket spread across with a napkin. From the fat of her butchered hog she made soap, standing in a drenching March rain beside her brawling iron kettle in the back yard till the task was done. Fifteen miles downriver at Parkersburg a waitress had short-changed her and that was a quarter of a century before and she had never gone to that town again.[42]

One sees in this description the key traits of an independent woman: autonomy from men, self-sustainability, and an ability to transcend traditional gender roles.

Rachel is able to provide for herself by taking on the kinds of physical labor once thought to be the primary domain of men. Her ability to raise and sell livestock and prepare meals for a minister's family impresses the reader with her nearly total self-reliance. The fact that she is able to take care of herself financially and prevent other livestock dealers from shortchanging her shows that she has no concerns about whether she has achieved equality with men. Even more impressive are her care and compassion for the displaced children Grubb depicts so movingly, showing how the community understands that Rachel is too good-hearted to turn away a child. "Many a dark-haired farm girl lost her wits to an August moon and the mouth of a cunning lover and found herself, after he had gone away to work in Pittsburgh or Detroit, with the fruit of their ecstasy squalling and unwelcome in her poor mother's kitchen. Once the child was weaned and toddling, it was to Rachel Cooper's door that he was carried . . . ."[43] As we see in the cases of John and Pearl, Rachel instills the values of hard work and integrity in the children, preparing them for the perils of life ahead.

As the novel progresses, Grubb prepares the reader for a showdown between the relentless Preacher and the heroic Rachel. Preacher is able to discover John and Pearl's whereabouts by playing on the vanity of one of Rachel's charges, the gullible Ruby. Preacher plays on Ruby's vanity to try to find John and

Pearl. The newly sexually active Ruby says she'll tell Preacher about the two children if she'll buy him a chocolate soda and a movie magazine. Notice the blend of childhood with adult life as she propositions Preacher, who realizes that her vanity is the quality to which he can make his appeal:

> What do you want now?
> She lifted her mouth and whispered it in his ear.
> What?
> Don't you want to? she mumbled. You can if you want to—
> Get away from me![44]

Once again, Preacher recoils from the mere mention of sexuality, but Ruby misinterprets Preacher's response, falling in love with him because she thinks that he is moral and not exploitative like other men.

Rachel prepares herself for Preacher's imminent arrival, for Ruby confesses her behavior to the old woman, who becomes "roused and fidgety with anger at the world's trifling men."[45] When Preacher arrives to retrieve the children, Rachel becomes the first person in the novel since Ben Harper to see through the villain and recognize that his pretended piety is an act. Preacher says that their mother took them away from him, and the children ran away to Rachel's place. Rachel then sets her trap:

> Where'd they run from? I mean, where'd you figure the woman took them
>   when she ran away from you?
> Somewhere downriver! he said, shaking his head grimly. Parkersburg, mebbe.
>   One of them Sodoms on the Ohio River!
> Rachel rocked fast and hard, her eyes twinkling and strong in her face.
> Right funny hain't it, she said, how they rowed all the way upriver in a ten-
>   foot john boat![46]

After John seems frightened of Preacher, Rachel gets her gun and tells Preacher to leave. She sees that he pulled his knife to use on John. From this point on, she realizes that a physical confrontation with Preacher is unavoidable.

In her defense of her home and of John and Pearl, Rachel shows no fear of Preacher, even after he comes back at night. Interestingly, she could have called for the assistance of state troopers, but she does not recognize the need for the protection of law enforcement: ". . . this was the last thing that would have entered Rachel Cooper's mind. She had a deep, bottomlands mistrust of civil law. If there was trouble at hand it could most always be settled by the showing of a gun muzzle and a few strong words."[47] In a highly suspenseful scene, she sends the children upstairs and waits as Preacher crawls near her, presumably hoping to stab her and take John and Pearl with him. Rachel wounds Preacher when he tries to attack her and then she calls the state police to capture him after he flees to the barn. By bringing Preacher to justice and by protecting John and Pearl from him, Rachel Cooper further establishes herself as the quintessential Appalachian independent woman.

The novel closes with a Christmas scene that is designed to provide a happy ending, but it also contains one last statement by Grubb on economic inequities. "Rachel reflected about children. One would think the world would be ashamed to name such a day for one of them and then go on the same way: children running the lanes, lost sheep crying in the wind while the shepherd drank and feasted in the tavern with never an ear to heed their small lament. Lord save little children!"[48] Grubb's outrage about children living in poverty is clear, but the passage which repeats the refrain "Lord save little children" reflects the author's tendency to inflate his rhetoric from time to time, without trusting his readers to draw the conclusion from the details of child poverty he has already presented. As Edwin T. Arnold has shown, Grubb's occasional lack of restraint as a writer contributes to the perception of his fiction as "uneven," but ultimately what shines through is that Grubb feels passionately about the ways in which economic hardship can demean a person, especially a child. The strengths of the novel clearly outshine the tendency to overwrite on occasion.

The novel balances tragedy and transcendence in ways that are directly related to the themes of gender and socio-economic class. Grubb's treatment of these themes reveal a great deal about what was expected of men and women in Depression-era West Virginia and how self-defeating it can be to conform to cultural norms. Ben's insistence upon being the traditional male provider for his family leads to his own death and endangers his family. Willa's conformity to conventional expectations of women of her time leads her to sacrifice her happiness and makes her an easy prey for Preacher. The tragedies of Ben and Willa are offset in the second half of the novel by the transcendence of Rachel. At the end of the novel, she has defeated Preacher and saved the children. The novel ends with the oft-tormented John falling into a peaceful sleep, free from fears of Preacher and the police officers who arrested his father, comforted by the tales and the support that Rachel has provided him. "But the night of the hunter was gone forever and the blue men would not come again. And so John pulled the gospel quilt snug around his ear and fell into a dreamless winter sleep, curled up beneath the quaint, stiff calico figures of the world's forgotten kings, and the strong, gentle shepherds of that fallen, ancient time who had guarded their small lambs against the night."[49]

Davis Grubb called *The Night of the Hunter* his "strange Appalachian song." It is an often somber tune that still resonates more than fifty years after its publication. While many fans of Grubb's work praise his ability to create suspense, that is only one impressive feature of the novel. The characters' fears that feed the novel's suspense are often linked with the author's tendency toward social criticism. Among Grubb's legacies is that he wrote about gender and sexuality with a frankness that anticipates the work of later West Virginia writers. Preacher's sexual hang-ups reveal his psychological issues that drive his motivations. In addition to the deft handling of suspense and sexuality, Grubb also gave a voice to the economic trials and the basic decency of the West Virginia people. As the author once commented, "If you write about West Virginia and its people, you particularly need this instinct for love, I think. For West Virginia is Appalachia—it is a state of poor people . . . . And for me at least only poor people, and, in my case only the poor people of West Virginia—are worth my efforts as a writer of tales."[50] *The Night of the Hunter* captures the values and mores of the Mountain State.

CHAPTER 2

Mary Lee Settle's
Beulah Quintet

Mary Lee Settle's *Beulah Quintet* takes on the ambitious project of chronicling the history of West Virginia. It traces the state's development from the ancestors of the first settlers of the Kanawha valley to the modern day citizens caught up in the continually changing economics of the coal industry in the twentieth century. It is a work of breathtaking skill and scope. In *Understanding Mary Lee Settle*, George Garrett calls the *Beulah Quintet* "an extraordinary achievement" and argues that "no other serious American novelist of Settle's generation—the generation which came to literary prominence in the years after World War II—has chosen to attempt anything so large and ambitious."[1] In his excellent critical work *Mary Lee Settle's Beulah Quintet: The Price of Freedom*, Brian Rosenberg shows how Settle's work focuses on the themes of class and gender. "Of particular concern to her are the relations between the empowered and the powerless, or the dispossessors and the dispossessed, that is, between wealthy and impoverished, governing and rebellious, Anglo-Saxon and non-Anglo-Saxon, male and female."[2] The first novel, *Prisons*, focuses on Johnny Church, a seventeenth-century ancestor of the settlers of Beulah, located in the Kanawha valley, who is battling for liberty in seventeenth-century England. The second volume, *O Beulah Land*, depicts life in eighteenth-century America during the time of the French and Indian wars, leading up to the American Revolution. *Know Nothing*, the third volume, focuses on the turmoil of the pre-Civil War years, while *The Scapegoat*, the fourth volume, explores a community in the midst of a coal strike in 1912. The fifth volume of the quintet, *The Killing Ground*, depicts the lives of upper and lower class West Virginians in the 1960s and 1970s, as well as its main character's search for the heritage that is covered in the five novels. Given that the *Quintet*, which should be read as a whole, runs over 1,400 pages, it could be considered the Russian novel of West Virginia literature. Through many different characters and situations, the quintet explores spiritual and philosophical issues, offers sharp political and social commentary, dramatizes key moments in the state's history, and celebrates the freedom and independence of West Virginians.

Mary Lee Settle's background prepared her to undertake this enormous project. The quintessential woman of letters, Settle was born in 1918 in Charleston, West Virginia. During the twenties, her father was responsible for worker safety in the mines, a position that provided his daughter with material for her fiction. After attending Sweet Briar, she briefly became a fashion model and auditioned for the role of Scarlett O'Hara in *Gone with the Wind*. Like Lily Lacey in *The Scapegoat*, Settle served as a military nurse—in Settle's case, the Women's Auxiliary of the Royal Air Force during World War II. When she returned to the United States, she landed a job at *Harper's Bazaar*. George Garrett describes a moment that was a turning point in Settle's life:

> One day in late summer of 1945 she came back to the office after a leisurely luncheon to find on her desk a layout of the Bronte country, together with a copy of the Modern Library Edition of *Wuthering Heights*, which she was supposed to put together appropriate captions for the pictures. A moment of literary epiphany. "I realized that Emily Bronte had written it and was dead by the time she was twenty-eight," Settle has written. "I had just turned twenty-seven. So I saw my two ways. Either I would still be sitting there, a well-paid fashion and arts editor at forty, still writing about other people's accomplishments, or I would plunge into the precarious world of writing myself."[3]

She tried her hand at plays before turning to fiction, finally seeing her first book in print in 1953, the novel *The Love Eaters*. All in all, Settle would write fifteen novels, in addition to memoirs and travel books. She arguably achieved her greatest artistic success in 1978, winning a National Book Award for her novel *Blood Tie*, about expatriates in Turkey. She said the award meant "a reunion with the literary world, advances seven times what they had been before, and the acceptance of what I was doing."[4]

Settle's achievements were not limited to her literary work. In 1980, frustrated by how the New York publishing establishment awarded literary prizes, she co-founded the PEN/Faulkner Award, a competition judged by writers, with the idea that "no favoritism would be granted to bestselling authors."[5] Settle also taught at the University of Iowa and the University of Virginia, strongly committed to the idea that writing and books can transform people's lives. After her death at the age of eighty-seven in 2005, many of her admirers praised her life and work. Matt Schudel wrote of Settle, "She was considered a 'writer's writer' whose well-wrought works—drawing on her worldwide travel, painstaking research and unerring ear for dialogue—brought her literary respect if not always public acclaim."[5] Denise Giardina called Settle her "literary mother" for showing her how to write about history, saying, "While much American fiction seemed to be turned inward, [Settle] let me know that it was fine to write about the rebels, the idealists, those who stand up for what they believe is right."[6] Susan Richards Shreve recalled Settle's determination to found the PEN/Faulkner award and praised the courage and curiosity of Settle's fiction, "She was a courageous writer doing the work she did against the grain, always wonderfully obsessed and impossible and captivating."[7] Joyce Dyer praised her ability to write international novels and regional novels as well: ". . . over and over, she returned to the familiar Appalachian soil of her own past that always yielded up enormous harvest for her, and for her readers."[8]

Settle's admirers often seem surprised that her work has not garnered more recognition and more attention from academic critics. In an overview of Settle's career, Brian Rosenberg describes how her first two novels—*The Love Eaters* (1954) and *The Kiss of Kin* (1955)—are "compact, bitterly ironic examples of contemporary social realism" and were "widely and on the whole favorably reviewed in England and the United States."[9] Then Settle made her first foray into historical fiction, and her reputation gradually began to suffer during the sixties, as the literary establishment discounted her historical novels as genre fiction. Rosenberg suggests that Settle had a problem with audience. Her historical fiction was not considered serious literature by some in academe, and yet her work is so demanding that she did not reach a wide audience. Furthermore, Settle's work is not easily categorized, and some would argue that writers, like all producers in the marketplace, need to have a recognizable brand. Rosenberg explains, "She is an American novelist who lived for many years in Europe and whose literary influences seem a mixture of the southern and the continental; she is a writer of novels set in centuries from the seventeenth to the twentieth and in locations from England to West Virginia to Turkey to Hong Kong . . . ."[10] Another potential explanation for her fiction being ignored is tonal. Rosenberg points out that her work lacks the ironic tone of much contemporary fiction and comes across as passionate and earnest. "The truth is that there are very few novelists today who approach their subjects in the manner of Settle and consequently few readers familiar with the sort of world she creates."[11] Her work engages the reader, explores the themes of class and gender, and chronicles the history of West Virginia, with little concern for cultural trends.

Interestingly, Settle did not originally plan the *Beulah Quintet* as a five-novel series. In fact, it was almost a trilogy. The publication history is complicated but intriguing. Settle published *O Beulah Land* and *Know Nothing*, the second and third novels of the series, in 1956 and 1960, respectively. Then came one of the greatest disappointments of Settle's career. In 1964, she published *Fight Night on a Sweet Saturday*, a novel that was considerably weakened, as Rosenberg puts it, by "some ill-advised editorial tinkering."[12] The novel received some negative reviews, and the author herself eventually expressed disappointment that her saga seemed incomplete. According to Garrett, Settle called the book "'a vicious failure,' adding, 'it came in the year that it was very chic among critics in New York City to absolutely trash books. And it was appallingly trashed.'"[13] Years later, she decided that she had not gone far enough back in history to trace the roots of the desire for greater liberty, and she published *Prisons* in 1973 as a sort of prequel to the other novels. Settle then felt inspired to reenvision *Fight Night* as two novels and published *The Scapegoat* in 1980 and *The Killing Ground* in 1982, thus completing one of the greatest multi-volume works of fiction in Appalachian literary history. Since Settle believed that the *Beulah Quintet* should be considered one work, I will treat it as such.

Brian Rosenberg uses a key phrase from the end of *The Killing Ground* as the subtitle of his book on the *Beulah Quintet*: "the price of freedom." Settle encourages her readers to reflect upon the sacrifices of our ancestors that have made possible our enjoyment of life, liberty, and the pursuit of happiness. However, she makes it clear that there are always threats to that liberty, and tension between the powerful and the powerless, as the former often tries to impose its will on the latter. In each novel in the *Quintet*, main characters attempt to reject or reshape an aspect of the culture's dominant ideology. The novels dramatize quintessential American subjects like freedom of religion and freedom of expression, the use of slavery, the exploitation of land and workers, and the snobbery of the upper classes. Each of these issues has at its core some kind of power struggle, often between social change and the status quo. Rosenberg writes that the book relies upon the repeated dramatization of "the agonized interdependence of the empowered and the powerless."[14] Settle's main characters often question what is accepted as just and proper by those who blindly accept the dominant ideology. The ensuing conflicts are often generational, with the younger characters hoping to avoid or even overturn the mistakes and excesses of their elders. Strong psychological forces enliven these works, in which children oppose their parents' will, and brother opposes brother. The tension between generations and the sense of conflict among family members are reflected in what Settle said, only partly in jest, "The price of freedom is to have everybody mad at you."[15] Settle brilliantly explores the dynamics that make a democracy work, in spite of its limitations and internal contradictions. She also captures historical moments in all their moral complexity.

In *Prisons*, the first novel of the *Quintet*, Settle reveals how self-interest, in the form of financial well-being or personal survival, often outweighs moral principle. As the novel begins, Parliament has been trying to check the power of Charles I, forming its own army to battle with that of the king. Some see the civil war as a battle for freedom, some as a religious war, and others as a means to secure wealth and power. The novel is narrated by Johnny Church, a twenty-year-old soldier who enlists in Cromwell's parliamentary army. Johnny finds the rancor over religious differences frustrating and even trivial. "In truth, I never saw religion as more than manners and politics and used as a stone wall of willful strength by my mother when I was a child."[16] For Johnny, the heroes of the time were men like John Lilburne, who bravely argued for individual liberty. Lilburne, known as "Freeborn Jack," was publicly punished, hauled in a cart from Westminster to St. Paul's and lashed repeatedly with a whip for disseminating a pamphlet that was critical of the church hierarchy. He bravely shouted his message until the whips overwhelmed him and he lost consciousness. Johnny is fascinated with Lilburne and with the political discussions at his home, but his father, who has risen from candle maker to land owner and who sympathizes with those who hope to curb the king's power, feels threatened by the prospects of overthrowing the established order. At one point, Johnny's father says, "Why, they'll turn everyone against all the nobility and clergy and gentry in the land and destroy the monarch itself. That is not what we meant when we started, but to chastise the king—to trim the tree, not strike so near the root."[17]

Johnny's relationship with his father is important to understanding gender dynamics in the novel. Their interactions are often formal and distant, and in fact, the young man enjoys little affection from either of his parents. At one point, he recalls the only time his father hugged him, when Johnny was leaving for Oxford. "It was the first time he had touched me with his hands except to whip me since I was a child."[18] His relationship with his uncle Sir Valentine and his lovely young aunt Nell offers a sharp contrast. Johnny is so drawn to Nell that the two of them engage in an illicit sexual encounter that produces an illegitimate child. As the novel progresses, Johnny's respect for his father diminishes. One of the major events of the book occurs when Johnny becomes angry with his father, who wants "to flood their village to make a lake and enclose the common up to Henlow Wood to run his deer."[19] The effect of this decision is that lower classes are driven away from his house, making it more difficult for them to survive. Full of democratic fervor, Johnny finds his father's decision elitist and exploitative. Johnny decides to make himself look more like a peasant, so he cuts off his long hair and the lace on his collar. When he refuses to kneel before his father and refers to him as "thee," his father slaps him and drives him from his home. In effect, Johnny is rejecting his father's worldview and condemning his self-important behavior. Johnny's summation of the event speaks to a major theme of the *Beulah Quintet* as a whole: "We must accept as hallowed the unblessings of our fathers."[20]

After Johnny joins the army, one could argue that Oliver Cromwell becomes a kind of surrogate father to him—or at the very least, a male authority figure he can idolize for a time. When he first sees Cromwell, Johnny is struck by the easy intimacy the men have with the legendary general, as Cromwell jokes with them and they refer to him as Oliver." Johnny is thrilled by this acquaintance: "Oh, Oliver, now turned great Cromwell, who knew first names and spoke among us as friends do, did you not know how much one boy had fell in love with you as you rode there, forgetting us, your back crouched in the saddle, your head down, as one listening for an inner answer he cannot hear."[21] Even more important than his personal warmth, the great general seems to embody the struggle for individual freedom that is Johnny's passion. By empowering the common man, Cromwell fans the flame of liberty for a time. Johnny romanticizes his first days in Cromwell's army, as ten thousand men from all stations of life joined together for a cause. "There was, for that moment, a streaming out of love as if all brothers, unknown to one another, had met in some vasty dream."[22] After their military victories, during which Johnny proves himself as a soldier and as a man, Cromwell's men enjoy a brief period of freedom of expression. Johnny says, "As I look back now, there was never a time like it, when every man had so much to say in his own destiny."[23] Clearly, Cromwell is able to effect change the young man's father could not even envision.

However, Cromwell eventually betrays Johnny and the men. Once Cromwell gets a taste of power, he makes a series of compromises that secure his position as one of the most important men in England. He agrees to disburse much of the Parliamentary army and is financially rewarded. "There was more and more parceling out of Cavalier lands among the new landowners of England. Even Cromwell accepted a huge tract from Parliament, a fine parcel, and a rich pension."[24] Cromwell cooperates in denying freedoms to those who are not landowners, and in a sense, people like Johnny have traded one oppressive ruler for another. Johnny and his fellow soldiers find themselves in a kind of limbo. Johnny says, "One day we were an army and subject to military law; on another we were free men with a right to speak."[25] Hope remains for a time that Cromwell will honor their dreams of liberty, even as he maneuvers to seize power after the execution of the king. Johnny and his best friend, the admirable Thankful Perkins, are elected as representatives of their unit to press for greater freedom. They travel to Burford, ostensibly to meet with Cromwell and his representatives to discuss their opposition to going to fight in Ireland. Threatened by the dissent of the soldiers who once admired him, Cromwell has Johnny and Thankful arrested. When the two young men refuse to recant, he sentences them to be executed. In a face-to-face encounter, Cromwell cruelly tempts Johnny with the issue of a father's love. Cromwell asserts that Johnny's father would have his son take his "rightful place in the country" and has "bragged so to me of your learning."[26] In a brief moment of weakness, Johnny feels a flash of validation that his father has praised him before realizing that Cromwell is merely trying to manipulate him into betraying political principles. Thus, ultimately Johnny rejects both his biological father and Cromwell, his surrogate father, and pays "the price of freedom."

Prisons raises a number of issues that descendants of Johnny Church must also address. To what extent can one break with his or her family's value system? What sacrifices are necessary to transform the dominant ideology so that society is less repressive? How does one even know, in some cases, what is right and wrong in a society in which the oppressed can eventually become the oppressor? In Settle's world, characters like Johnny Church make individual liberty possible. However, a free society is characterized by ongoing tensions between the empowered and the powerless, as the former tries to impose its wishes on the latter. Settle believes that sometimes the lost cause makes possible the eventual progress and that a group that is empowered one day may be disenfranchised the next, as is the case in *Prisons*, where the seed of American democracy is planted. Settle said in an interview with Rosenberg, "Are we a band of brothers, or do we have a paternal leader? We have daddy presidents all the time. Then we balance again and have a strong legislative band of brothers, and so it goes. American democracy is a fascinating revolutionary form of government. It always fails, and it always succeeds. It's crazy, isn't it?"[27] Settle explores this constant shifting and balancing of power throughout the *Beulah Quintet*.

In *O Beulah Land*, the second novel in the *Quintet*, Settle explores the origins of the ideology of the American dream, focusing on Jonathan Lacey's rise from an officer in the British army to his settlement of Beulah, Settle's fictional version of the Kanawha valley, to his election to the House of Burgesses just before the Revolutionary War. Like Johnny Church, Lacey is a man of principle and pragmatism, avoiding the political excesses of many of his contemporaries but exhibiting the principled self-reliance that proves his worth. The novel traces Lacey's life and the evolution of his thought from 1755-74. In battle, he does not adopt the superior airs and misplaced masculinity of some of the British army that leads to its defeat in the Battle of the Monongahela in 1755. While questioning the wisdom of those from the eastern colonies who want to break ties with King George III, he defies the restrictions placed on settlements in western Virginia by the king's Proclamation Line of 1763. Lacey stakes his claim and founds Beulah, with the help of a number of rugged settlers. He defends his settlement from the raids of border ruffians and the attack of angry Indians. When Beulah is incorporated into a county, Lacey enters politics and begins his rise in Virginia society. Throughout his experiences, Lacey distinguishes himself with his sound judgment and personal strength. One of Settle's greatest strengths in the *Beulah Quintet* is her ability to capture the fluidity of political processes and to dramatize the struggles of main characters who must navigate the troubled waters of their times. As Jane Gentry Vance points out, "*O Beulah Land*, like the other books of the Quintet, probes events of the American past by purging them of the generalizations and the mythifications of history."[28] We see in Jonathan Lacey a man who can understand the moral complexities of pre-revolutionary America. He correctly judges when revolution seems unwise and when the British government oversteps its bounds and necessitates the pursuit of American liberty.

Jonathan's worth shines through in several key moments. During the French and Indian War, he contrasts sharply with the ambitious Captain Orme, who serves as chief advisor to the ill-fated General Braddock. Orme lords his powerful position over the other men, at one point unfairly questioning Lacey's courage. Jonathan remains self-assured, and unlike Orme, he recognizes the inevitability of defeat on the Monongahela. In many ways, Settle portrays Braddock's defeat as resulting from misplaced masculine pride, as the general refused to retreat when the opposing force had the advantage. Jonathan looks at the defeat honestly, unlike Orme, who tries "to catch and save in hollow words some kind of reputation from the disaster."[29] This ability to see reality clearly and to maintain personal integrity becomes one of Lacey's key character traits. He remains a loyal colonist until the British no longer deserve his fidelity. He defies the king's orders about settling west of the Proclamation Line, and later when he wins election to the House of Burgesses, he becomes understandably upset about a member of Parliament who wants to require American elected officials to swear allegiance to the king. Finally, the reader admires Lacey's ability to organize and defend the vulnerable settlement of Beulah from aggressors. He tells his friend Jarcey of his vision for Beulah: "I've thought for a long time and I've concluded to farm. That and the salt trade, and for a while I intend public house keepin, and a little boat-buildin, for I see the day when they'll be plenty of jobbers comin down the valley to the Ohio."[30] As a determined and effective settler with respect for cultural and philosophical diversity, Jonathan Lacey embodies many of the best qualities of early American patriotism.

Class issues dominate much of the novel, as Settle demonstrates not just the growing political strength of the colonists against a powerful empire, but also the humble origins of the future affluent families of West Virginia. Some of the eastern Virginians, like Jonathan's wife Sally, see themselves as the superiors of the western Virginians. After relocating to Beulah, she tries to bring culture to the women of the settlement by serving them hot chocolate in fine china. Her hopes are thwarted when one woman complains that the drink lacks liquor and another steals one of her cups. When her daughter Sara is forced to marry the decidedly lower class Ezekiel Catlett, Sally feels shamed and defeated. Ezekiel's parents both came to America in desperate situations. Jeremiah was sold into servitude as a child, and Hannah came to America after being sentenced in England to be transported to Virginia for petty theft. For many years, they live in the wild, struggling for survival and eventually settling in Beulah. Even after Sally experiences a sense of triumph because Jonathan's election means she will be able to attend the Governor's Ball, it is ultimately the Catletts who prevail. At the end of the novel Jonathan and Sally's son, Peregrine, becomes a ruthless Indian killer, "drunk with killin',"[31] a man who disgraces his father with his bigotry and bellicosity. After Jonathan disowns Peregrine, the Beulah settlement is willed to Sara and thus will ultimately fall into the hands of the Catletts, a family of low social standing, as Rosenberg writes, "scarcely a decade after its founding."[32]

If Sally Lacey represents the kind of privileged woman who sees herself as upholding the standards of the genteel class, Hannah Catlett offers the stark contrast of a lower class woman who has had to struggle for survival. We are introduced to Hannah in the breathtaking prologue, in which she travels through the wilderness alone, surviving by gathering fruit and catching small game and fish. Early on, her toughness and determination are established:

> The woman who woke up, weak as she was, was new, made free for a time of haunting memory by shock, a different woman from the one who had blundered into the thicket. She had been a haunted, chased creature, mindless with panic, in the two weeks she had been driven east by her own fear, kept alive only by some boundless miracle that lets the nervous fawns alive, or the silly vulnerable fish. Now she was no longer running from the west, too scared to scream, with the devil at her heels. She was headed east, ready to meet the sun as it rose to guide her.[33]

George Garrett justly calls the prologue virtuoso writing. Hannah finally arrives at the home of Jeremiah Catlett, who revives the malnourished Hannah. She ends up sharing his cabin with him, along with his sow Hagar and her piglets. After she and Jeremiah settle in Beulah, she assumes responsibility for arranging for them to acquire their own land by talking to Jonathan about how her religiously fanatic husband believes that God has led them to this land. Lacey trades her the land for a bright red stone and a fancy riding crop that are subsequently passed down through the generations. Like Jonathan, Hannah possesses the practicality to survive many difficult years in the wilds of western Virginia.

At the wedding of her daughter to Zeke Catlett, Hannah and Jeremiah's son, Sally behaves arrogantly toward the Catletts, annoyed that the groom has chosen not to wear the suit she lent him and frustrated that no one notices the candles she saved for such an occasion. Obviously, Sally is out of her element in rugged western Virginia. Jonathan says at one point, "I sometimes think I done her a great wrong, bringin her from what she was used to. I've made here what she wanted, but she don't see it. She clings to a dream instead"[34] By going to Richmond as the wife of an elected official, Sally escapes what she sees as a demeaning way of life. And one senses that the inhabitants of Beulah are happy when she leaves. Still, she is given the novel's last word, as Sara, living in Beulah, recalls how her mother used to fight against poor manners and ill breeding. The daughter thinks of her mother realizing that "there were more kinds of conquerors for a new heaven and a new earth than one fool gal could reckon."[35] Brian Rosenberg rightly points out how Sally Lacey, in many ways, provides the model of the class consciousness that many subsequent Beulah matriarchs would emulate. "Sally's class-consciousness, apparent in her advice that 'ye can be polite and friendly but 'tis as well to show the lower class of people right off the ways ye're used to,' contains the seeds of the antebellum society portrayed in *Know Nothing*."[36]

In *Know Nothing*, the third novel of the *Quintet*, Settle explores the personal and political issues of a slave-owning family at Beulah. Book One takes place in 1837, when Johnny Catlett, the novel's main character, is seven years old. Book Two finds the extended family in the fashionable resort Egeria Springs in 1849, fleeing a potential cholera epidemic and hoping to meet suitable prospective spouses for the unmarried young people in the entourage. Book Three focuses on Johnny's return home from his adventures out west, and covers the years 1857–61. Since his brother Lewis has become an abolitionist, it falls upon Johnny's soldiers to manage the family's holdings in Beulah, including its slaves. Johnny is an intriguing figure, a moral and likable person who allows his sense of family obligation to pressure him into making poor choices. He ends up joining the Confederate army at the end of the novel and participating in the Battle of Philippi in then-western Virginia, which historians consider more of an embarrassment for the rebel forces than a full-fledged battle. In this novel, Settle explores how southern attitudes were sustained and justified, particularly in relation to the immoral institution of slavery. The novel takes its name from the political party that feared foreign influence from immigrants, especially Catholic influence, but whose members denied any knowledge of the party's existence when asked about it. Settle uses this title to indict the ignorance of many of the region's citizens at that time, and to show how ill-conceived the system was that allowed for the ownership of human beings.

Not surprisingly, class issues provide much of the thematic material for the novel. In 1837 Brandon and Sally Lacey visit "their backwoods Catlett kin" to ask Johnny's father for money. At dinner one night, the conversation reveals the families' pretensions and prejudices. Old Mrs. Catlett claims her family name is French, and that her relatives "laid claim to Beulah with a ruby ring and a silver riding crop. She even claims that her ancestors "came over to England with William the Conqueror."[37] Readers of *O Beulah Land* know how absurd these claims are. Jeremiah and Hannah Catlett's origins were far from aristocratic, and Hannah found the ruby rather than inheriting it. Their son became the heir of Beulah after impregnating Sara Lacey and marrying into a family with a much more honorable lineage. Then the conversation turns toward the xenophobic, as Mrs. Catlett refers to the Catholic church as "the Whore of Babylon" and her daughter-in-law, Leah, a Cutwright and thus a descendent of the crudest characters in the previous novel, claims: "I saw the immigrants in Cincinnati, all paid by the Pope to take over the west from the Americans."[38] Then they discuss the fears of a slave uprising aroused by Nat Turner, "the name and the fear seeping on and on around the table."[39] Settle's point is masterfully rendered. The characters at this dinner "know nothing" of their true heritage and mistakenly think of themselves as descendants from the upper echelon of society. Their paranoia about popish plots and slave uprisings all relates to preserving what little wealth they have remaining. Living under a corrupt system, they engage in twisted logic and far-fetched fears.

Class pretensions become even further revealed in Book Two, which chronicles the trip to Egeria Springs, a place which aspires to be a sort of American Bath, a resort where the fashionable go to socialize and derive medicinal value from the spa. As was the case in Bath, England, there is at Egeria Springs a master of ceremonies, an Englishman named Wellington Smythe, who introduces wealthy individuals to each other. Smythe understands that many of the visitors lack sophistication, but profits from pretending otherwise. His comments about Sally Lacey reveal his condescension toward the southern women and their pretensions:

He knew her kind; perpetual, useless aunts he had to flatter from time to time. "You'll find us very English here." That's the first thing she had said to him, as he knew she would, as they all did, and told him about how in Papa's time they'd served toddies in silver cups on a big tray that came from England, on an English sideboard. With such ladies the great days had always been in their papas' time, and would be again, if they had their way, in their sons-in-law's time. He hated pretentious poverty.[40]

The Sally Lacey of this novel reminds the reader of the character by the same name in *O Beulah Land*. However, as Brian Rosenberg has shown, "This novel's Sally Lacey is a debased version of the first, all manners and vanity with little underlying strength, but she is also as much a product of southern culture as is cotton or tobacco."[41] She tries to secure a wealthy husband for her unfortunate daughter Sara and fails to see how she commodifies other human beings, not just the slaves, equating everyone's self-worth with financial worth. The irony, as Settle points out, is that characters like Sally Lacey are themselves on the verge of losing their financial footing, though they do not fully realize the implications of their shifting socio-economic status.

If capitalism is one dominant ideology in the novel, romantic love is another, and readers find themselves rooting for the worthy, socially inferior heroine, just as they do when reading Jane Austen. The worthy young woman in *Know Nothing* is Melinda Lacey, an orphaned cousin who lives with the Catletts. She fears becoming like Cousin Annie, an older relation who depends upon the family for economic survival. Accustomed to feelings of inferiority in comparison to the privileged Catlett daughter, Lydia, Melinda nevertheless impresses the Catlett boys. Even Johnny's brother, the taciturn Lewis, respects Melinda's independent spirit, admiring how "she wasn't afraid of the devil and hell . . ." and acknowledging that "she was the only one he couldn't make do what he told them."[42] However, it is she and Johnny that develop a mutual attraction that promises to turn into something more at Egeria Springs, except that he remains aloof, apparently fearing the disapproval of his parents who make it clear that they would oppose such a union. Romance finds Melinda in spite of Johnny's apparent rejection of her, in the person of Crawford Kregg, a wealthy distant cousin. The Egeria scenes are among the most beautifully written passages in Appalachian literature. Aware that the other ladies at the ball will have fancier gowns than she, Melinda decides to fashion a garland of rosebuds for her hair. She says, "There comes a time . . .

when a gal of spirit has to be her own fairy godmother."[43] The allusion to Cinderella proves prophetic when Wellington Smythe, recognizing that "the dear girl had a spirit which had made her strip her cheap white dress and deck herself with rosebuds so that she looked quite elegant,"[44] selects her to lead the dance at the ball. She rises to the occasion and impresses with her poise. Of course, the fact that the other, richer young women are rejected in favor of a dowryless orphan allows Settle to use the ideology of romance to subvert the ideology of class consciousness. When a little later in the novel Melinda entices Crawford to kiss her and propose during the cave expedition, she finds herself on the brink of wealth that would have been inconceivable a few days earlier.

Melinda finds herself torn between choosing a financially lucrative match or following her heart. When she offers Johnny one more chance to declare his love, his response suggests a desire to wait until he can be less dependent upon his parents. He tells her, "I don't want to marry anyone yet . . . . Cain't you give me time, Melinda?"[45] Later in the discussion, she explains, "I'm scared. I don't want to end up like Cousin Annie. You don't know what it's like for a woman to have nothing, and all the other women to treat her like a poor relation."[46] Interestingly, both characters feel the pressure of social class for the same reason: they are seeking to escape from their dependence upon Johnny's parents. Knowing that she loves Johnny more, Melinda realizes that she would be a fool to turn down a proposal from an honorable, wealthy man like Crawford. After Johnny lets Crawford win a riding competition, Crawford, as the winner, crowns the woman of his choice the Queen of Love and Beauty. When the engagement between Crawford and Melinda is announced, her triumph seems complete to all in attendance. However, the reader knows that she still harbors feelings for Johnny. Therefore, once again, Settle reveals how financial pressures force individuals to make choices that go against their sense of right. As mentioned before, Johnny, in particular, becomes a victim of his own choices. His devoutly religious brother Lewis becomes an abolitionist, and thus incapable of managing the family business, even though he has always treated the slaves with less respect than his brother. Thus, Johnny honors his father's dying wishes and tries to maintain the family business and perpetuate the use of slave labor. In an interview, Settle addresses how the choices of people like Johnny have such tragic consequences: "In *Know Nothing* Johnny Catlett fails. He doesn't pay the price of freedom. The result is, and, God, this reverberates so, we have a Civil War.

In other words, that failure to pay was embodied in *Know Nothing* in one person's decision to when it was the decision of thousands."[47] Settle's achievement in historical fiction rests largely in her ability to make one character's choices representative of those of many individuals at that point in history.

With *The Scapegoat*, the fourth novel of the *Beulah Quintet*, Settle focuses on a coal miners' strike in 1912. With its intricate use of multiple points of view, this novel possesses a higher degree of technical complexity than the other works in the *Quintet*. The use of multiple perspectives seems appropriate to a narrative that portrays a situation about which so many characters disagree. As Rosenberg points out, "Eighteen different characters serve at least once as the narrative's central consciousness, or the viewpoint through which the third-person voice is filtered . . . . *The Scapegoat* is comprised less of a story or series of events than of a set of simultaneous, overlapping, but subtly different stories, none of which has any special claim to accuracy or reliability."[48] However, if there is a main character, it is probably Lily Lacey, the oldest of three daughters of the owner of the Seven Stars mine. She is a character who observes and interacts with the many diverse groups of people in the novel. Mining company executives meet at her home, she hears part of Mother Jones's speech to the women from the miners' community, and she has a romantic interest in Eduardo Pagano, an Italian immigrant. She is the daughter of a mine operator, but she is an aspiring suffragette, with socialist leanings.

As with the other novels, class issues pervade *The Scapegoat*, and friends and family take opposite sides on the key moral and political issues. The novel begins with an image of a Gatling gun on the porch of Beverley Lacey, Lily's father. The local miners have been forced into a tent colony as a result of a labor dispute. Mother Jones, the famous labor organizer, has arrived on the scene, as have some powerful out-of-state businessmen, whose companies own the neighboring mines. The Imperial corporation would like to buy Mr. Lacey's mine. Ten years earlier, in 1902, an agreement had been reached between the mine operators and the workers, but that was when the mines were almost all owned by local businessmen who knew the miners personally. "But all that ended when Imperial came, and nobody knew the owners anymore."[49] In this kind of tense environment, where, as one of the businessmen says, the issue is "greater than what's going on in one little valley in West Virginia,"[50] it is not surprising that the conflict escalates. One of the miners accidentally wounds one of the Baldwin detectives, a group of armed men hired to enforce the coal companies' will. The Baldwins turn the Italian families out of their company homes. Mother Jones leads a comical prayer meeting with the miners' wives to protest the use of scab workers. Eventually, the Baldwins kill one of the Italians, and as one of the characters recognizes, "nothing was ever going to be the same."[51] As she does in the previous novels in the *Quintet*, Settle takes us to the brink of a major conflict without depicting the conflict itself. In this case, she examines the events leading up to the Baldwin detectives firing machine guns into the miners' tent colonies.

The coal companies' strong-armed tactics and the miners' strike provide the context for the novel's commentary on class issues. Lily's father, Beverley Lacey, is an important character in this regard because he knows he is dying, and his passing will mark the demise of one of the last independent mine owners. As a neighbor of the miners, he strongly opposes the coal companies' practice of turning out striking miners from their homes. When he meets with the corporate executives, he refers to the miners as "my people" and says, "They have lived here many years."[52] The businessmen think he is too sentimental. Mr. Lacey feels his influence fading, and he realizes he is powerless to stop the eventual corporate control of the mining industry. He compares feebly with his powerful father, who "had opened a coalfield, made money and lost money, made decisions, used all his mental and physical muscles, been to war."[53] Old Man Lacey would have found a way to settle the strike. Beverley no longer has the money to take his family to Europe on vacation, and when his doctor diagnoses tuberculosis and advises him to seek further treatment in Cincinnati, the narrator reveals that Beverley "didn't have enough ready cash to go across the creek, much less Cincinnati."[54] With Imperial pressuring him to sell his mine, and his wife pressuring him to take the offer, the out-of-state corporate interests seem well on their way to controlling West Virginia's coal. As Beverley's longtime friend and sometime adversary Jake Catlett points out, Imperial can always just close Beverley's mine and thus break the union. In other words, more power rests with the corporate interests than with the local citizens.

However, with Mother Jones on the scene, it is unlikely that the miners will back down. Jones is another pivotal figure in the novel. By 1912, she had already earned her reputation as "The Angel of the Miners."[55] Jake Catlett recalls how in 1902 she stood in the creek to sign up miners for the UMW because waterways were in the public domain, and the creek banks were company land, "My God, he could still see her, that little old thing with the water in winter up to her ankles, and in the spring up to her knees, and her with her black skirt tucked up to the waist, showing the lace on her bloomers and not giving a tinker's dam."[56] She inspires the women in the tent colony to join the cause. Mother Jones's ability to inspire the courage to question authority is captured in this excerpt:

> Now I don't say nuthin' about your church as such. But it ain't your church. It's company church, you can't even use it to git berried from when there's a strike. It don't belong to God. It belongs to a company with a company Jesus. Why, I set in one of them churches and I seen sixteen hundred dollars of your money sent out to teach Chinese heathens about Jesus. Why, that company Jesus don't know more about you than a dawg does its father! Jesus never saw a penny of it and never will. You don't need company Jesus up this holler. You got the UNITED MINE WORKERS DISTRICT SEVENTEEN! QUIT YOUR BELLY-ACHIN'! ORGANIZE![57]

The next morning, she leads the women to the mine and holds a prayer meeting for the scab workers, asking God not to let them "git blowed up" or "mashed in the mine," "crushed and bleeding," with their "legs severed."[58] By the time she has finished, she has broken the wills of the replacement workers. Time and again, she shows the coal company and the Baldwin detectives that she has the ability to keep the union strong.

Some of the novel's strongest comments on gender involve masculinity and violence. In a conversation late in the book, Jake admits that his attempt to scare the Baldwins by firing at them was "a damned fool thing to do," and Beverley Lacey admits the same thing about setting a Gatling gun on his porch.[59] Many of the men's attempts to assert their power through a show of violence prove self-defeating and lack the imagination of some of Mother Jones's plots. When Dan Neill leads some of the Baldwin detectives into the tent colony one night to warn against public meetings, the men and the horses end up tangled in clothesline with Mother Jones mocking them. She says to Neill, "Well, Captain, you better git your pretty little butt out of here before these women take your jewelry."[60] The attempts to prove his masculinity lead to the senseless murder of an innocent Italian boy, Carlo Michele, the scapegoat of the title, and more violence becomes inevitable.

A key character in the portrayal of women's roles is Lily Lacey. A beneficiary of an affluent upbringing, including an education at Vassar, she desperately wants to change the world for the better. However, given her youth, some of her schemes amuse the reader. For example, she tries to improve the mind of the handsome Italian coal miner Eduardo Pagano, and insists that her intentions are pure, in spite of the physical attraction she feels. "She had long had the habit of luring him, not like a woman lures a man . . . , but as a Muse, for instance, would lure a poet, out of his feral shyness." She romanticizes Eduardo's physically demanding work. "She told herself about how exhausting manual labor was and resolved to experience it sometime."[61] Lily daydreams about becoming an important figure in the struggle for women's equality when she returns to New York. "She saw herself marching right down Fifth Avenue with Mrs. Belmont and Mrs. Peabody and Carrie Chapman Catt, carrying the banner. VOTES FOR WOMEN. LILY LACEY, huge red letters."[62] Desire to feel empathy for the miners and their families leads her to go inside a mine at night and to travel down to the tent colony in what she sees as a show of solidarity with the workers. Lily thinks she has found a role model in Mother Jones, after she sees the labor activist confront the most vicious of the Baldwin detectives: "Lily saw Florence Nightingale and Joan of Arc and herself in her visions standing there with the whole crowd of them reined in by her voice. Mother Jones was the Miners' Angel. Lily knew what it was to be in love."[63] Alas, the love is not reciprocated because later Mother Jones and many of the other characters make it clear that they see Lily as a spoiled rich girl. Indeed, there are many times when her hopes seem like idealistic dreams of grandeur.

And yet the reader who dismisses her as simply a naïve daughter of privilege risks overlooking some of her character strengths. In some ways, she serves as her father's conscience, calling the Imperial Land Company "bloated capitalists"[64] and ruffling his feathers by bringing a Eugene Debs pamphlet into the house. Her intentions, while overly romanticized, exemplify purity and principle. Her decision to volunteer as a nurse during World War I reveals a maturity that had eluded her as an adolescent idealist. Settle closes the novel with a moment of triumph for Lily, who decides to strike out on her own, accompanying Eduardo as he escapes the Baldwins. When he gets off at the train station in Covington, we see her pursuing the possibility of achieving her goal of making a difference in the world. "She couldn't worry about [Eduardo]. She was dropping away the miles behind her. She didn't know where he was going when he got off at Covington, but she knew at last where she was going. She leaned back and dreamed . . . . There was clarity in dreams, too. She dreamed, lulled by the train, of getting off at heaven or New York City, whichever she got to first."[65] It is fitting that the novel ends with Lily, a character who has observed and absorbed so many of the novel's key moments, a character who has grappled with issues of class and gender. At the end of the novel, Settle portrays a young woman who is capable of making her own decisions and of pursuing her own dreams.

Set during more contemporary times (1960-1980), the final novel of the *Quintet* focuses on the attempts of another woman to fight for her independence, while continually being pulled back to home and family and thus the obligations and expectations of the past. *The Killing Ground* depicts the attempts of a writer named Hannah McKarkle to make sense of the past, particularly the death of her brother in 1960. In the first section of the novel, set in 1978, Hannah, now a successful writer, returns home to deliver a lecture at a fundraiser. During her remarks, she reveals herself to be the author of the first four books of the *Quintet*. Thus, we experience a kind of metafiction, in which the narrator comments on the process of writing. Like Lily Lacey before her, Hannah has left home to pursue an independent lifestyle that was out of the norm for women of the time. (Interestingly, Hannah's mother is a Neill, and Dan Neill married Lily's sister, Althea.) However, with a vehemence that Lily could never have mustered, Hannah questions the upper-class society into which she was born and mocks the classism inherent in the affluent culture of Canona, Settle's fictional name for Charleston.

As previously mentioned, Hannah becomes fascinated with discovering an explanation for the murder of her brother, Johnny, who hits his head on an iron bench after being punched in a "drunk tank." Johnny is a tortured soul, and Hannah blames his death on their possessive mother and the expectations placed on Johnny as a member of the upper class. Their mother, Sally Brandon Neill McKarkle, had idolized her father, who had given her a glimpse of high society life before his eventual financial ruin and suicide. She tries to project her romanticized image of her father onto her son and thus seems to celebrate the young man's womanizing, perhaps because it means no one woman will become her rival. Hannah explains her brother and mother's relationship as follows: "Out of a fear of hurting Mother which they both thought of as love, he developed an insolent charm to please her and make her smile and say he was like her father, that ghostly dandy, Mother's model of a gentleman, who, she said, could have charmed the birds from the trees, and who had gone back to a Beulah he no longer owned in 1908, and blown his brains into the grass, and left Mother fourteen forever, inside the armor of her rigid body."[66] In his bedroom, Johnny pastes "photographs of a long history of girls that Mother would say proudly just ran after him like the girls after her papa."[67] One character suggests that Mrs. McKarkle approves of her son's drinking, "That way he stayed guilty and he stayed home."[68] Of course, in public he can only become romantically involved with rich women, who "are trotted before Johnny, with one thing in common, the smell of money."[69] However, most of the time it seems clear that she enjoys him staying single into his thirties, living at home, under her control.

Most of Hannah's own disagreements with her mother involve gender and class. While Hannah has moved to New York City to pursue a career as a writer, Mrs. McKarkle wishes her daughter would live up to the traditional expectations of a woman of her social class. In a way, the matriarch has warped both Hannah's and Johnny's attitudes toward sexuality, which they used as a "weapon to 'marry well,'" or for gratification in "secret rooms," as Hannah states, with lovers who "as our mother pointed out, didn't have our background."[70] Clearly, Hannah seeks more from a relationship than status or sex free of emotional intimacy, but these seem her only options in Canona. Her mother believes that an affluent upbringing demands Hannah's obedience: "We sent you to Sweet Briar. What more did you want? Running off to Europe. Staying up there in New York not doing a damn thing."[71] Mrs. McKarkle resents her daughter's independence and acts as if a woman who pursues her own dreams is behaving abnormally. After Johnny passes away, Hannah's mother orders her to not go back to New York and to live in Canona. "Come home where you are needed. There really is no reason for you not to. It isn't as if you were *married* . . . ."[72] When Hannah refuses to allow her mother to control her life and decides to leave home again, Mrs. McKarkle threatens to disown her. Ultimately, Hannah, like Johnny Church and Lily Lacey before her, decides that, as Settle said, "The price of freedom is to have everybody mad at you."[73]

The key to understanding *The Killing Ground*, and the entire *Beulah Quintet* for that matter, is Hannah's exploration of the motives of her brother's killer, a distant relative who has fallen upon hard financial times. The unintentional murderer is the younger Jake Catlett, son of his namesake in *The Scapegoat*. When Hannah questions Jake about his motives for delivering the fatal blow, she discovers a type of class resentment that has long nagged at the assailant. He tells Hannah, "You people make me sick. When you spit you hawk coal dust the same as us."[74] Jake talks about how the rich people relocated the country club after industrial fumes spread through the upper class community. "When you people came up and built that there golf club right in our faces, it was like them fancy cars was chasin' me right off my own doorstep. Not a covey on the place no more. Wouldn't even let us hunt squirrels on land we knowed every tree on. It wouldn't have been so bad if we didn't feel like we'd been plowed under like a bad crop."[75] Eventually, Hannah realizes that one's financial background does not determine a person's self-worth. Ultimately, she reflects upon her and Johnny's behavior and concludes that they had "strip-mined every stranger" that had shown them kindness.[76]

In each of the novels of the *Beulah Quintet* characters try to rise above the limitations of their situations. Some characters transcend their issues fleetingly, others more completely. Some of the characters' efforts to transcend their limiting situations end in tragedy. In *Prisons* Johnny Church becomes desperate to escape a culture in which the lower classes are exploited and briefly realizes a vision of a more equitable society by joining Oliver Cromwell's army until becoming a victim of Cromwell's ambitions and the firing squad. Unlike Johnny Church, Jonathan Lacey in *O Beulah Land* transcends all of the threats to his ambitions and realizes his dream of establishing a new community located in what would become West Virginia, in which liberty and the pursuit of happiness become possible. Hannah Catlett also transcends her limiting situation, surviving abject poverty and a dangerous trek through the wilderness and ultimately see her son marry into Jonathan Lacey's family. In *Know Nothing* Melinda Lacey rises above the limitations of poverty and wins the hand of the wealthy Crawford Kregg, though she does not marry the man she loves, Johnny Catlett. The character who makes tragic choices in the novel, Johnny tragically does not follow his heart and declare his love for Melinda and makes the even more tragic decision to obey his father's wishes and perpetuate slavery on his land. In *The Scapegoat* Lily Lacey rises above the limitations placed upon a woman of her time, even one of the upper classes, by making a difference as a nurse during World War I. Finally, in *The Killing Ground* Hannah McKarkle escapes her mother's attempts to control her life, in a way that her brother Johnny was not able to do. Hannah becomes a successful writer and avoids becoming the traditional woman her mother wanted her to be. These novels all show that individuals must make difficult decisions if they are to rise above the limitations of their situations.

In his book *Understanding Mary Lee Settle*, George Garrett offers the following summation of the themes of the *Beulah Quintet*. Among them, he names "the never-ending conflict between liberal conscience, the youthful dream of liberty, and the power of authority," and he points out that "those who are wicked and unworthy (to one degree or another) are those who are cruel or over privileged and too comfortable or too weak to hold any serious beliefs."[77] In *The Killing Ground* an independent woman discovers that she does not need the approval of the upper class society to become fulfilled. Ultimately, Hannah chooses to follow her conscience and reject her parents' worldview. In doing so, she discovers the connection between herself and the previous generations. "Finally, I knew that I had joined the wanderers, from Johnny Church, through the old Hannah, lost in the woods below, Jonathan Lacey who had brought us there, Johnny Catlett, Carlo Michele, Eduardo Pagano, and Lily; all of those who have set out alone, perhaps self-deluded by necessity." Hannah concludes with a statement that encapsulates Settle's belief about the nature and value of life in a democracy: "Deep within us there had been instilled an itch, a discontent, an unfulfilled promise, perpetually demanding that it be kept. Johnny and Thankful, and all of us, would always fail and always win, and eternal vigilance and our sense of loss, of being unblessed, were the price of freedom."[78] Just as Hannah rejects the class snobbery of her parents, so does Settle seem to believe that the truly worthy individuals are those who work to maintain the possibility of personal liberty for everyone. In breathtaking scope, the *Beulah Quintet* explores the insistence upon freedom and self-reliance that are central to West Virginia's identity.

CHAPTER 3

Breece D'J Pancake's
Short Fiction

The Stories of Breece D'J Pancake is the one of the most influential books in the history of West Virginia literature. Irene McKinney and Pinckney Benedict have both credited Pancake with making it possible for West Virginia writers to write more freely about the dark side of the state's economic challenges, the desperation of poverty, and the search for validation in the depths of hardship. Upon its publication in 1983, the collection received an enthusiastic critical response. As Albert E. Wilhelm points out, "The thin volume was reviewed (almost always favorably) in over one hundred journals and newspapers . . . ."[1] Pancake biographer Thomas E. Douglass has summarized what the critics praised about the book: "Reviewers uniformly praised Pancake for his artistry, his ability to unify sharply honed sensory detail, his talent for making sound and meaning converge, his imagery, dialogue, and his fine sense of drama. They noted the tremendous emotional compression and the stories and the minimalist style which begged comparison with Raymond Carver. . . ."[2] The book earned the praise of some of the biggest names in contemporary fiction. "This is an exceptional voice," wrote Margaret Atwood, "gritty, mordant, invested with the texture of stroked reality; urgent and haunting."[3] On the book jacket, Jayne Anne Phillips calls the book an "American *Dubliners*" adding, "We find here a landscape preserved in rich sadness because it is forgotten, a people whose lives are informed by loss, wrenching cruelty, and the luminous dignity which marks the endurance of all that is most human."

Sadly, Pancake's tragic life story threatens to overshadow his literary accomplishment. A native of Milton, West Virginia, he was working on a Master's degree at the University of Virginia at the beginning what promised to be an impressive career as a writer, when the prestigious *Atlantic Monthly* accepted two of his stories. When the story "Trilobites" was published, Phoebe-Lou Adams, an *Atlantic Monthly* editor, said, "In thirty some years at *The Atlantic* I cannot recall a response to a new writer like the response to this one. Letters drifted in for months asking for more stories . . . ."[4] Always hard on himself, battling a sense of inferiority, Pancake did not seem to recognize or find solace in his budding talent. His mentor at the University of Virginia, John Casey said, "Breece didn't know how good he was; he didn't know how much he knew; he didn't know that he was a swan instead of an ugly duckling."[5] After losing his father to multiple sclerosis and a friend to a car accident within a three-week period after his fiancée broke off their engagement, Pancake committed suicide in 1979, at the age of twenty-six. At a memorial service, Father Pat O'Connor warned that dwelling on his loss would "make Breece's death larger than his life.'"[6] Pancake's mother and Casey were determined to make his fiction his legacy. They shopped his stories around to literary magazines in hopes of publishing a collection of his short fiction. The collection is Pancake's only book, but it established him as a true talent.

The stories display a style that was mature beyond Pancake's years. They feature a compact, descriptive prose that renders a sense of place succinctly and vividly. They also present main characters who truly embody Faulkner's maxim about depicting "the human heart in conflict with itself." Pancake's protagonists lead desperate lives, trying to convince themselves that some kind of fulfillment is possible, while almost always falling short of their dreams. As Douglass has pointed out, "What one first notices in a Pancake story is the careful attention to concrete detail but underneath lies the drama of the story where he works the extremes of internal experience."[7] Pancake was writing at a time when West Virginia's economy was in dire straits, and so his main characters often battle a sense of diminished self-worth that is related to poverty. To compensate for feelings of inferiority, they often try to take bold action, usually in the form of some kind of misguided male bravado, only to realize how far away true fulfillment really is. The collection marks one of the most impressive debuts in Appalachian literary history.

Pancake's stories brought attention to literature of the region. Douglass has described the impact of the book: "Nominated for a Pulitzer and a Weatherford Award, *The Stories of Breece D'J Pancake* announced a revival in regional interest, and its publication focused national attention on an unusually large number of emerging writers from Appalachia . . . ."[8] In an interview with Jeff

Mann, Irene McKinney spoke about Pancake's importance to other West Virginia writers in terms of providing a model of how to write about the region:

> . . . that's a very basic lack which we all had. When I teach Appalachian lit, one of the things I try to emphasize about Breece Pancake is that he invented this place. As far as I'm concerned, that's the first real fictional voice that showed us the struggles of poor, rural West Virginians, by someone who'd grown up there . . . . [W]hat he finally won through to was claiming a literary space that hadn't been claimed before. And I remember feeling that lack [of role models] very much when I was growing up, especially when I first started writing seriously. I remember talking to Maggie Anderson and Jayne Anne Phillips about that, about who do we look to, who came before us.[9]

Like other writers, McKinney had never encountered anyone who wrote about West Virginia like Breece Pancake did. In interviews with Thomas E. Douglass, Denise Giardina says that "Pancake made a big impact on me,"[10] and Pinckney Benedict acknowledges how Pancake freed him to write about West Virginia: "I do owe a great deal to Breece Pancake. I had discovered his work when I was a freshman at Princeton University. His work to me was like a homecoming. His stories were a return to some places I knew about . . . . So my stories, similarly, were a way for me to return imaginatively to these places."[11] Of all West Virginia writers, Pancake probably influenced Benedict the most. In addition to helping him find his voice, Benedict credits Pancake with helping battle homesickness while at Princeton: "So I owe him a great deal spiritually, and his stories were literally an inspiration to me . . . ."[12] Clearly, in terms of subject matter, theme, and style, the publication of Pancake's collection marked a turning point in West Virginia literary history.

Like Jayne Anne Phillips and Irene McKinney, Pancake writes about the tension between staying in West Virginia and leaving the region for better opportunities. This is an important theme in several of his greatest stories—for example, "Trilobites," "Fox Hunters," "In the Dry," "The Honored Dead," and "The Salvation of Me." The resolution of the "should I stay or should I go" theme is never simple. The characters in Pancake's work can never solve their problems just by changing their location. Place and problems may be interwoven, but the answer is never as simple as either leaving or returning home.

In terms of the theme of gender, Breece Pancake's work focuses on masculinity—in particular the kind of Appalachian male who finds his manhood in some way questioned and who tries to compensate for feelings of inadequacy. Often in Pancake's fiction, the main character indulges in self-defeating behavior. Among the stories involving males who have no immediate solution for their problems, we find three main categories: those who have no immediate chance of rising above their current situation and who have lost much of their dignity, those who have no immediate chance of rising above their current situation but who do maintain a measure of dignity, and those with some hope of transcending the limitations of their situations.

In the first category, men with little hope and a loss of dignity, Buddy from the story "Hollow" best exemplifies a character who lacks any chance of rising above his current status and possesses little individual dignity. To a large extent, Buddy feels oppressed by his poverty and believes that a little money can solve all his problems. To compensate for his economic struggles, he tries to assert his masculinity through violence and aggression, but he moves from one senseless, wasted effort to another. At the beginning of the story, as Buddy and his coworkers work the coal in what proves to be a small-time mining operation, Pancake introduces Buddy's antagonist, Fuller. During a break, Fuller demeans Buddy's girlfriend, asking, "Is Sally goin' back to whorin'?"[13] From that point on, Buddy is determined to fight, challenging Fuller to meet him at a local bar later that night. The reader begins to see that most of Buddy's personal issues revolve around his sense of inferiority as a member of the lower class. For example, he feels that Fuller has gained a sense of empowerment because he recently acquired a car. When Buddy walks home to the trailer, he remembers how he has hated Fuller since childhood for calling him a ridge runner. Thus, from the first pages of the story, we see that Buddy's sense of inadequacy comes from his belief that his lack of self-worth is related to his lack of financial worth. We also see that he tries to compensate for his lower-class social standing by resorting to physical violence or the threat of physical violence.

This pattern of using violence to compensate for a feeling of inferiority continues when he goes home to his trailer. "Sally sat by the window, looking, waiting, but he knew it was not for him." She has prepared dinner for him, and almost instantly, the conversation becomes tense as Buddy looks in the pot on the stove and asks, "No meat?"[14] A moment later, he tells Sally that he thinks his financial situation is about to improve, and she responds with skepticism:

"They's gonna be money, Sal."

"Don't start up. They's al's *gonna*, but they ain't never any."

"This time's for sure. Estep an' me, we worked that stuff today. A D-9 dozer
an' steamshovel'd a-fixed us real quick. Curt's got the deed an' all."

"Thought yer folks settled these here ridges."

He remembered standing in the sun at a funeral—he could not say whose,
but the scent of Vitalis from his father's hands had turned his stomach,
and his new shoes pinched his feet.

"Never had a pot to piss in, neither. Stick 'round, Sal."

With her fork, Sally drew lazy curves in her bean-soup, and shook her head.
"Na I'm tired of livin' on talk."

"This ain't talk. What made ya stay with me this long?"

"Talk."

"Love? Love ain't talk."

"Whore's talk," she said.

His hand flashed across the table, knocking her head askance, and she flushed.
She got up slowly, put her plate in the sink, and walked down the hall to
the bedroom.[15]

In this scene, we see the pattern that Buddy repeats throughout the story. As Douglass has written about the protagonists in Pancake's work, "The emotional descent of his characters is like a deep echo and each echo suggests a farther fall."[16] Buddy's poverty makes him feel diminished as a human being, and he responds by asserting his masculinity through physical violence. Each act of violence serves no real purpose, and at its worst becomes self-defeating. In this case, he is trying to convince Sally to stay with him, and when she mocks the idea that their relationship is based on love not sex, he hits her.

Buddy's violent tendencies again are revealed in the next scene after Sally has left him in the kitchen. His dog Lindy is in heat, and a number of male dogs are circling and climbing underneath the trailer. The symbolism is clear. The dogs coming around the trailer symbolize the men that Buddy fears are pursuing Sally. He grabs his rifle and shoots one of the dogs. "The dogs scattered into the brush beyond the road, leaving the thrashing spitz to die in the yard."[17] It seems unlikely that killing one of the dogs will solve the problem, but Buddy gains a sense of superiority by engaging in a violent act. However, the senseless killing of a defenseless animal, in some ways, helps define Buddy's character. Later in the story, Buddy kills a doe, and when he dresses the deer, he discovers a fetus inside. Pancake uses the destruction of the unborn deer to underscore the unnecessary violence inherent in Buddy's character. Albert Wilhelm points out how "Buddy has been guilty of hunting out of season" and then adds, "Through his untimely killing of the doe, Buddy not only ends an individual life but also destroys the potential for future life."[18] In Appalachian literature, violence is used in one of two ways. It can establish a character's strength, physically and morally, when violence is necessary. However, it can also reveal how unprincipled characters use violence as a way of feeling superior to other humans or creatures. In Buddy's case, his use of violence calls into question his moral character and reveals him to be a person who tries to repair his self-image by hurting others.

Another story that presents a man who expresses himself through violence is the narrator of "Time and Again," an older man who drives a snowplow to clear the highway. One night, he picks up a hitchhiker, a young man who reminds the narrator of his son who has disappeared. The young man talks about how a number of hitchhikers have been killed along Route 60, and the reader begins to suspect the narrator of violent tendencies because of something he says when he first climbs into his vehicle: "The lug wrench is where it has always been beside my seat."[19] This sentence, placed in the middle of the story's third paragraph, seems out of place until the young man provides the context of the murdered hitchhikers. During the course of their conversation, the narrator talks about the snow in France in 1944 and about how his unit took a farmhouse without firing a shot. When the hitchhiker asks, "Did you knife them?" the snowplow driver's response is haunting: "'Snapped their necks,' I say, and I see my man tumble into the sty. People die so easy"[20] The last line, "People die so easy," reveals him to be the killer of the hitchhikers, but he decides not to kill the young man, probably because of several similarities with the narrator's son.

Douglass explores whether the sparing of the young man's life constitutes redemption and considers the story from two possible perspectives. Douglass correctly states that ". . . the redemption sought by the man who drives the snowplow along Route 60 in 'Time and Again' turns out to be only a temporary stay of anguish and psychosis."[21] However, Douglass later adds, "It is a kind of redemption, a payment of dues, that he refrains from killing the young hitchhiker (although he would dearly love to) for the sake of his son and for a memory of the past."[22] Douglass makes an interesting point, but I think his first statement is more accurate because of what the narrator says when he decides not to murder the young man. He asks the hitchhiker to search under the seat for a flashlight, presumably as a prelude to killing him with the lug wrench. Then he says of the young man, "He bends forward, grabbing under the seat, and his head is turned from me. But I am way too tired now, and I don't want to clean the seat."[23] Therefore, this statement suggests that the desire to avoid the messy task of cleaning the seat, not "a kind of redemption" that spares the young man his life.

Some of Pancake's critics have voiced concern about his portrayal of lower class Appalachians. For example, in writing about Pancake and Pinckney Benedict, Angela B. Freeman argues that reviewers of the two writers' work from outside the region develop distorted perceptions of Appalachia. She writes, "These authors are not blasphemous in their depictions of the state; however I was unprepared to discover that, in the minds of most literary critics, their fiction serves to reaffirm only negative impressions about West Virginia."[24] Freeman points out how Joyce Carol Oates, writing in *The New York Times*, made an uncharitable comment about Pancake's male characters. "It goes without saying that they drink a good deal and are brutal to women, including their wives." Indeed, one can find reviews, like the one in *Publisher's Weekly*, that treat West Virginia as if it were a remote, underdeveloped nation: "The world he writes of is the harsh lonely one of mountain hollows, coal mining, hard living, desperation. . . ."[25] However, if such distortions appear in the reviews of the works of Appalachian writers, that is the fault of the reviewers, not the authors, and since most reviews appreciate the realism of Pancake's portrayal of poor West Virginians, the state is richer for his fiction. Douglass quotes Denise Giardina on the necessity for an author to present a positive portrayal of a region: "There's no responsibility to put the best face on everything . . . . That's not the writer's job. The only responsibility I have is to tell a story the best way I can."[26] Unconcerned with whether his depictions of West Virginia appeal to every reader's sensibility, Breece Pancake demonstrates the same commitment to the integrity of his art.

However, as we will see, many of Pancake's protagonists do achieve a measure of dignity. Critics have compared Pancake's work to that of Flannery O'Connor, especially in its depiction of lower class characters. In her work, O'Connor often satirizes the ignorance and inconsideration of poor rural characters in stories that feature a wicked sense of humor. In a review of Pancake's collection, John Domini wrote that "the subject matter smacks of Flannery O'Connor, her half-mad families trapped by the ultimatums of time, place, and morality."[27] However, while the subject matter might have some occasional parallels, the two authors' tones differ greatly, with O'Connor by far the more comic of the two. Still, the comparison with O'Connor offers one helpful parallel. Since both writers sometimes use violence as a way of revealing character, O'Connor's comment in *Mystery and Manners* suggests a way of approaching Pancake's work. "I suppose the reasons for the use of so much violence in modern fiction will differ with each writer who uses it, but in my own stories I have found that violence is strongly capable of returning my characters to reality and preparing them to accept their moment of grace. Their heads are so hard that nothing else will do the work."[28] In the following sections, we will see how some of Pancake's characters experience "moments of grace," brief instances of time in which they momentarily transcend their difficult situations.

In this second category of masculinity, men with little hope but some dignity, the male characters find themselves in desperate situations with little hope of escaping their problems, but who nonetheless possess some degree of dignity. Douglass links the characters' hope of dignity with stories that are "more open-ended," suggesting that while the protagonists cannot resolve all of their issues in the short story format, they imply "an imaginative search for some sort of resolution that promises either escape or moral affirmation."[29] One character who engages on such a search and who best exemplifies this category of males in seemingly inescapable situations, but who achieve some measure of dignity is Skeevy from "The Scrapper." Unlike Buddy in "Hollow," Skeevy reveals that he possesses a conscience from the beginning of the story. He remembers how he awoke from a bad dream about a fight, "too much like the real fight with Bund, and he wondered if he had really tried to kill his best friend."[30] After Skeevy's mother had begged him to promise to curtail the violence, saying, "Don't never hurt nobody again," he promised to try to honor her wishes. He rises from bed, careful not to wake his girlfriend, Trudy, and goes into the town of Clayton to a diner that "still smelled of sweat and blood from the fight the night before."[31] The fight, pitting men of Clayton against those of nearby Purserville, had spilled into a church, where an old deacon, "sweeping bottles from between the pews," tells Skeevy, "Ain't right, drinkin' in a church."[32] Clearly, this is a community in which violence offers men a chance to assert their masculinity.

Skeevy's relationship with Trudy reveals how he considers it a surrender of his masculine control to develop an emotional attachment with her; again we see that he is only comfortable expressing himself physically. At the beginning of the story, Pancake writes, "He felt empty talking to her, and did not want to be there when she woke up."[33] Later, at the diner, Trudy teases him about sneaking away from her that morning: "You don't show me no respect. Just up an' leave without a good-mornin' kiss." In response, Skeevy turns even the idea of respect into physical expression. "I bet you respect real good. I'd respect you till you couldn't walk."[34] In their conversation, a pattern emerges in which she alludes to an emotional attachment between them, her desire for respect, and he shifts the conversation to the physical realm. He continues this pattern later during a conversation when they talk about what they might do with the $200 he will win in a fight:

"You reckon that money would do for a weddin'?" she asked.
"Maybe," he said. "We'll think on it."
They ate.
"Did I ever tell you 'bout the time me an' Bund wrecked the Sunflower Inn?"
"Yeah."
"Oh."[35]

Through this brief conversation, Pancake masterfully establishes the essential truths about these characters' relationship: she longs for an emotional attachment, and he is more comfortable with physical expression.

The extent of the violence among the men in this impoverished community becomes clearer when Skeevy volunteers to sell liquor at a local cockfight for his friend Tom Corey. Apparently, during the fight the night before, Corey had taken a club to Jim Gibson from Purserville. Gibson is looking for revenge. Corey proposes that Skeevy "stand in" for him and fight Jim Gibson for him. Immediately, Skeevy recalls the promise he made his mother, a promise he has not revealed to anyone because "he knew they would laugh."[36] It is interesting to note how Skeevy's lower class socio-economic status becomes the main factor in his decision to fight Gibson. First of all, Skeevy needs the $200 Corey offers him to box Gibson, hoping to send the money to Bund for medical expenses. However, one of the greatest indications of Skeevy's sense of class inferiority can be seen in his interactions with Cally, the beautiful young college student whose father, Jeb Simpkin, is hosting the cockfights. Here is Skeevy's description of her:

He had heard Jeb talk of her at work and knew she had been to college in Huntington; he believed Trudy when she said college girls were all looking for rich boys. He watched her clomp down the steps in chunky wooden shoes, and as she crossed the yard between them, he saw how everything from the curve of her hair to the fit of her jeans was just too perfect. She looked like the girls he had seen in *Playboy*, and he knew even if she stood beside him, he couldn't have her.[37]

Given that he is asked to fight Gibson in front of Cally, it seems likely that Skeevy is trying to compensate for his socio-economic discomfort with a masculine willingness to throw punches.

Skeevy's class inferiority results not just from the knowledge that Cally is out of his league, but also from his ignorance of university life. Cally mentions how she has heard that Skeevy is related to Machine Gun Kelly, a relative of whom Skeevy seems ashamed. However, the next part of his conversation further decreases his sense of self-worth:

"I thought you might know something. I'm doing a paper on him for Psych."
"Say what?"
"A paper for Psychology."
Skeevy wondered if she collected maniacs the way men collect gamecocks.[38]

Later, on the day of the fight with Gibson, Skeevy's resentment of superior college students grows when he sees Cally with a "longhair." He begins to feel that Cally and her friend view him as some kind of circus freak. At one point, ". . . the longhair took a picture of Skeevy, and Skeevy wanted to kill him."[39] In each of these scenes, Skeevy feels diminished by his interactions with people he assumes are superior to him socio-economically. As a result, he tries to compensate through physical toughness.

In a case of situational irony, the fight with Gibson threatens to mock Skeevy's hopes of asserting his masculinity. Skeevy's strategy—to dodge Gibson's punches until his opponent weakens by "punching himself out"—is thwarted by an apparent plot to give Gibson an unfair advantage. The entire fight is described succinctly, in less than a page. The effectiveness of Skeevy's strategy and the proof that the fight is fixed are revealed in a few sentences: "Skeevy tried to go low for the sagging belly, made heavy contact twice, but was disappointed to see the results. He danced some more, dodging haymakers, knowing Gibson could only strike thin air a number of times before weakening. When he saw the time come, he sighted on the man's bruised temple, caught it with a left hook, and dropped him. Then came the bell."[40] The reader understands that the person ringing the bell has plotted not to end the round as long as Gibson has the upper hand, but as soon as Skeevy gains the momentum, the bell sounds, ending the round and providing Gibson with an opportunity to rest and recover from Skeevy's punches.

At the end of the story, as we begin to see that Skeevy will lose the fight, he does capture a measure of dignity. He remains faithful to his code of behavior, which holds that a true man will not accept defeat even when it seems as if he has been beaten. When the second round begins, Skeevy initially seems determined that he can maintain the momentum in the fight. As Gibson breaks his jaw, Skeevy thinks about how he wants "to tear the eye out and step on it." Then, in the story's conclusion, even after Gibson knocks him down, Skeevy's mind flashes back to when he beat up his friend Bund, but Skeevy remains determined:

> As he went down he could hear Trudy screaming his name above the cheers. He lay for a time on the cold floor of the Sunflower Inn: the jukebox played, and he heard Bund coughing.
> He rolled to his side.
> Cephus threw water on Skeevy, and he spat out the bitten-off tip of his tongue. Gibson waited as Skeevy raised himself to a squat. His head cleared, and he knew he could get up.[41]

In some ways, the decision to fight Gibson seems self-defeating. After all, it is not Skeevy's fight; he accepts because he needs the $200. However, if we consider the story a different way, Skeevy has managed a moral victory by revealing his toughness during the fight. And returning to Flannery O'Connor's concept of a "moment of grace," we see that at least for a brief instant Skeevy achieves a measure of dignity.

The story "In the Dry" features another male character whose life offers little hope, but who does achieve a kind of "moment of grace" at the story's end. The main character of "In the Dry," an independent trucker named Ottie, returns to West Virginia to visit one of his former foster homes. Shelia Gerlock and her mother seem happy to see him, but Old Man Gerlock clearly is not, calling Ottie "a murderous devil" at one point in the story.[42] Personal tragedy darkens his history with the Gerlock family, for Ottie was injured in an automobile accident with Shelia's cousin, Bus, whom the accident turned into an invalid. Mr. Gerlock blames Ottie for the accident and keeps asking him if he can remember details from the car wreck. The relationships are further complicated by the jealousy Bus felt for Ottie years ago for "a day forgotten" when Shelia hugged Ottie by the fishing hole. Ottie quickly summarizes what he remembers about the day of the accident: "Just me and Shelia fishing and Bus coming to say he wants me to ride with him and listen for a noise."[43]

However, that fateful day destroyed any semblance of family happiness and scarred Ottie physically and psychologically. After he arrives at the Gerlock home, he freshens up and looks at himself in the mirror. "Combing out his hair, he sees how thin it has gone, how his jaw caves in where teeth are missing. He stares at the knotted purple glow along the curve of his jaw—the wreck-scar—and knows what the Gerlocks will think, wonders why it matters. No breaks are his; no breaks for foster kids, for scab truckers."[44] Ottie has entertained the notion of leaving the road and working in Chicago rebuilding trucks—and of asking Shelia to come live with him. "He has half hoped, kept the hope just a picture of thought, a thought of sending Shelia the fare and working regular hours. Now he puts it away, seeing too soon how dim it gets." Ottie realizes how Shelia has grown unhappy with age: "Now he sees her an old maid in a little town, and knows her bitterness."[45] Toward the end of the story, he rejects her and the Gerlock family as incapable of coming to terms with the past and ever giving him his due. He leaves in the middle of the night.

As Douglass has pointed out, the description of the landscape and the use of biblical allusion give the story a mythic quality. At the beginning of the story, as he is driving his truck, Ottie notices the seemingly impossible dryness of the land, given that it is summer: "Jolting along the Pike, he looks at withered fields, corn tassling out at three feet, the high places worse with yellowish leaves. August seems too early for the hills to rust with dying trees, early for embankments to show patches of pale clay between milkweed and thistle. All is ripe for fire."[46] Douglass has aptly shown how the story "reminds us of the mythic wasteland,"[47] and indeed the line "all is ripe for fire" suggests a need for redemption. At one point, Mr. Gerlock reads from the gospel of Luke: "For if they do these things in a green tree, what shall be done in the dry?"[48] The landscape, so clearly "in the dry," reflects the need for some kind of salvation. However, Ottie recognizes that Mr. Gerlock, incapable of forgiving Ottie for some imagined wrong, is the wrong messenger for such an apocalyptic text, as Ottie "hears false power in the preacher's voice."[49] Mr. Gerlock may think that redemption is imminent, but his inability to come to terms with the past keeps any hope of redemption far away. The Gerlock family's refusal to accept Ottie as an equal negates all hope of happiness and necessitates his departure.

Ottie's moment of grace comes not only when he leaves at the end of the story, but also when he allows Mr. Gerlock to persist in believing that Bus is innocent and Ottie is guilty in the car accident. What Mr. Gerlock does not know is that Bus' resentment of Ottie reached unspeakable levels. Years ago, Bus vowed, "I'll show you something" and killed Ottie's dog Beagle, and as Douglass has shown, "The 'pink-lipped wound in one dimple of Beagle's chest' hints at Ottie's deeper wound of rejection and lovelessness, and, since his return to the Gerlock farm, he becomes aware that the wound has not healed and the drought of love and life will continue . . . ."[50] Out of jealousy about Ottie's relationship with Shelia, Bus again had vowed to show Ottie something by slamming his rival's side of the car into the railings of the bridge. "He saw Bus's face go stiff to fight, saw the sneer before that hand twisted the wheel a full turn and metal scraped and warped against bridge sides."[51] Ottie earns a measure of dignity by not telling the old man the truth about Bus. Furthermore, he resists the loveless, sexual temptations of Shelia and the even greater temptation of having to be seen as in the right. His restraint redeems him and allows him to escape the deceit and falsehood that corrupt the Gerlocks.

The male characters in the final category, males who possess both hope and dignity, also face tribulation. However, they manage to demonstrate not only some dignity for themselves, but also create a sense of hope for themselves somewhere in the future. These characters possess a moral center that Buddy in "Hollow" lacks and a sense that better days lie ahead for them, not immediately but in the foreseeable future. This section will focus on two characters from two of Pancake's most accomplished stories: Colly in "Trilobites" and Bo in "Fox Hunters."

Colly's issues in "Trilobites" involve his perceived failures in masculinity, related to his four biggest concerns: the recent death of his father; Colly's sense of inadequacy in running the family farm; his uncertainty about what to do after his mother sells their land and moves to Ohio; and his lingering romantic feelings for his ex-girlfriend Ginny, who has moved to Florida. "Trilobites" is a story about the common Appalachian inner conflict: whether to stay in the place one calls home or leave the region in search of better opportunities. Colly feels an extraordinary connection to the local area. With his interest in geology, he understands how the land has evolved over time, and he has spent time looking for trilobites, or fossils of extinct marine arthropods. As Geoffrey Galt Harpham has suggested, "Trilobites become a synecdoche for a pastness, which, if he could apprehend, would make the present possible."[51] Instead, like the trilobites, Colly seems frozen in time. In the first paragraph of the story, he says, "I was born in this country and I have never much wanted to leave." However, he both envies and resents Ginny for fulfilling what had once been their dream—to go to Florida. Colly had written in Ginny's yearbook: "We will live on mangoes and love."[52] While understanding why she left, Colly at some level clearly feels abandoned by her. The reader sees early in the story that Colly feels a connection to the land that Ginny does not, perhaps because he feels he owes it to himself and to his father's memory to try to keep the family farm in operation.

Colly feels that his masculinity has been called into question by the death of his father. It is clear that Colly worries about whether he can prove himself to be the man his father was. Pancake underscores the protagonist's concerns with a depiction of the land as remarkably barren, as critics have noted. Harpham wrote of Pancake's collection, "The barrenness of the land is a state of mind in these stories, an all pervasive fact."[53] Colly internalizes the failure of the land to produce and thinks of it as his own failure to live up to his father's agricultural achievements. As Douglass has pointed out, ". . . Colly's inability as a farmer is exacerbated by a blighted, dry, and infertile landscape . . ."[54] At one point, Colly drives the tractor around the farm to take stock of the situation. He notices the spot where he had discovered his father's dead body. He winds up at the locust post that his father used to mark the property line. Colly says to himself, "I'm just no good at it . . . . It just don't do to work your ass off at something you're not good at."[55] In addition to feeling less adequate as a farmer, Colly also feels inferior about the level of adventure his father experienced—his "hobo and soldier days." His father had been wounded in World War II and had ridden the trains to Michigan as a hobo. Clearly, Colly feels as though his father has lived life more fully, and this adds to his feelings of inadequacy. Part of Colly's incentive for leaving the region is that his father experienced the excitement of life away from home, something Colly has not known. However, Colly also admires how out of all the people who left the region, "only Jim [Colly's father's best friend] and Pop came back to the land, worked it."[56] The result of all this is that Colly, like many characters in Appalachian literature, is genuinely torn about whether to leave the region. This is an important theme for Pancake. Douglass has eloquently explained how Pancake creates the protagonists' dilemmas in his fiction. "Characters are held tightly in place, haunted by the ghost of the father and/or other ancestors, which in this instance irrevocably chain Colly to family and the past where he cannot escape the 'dead eyes' that remind him of guilt, grief, and his own future mortality."[57] Clearly, Colly seems trapped between the memories of what he knew when his father was living and an uncertain future after his death.

In contrast with his feelings of respect for his father, Colly resents his mother for being "on the warpath to sell the farm."[58] In some ways, his mother's resolve gives an air of finality to Colly's inability to make the land produce: If there's no farm left, he must have failed. However, Colly may resent her most for not feeling a connection to the land. It is difficult not to see selling a family farm to make way for a housing development as a way of "cashing in," and clearly Colly has fonder memories of his home than his mother does. She dreams of selling the land and moving to Akron, where some of her family live. A potentially pleasant conversation turns into a tense encounter. When they share a laugh about his father's playful use of language, Colly clearly resents her note of sentimental finality after she recalls her husband's linguistic approximations:

> "He had some funny names all right. Called a tomcat a 'pussyscat.'"
> I think back. "Cornflakes were 'pone-rakes,' and a chicken was a 'sick-un.'"
> We laugh.
> "Well," she says, "he'll always be a part of us."
> The glommy paint on the chair arm packs under my fingernails. I think how
> she could foul up a free lunch . . . .
> "I ain't going to live in Akron," I say.[59]

Colly regrets his comment when he hears his mother crying. He realizes that this is the first time he has talked back to her.[60] Clearly, he resents what he sees as his mother's insensitivity to his father's memory and Colly's connection to the place.

Colly's attempts to preserve, or at least understand, the past undergo another setback when he realizes that he has grown more distant from his exgirlfriend, Ginny, than ever before. Romanticizing his past with her, he fails to realize that she has moved on. He even resents the way she has lost her Appalachian accent. When he first talks with her when she comes home, he says, "I wanted to tell her Pop had died and Mom was on the warpath to sell the farm, but Ginny was talking through her beak. It gave me the creeps."[61] Later in the story when they go for a drive together, Colly again notices how she has changed. "She looks different. I've never seen these clothes, and she wears too much jewelry." When Ginny suggests, "Let's park for old times' sake,"[62] the evening takes a downward turn. When they go to the depot, he points out her family home, and she stares at him in recognition that he has looked at her home many times and is truly living in the past. Ultimately, Colly realizes that Ginny no longer has romantic feelings for him, and he angrily decides to have sex with her. "She isn't making love, she's getting laid. All right, I think, all right. Get laid."[63] As Douglass has pointed out, "When love is unavailable [in Pancake's stories], relationships become sexually lurid, forbidden, animalistic, driven by physical domination and/or possession and reduced to appetite."[64] Annoyed by his sullenness and his insensitivity, Ginny abandons him at the depot. This turns out to be the proper place for Colly to be because as a train flies past, he realizes that hopping a train like his father once did is no longer a possibility: "I watch her [the train] beat by. She's just too fast to jump. Plain and simple."[65]

In some ways, it would seem that Colly has been defeated by the action in the story. His mother has decided to sell the farm; Colly's connection with Ginny has been severed. However, contained in the conclusion of the story is the suggestion that Colly will survive. "I get up. I'll spend tonight at home. I've got eyes to shut in Michigan—maybe even Germany or China, I don't know yet. I walk, but I'm not scared. I feel my fear moving away in rings through time for a million years."[66] The tone is hopeful, and Colly seems to possess the strength of character that will help him find a better path. For the short term, the future is uncertain, but unlike Skeevy in "The Scrapper," Colly has a more promising future.

Bo, the main character of "Fox Hunters," faces much adversity during the course of the story. Like Colly, Bo has lost his father, but the circumstances of his home life make his life much bleaker than Colly's. His mother seems to have given up after the death of Bo's father in a mining accident. "The doctor told her to rest eight years ago, when her husband died. Miner's insurance paid her to rest until the rest sapped her strength."[67] Bo does the cooking and works at Enoch's garage. His mother offers him little but a sense of responsibility, for Bo takes care of her while she rests. Unfortunately for Bo, he is ostracized by many people in the town. His only friend is Lucy, an older woman who runs a diner and a boarding house. When he complains, "Nobody wants to talk to me, Lucy," she reassures him and encourages him to try to be more sociable.[68] With a growing awareness of the emptiness of his life, he pins his hopes on the broken down Chevrolet Impala in his back yard that he hopes to rebuild. He boasts to Lucy that one day he is going to leave, "gonna break out like gangbusters,"[69] but his life seems unfulfilling and unpromising.

Bo's situation is complicated by his interactions with his boss Enoch, a man of questionable morals. Two of Bo's female classmates die in an automobile accident, and Enoch crassly suggests that Bo could use the parts on his Impala. Fearful that Bo knows something about his sexual exploits, Enoch offers to be a surrogate father to the young man. Toward that end, Enoch invites Bo to go fox hunting with him and his friends. Desperate to fit in, Bo drinks bourbon and fabricates a sexual conquest. After a great deal of drinking, he finds himself on the verge of falling asleep, "torn between passing out and taking another drink."[70] In his intoxicated state, he hears the men discussing the two young women who were recently killed in a car accident. The men's conversation suggests that they committed sexual assault with the girls. Cuffy says, "She coulda hung us all if'n somebody didn' marry her. No-sir, I'm glad she's dead."[71] Even in his drunken state, Bo seems to recognize the true nature of these evil men. When a dog chases a fox near the men, Bo pulls out his pistol and tries to shoot the dog. The men angrily yell at Bo, who slurs an explanation that he was "try'n save foxie."[72] As Douglass states, "It is at that climactic moment when young Bo awakens from his stupor and his indecisiveness and declares himself opposed to all that these men have done and will do."[73] This incident symbolically suggests that Bo recognizes the men as exploiters and he chooses to side with the victims.

In some ways, Bo's situation seems so devoid of happiness that it is difficult to see any glimmer of dignity or hope in his life. However, the ending of the story offers a little of both. First of all, he rejects the immorality of the men whose approval he briefly desired. Secondly, he begins to see the Impala as his way out of his situation. The fact that his dream of leaving home seems more certain constitutes a victory for Bo. Some readers find Pancake's fiction bleak and grimly realistic, but as we can see in "Fox Hunters," that his work also possesses a sharp moral sense. Bo eventually rejects the kind of sexuality that preys upon the innocent. In Pancake's biography, Douglass discusses the author's sexual values: "He wanted to believe that sex was not something consumed but was rather the physical expression of a deeply humane and spiritual bond . . . ."[74] Douglass also correctly emphasizes that in spite of "the dominating effect of his mimetic rendering of place and character" that Pancake "was more concerned with his characters' moral condition than with the fact that they may be living in a rundown trailer in a hollow or seeking shelter in a cheap hotel room."[75] Pancake portrays a world that is full of corruption as desperate characters behave in desperate ways, but embeds a moral value as well. To miss the potential for redemption in some of his characters is to miss an important facet of his work.

In Pancake's depiction of masculinity, we see that his least admirable male characters, like Buddy in "Hollow" and the narrator of "Time and Again," express their masculinity through violence and that the more evolved men, like Bo in "Fox Hunters" and Ottie in "In the Dry," avoid the self-defeating impulses that can result from traditional male attitudes. Bo rejects the evil represented by Enoch and his friends, and Ottie rejects the self-deception of Shelia and the Gerlock family. Throughout his fiction, Pancake portrays Appalachian men engaging in desperate acts, but also allows his characters opportunities for "moments of grace." While the stories sometimes allow for the possibility of transcendence in the characters' futures, most of Pancake's protagonists remain defeated, unable to rise above the limitations of their situations.

Breece Pancake's brief literary career made a profound impact on other writers. The artistic success of his one short story collection made it possible for other West Virginia writers to find their way into print, but he also made it easier for them to depict the desperation of poverty with the determination of the Appalachian spirit. In describing Pancake's subject matter, Albert E. Wilhelm said, ". . . Pancake documents physical poverty, but he is even more concerned with exploring the poverty of spirit which frequently accompanies it."[76] Wilhelm acknowledges that the realism of Pancake's world is "not pretty, but poverty and its consequences seldom are. Nevertheless, Pancake's vision did not waver. His depictions of poverty are surely among the most moving to be found anywhere in American literature."[77] Indeed, the stories of Breece Pancake reveal the debilitating effects of poverty, particularly on his male characters.

CHAPTER 4

Denise Giardina's
Storming Heaven

As social criticism, a love story, and historical fiction, Denise Giardina's *Storming Heaven* (1987) is an impressive Appalachian novel. It focuses on the events leading up to the Matewan Massacre and the Battle of Blair Mountain and depicts the rugged independence of the Appalachian people and the uneasy relationship between the state's people and the coal mining interests. The novel won the Weatherford Award, a prize honoring books that "best illuminate the challenges, personalities, and unique qualities of the Appalachian South."[1] It also enjoyed a warm critical reception. *The Chicago Tribune* called it "an excellent book, full of fine observations and vivid characters," and *The Cleveland Plain Dealer* raved, "If we are very lucky, every few years there arrives a novel that is so moving, so instantly successful . . . that it towers high over much else that is being published. *Storming Heaven* is that novel." *The Tennessean* offered perhaps the most glowing praise. "In scope, it encompasses the spirit of humanity, from the heights of greatness to the depths of suffering with a fullness of emotion devoid of sentimentality. The beauty of the language makes us believe. The lump in our throats makes us believe." Giardina's fellow writers praised the novel as well. Jayne Anne Phillips said, "The book's triumph lies in the authenticity of these voices, in their ability to make real these undiminished lives." Annie Dillard wrote, "Denise Giardina tells the miners' stirring story with a fierceness and passion. This is a fine, moving book.[2]

As these reviews suggest, the novel possesses considerable merit, and *Storming Heaven*, like most of Giardina's work, could be classified as historical fiction. In most of her novels, she uses historical figures or historical events to dramatize moral and political issues, but she does not limit herself to writing about Appalachia. Her work reflects a broad range of historical knowledge and interest. Her first novel, *Good King Harry* (1984), focuses on the life of King Henry V of England. Then she turned to the Mountain State's uneasy coal mining history for her next two novels—*Storming Heaven* (1987) and *The Unquiet Earth* (1992). After the two Appalachian novels, Giardina published *Saints and Villains* (1998), which explores the life of German theologian Dietrich Bonhoeffer. *Saints and Villains* received rave reviews, with Annie Dillard calling it "a masterpiece." *Fallam's Secret* (2003) marks the author's foray into the fantasy genre in a novel that involves time travel. Her most recent novel is *Emily's Ghost* (2009), which explores the life of one of the author's literary heroes, Emily Bronte, a writer whose presence is felt in a number of Giardina's works. Still, labeling her work as historical fiction overlooks the literary merit of a novel like *Storming Heaven*.

The novel chronicles the coal companies' exploitation of the Appalachian region in the late nineteenth and early twentieth centuries. The companies took land from its rightful owners, they paid workers in scrip that they could only use in company stores, they underpaid them by underweighing the coal they mined, they created life-threatening working conditions, they utilized child labor in the mines, they refused to remedy unsanitary living conditions, and they created their own police force to intimidate those who dared to protest. The novel tracks the outrage and resistance of several tough and proud Appalachians, culminating in a battle that history books have often overlooked, as the U. S. government revealed its willingness to use the nation's military power against private citizens. The harsh critique of the injustices of the time made it difficult for the novel to find its way into print. On her website, Giardina states:

> I wanted *Storming Heaven* [to] be my first novel, because I wanted most of all to tell the world the story of the West Virginia mine wars. The publishing industry at that time indicated a lack of interest. No one in the early 1980s wanted a novel about labor struggles in West Virginia. The history of poverty and exploitation in the Appalachian Mountains is the history of the coal industry. Although I grew up in southern West Virginia, in the coalfields where the events occurred, I had never heard of the mine wars when I was in school. Then I discovered obscure self-published accounts in the back of a local bookstore, and realized West Virginians had fought back against their oppressors.[3]

Giardina's upbringing in the West Virginia coalfields developed her interest in the kind of social justice that she has championed in her life and in her writing. She attended West Virginia Wesleyan College, earning her B.A. in 1973, and then earned a Master of Divinity degree from Virginia Theological Seminary in 1979. Giardina told *Contemporary Authors* of her interest in the links between Appalachia and "other exploited places" and added, "I am also interested in writing that includes the political and spiritual dimensions of life and am not much interested in fiction that pretends these areas do not exist."[4] Giardina has devoted her life to her interests in the spiritual and political. She was arrested in 1989 as part of a protest of the Pittston Company's treatment of union miners. Giardina has vehemently opposed mountaintop removal, and for her it is a spiritual issue. She once wrote, "I will be as blunt as I can be. Mountaintop removal is evil, and those who support it are supporting evil. The mountains of West Virginia are God's greatest gift to West Virginia. To destroy the mountains is to spit in the face of God Almighty."[5] Giardina is a licensed lay preacher in the Episcopal church, and she also ran for governor of West Virginia in 2000, as the nominee of the Mountain Party. In addition to her religious and political activities, she has published six novels. In her fiction, she explores "how people with a conscience deal with the compromises they have to make."[6]

Socio-economic class is a dominant theme in *Storming Heaven*. Giardina does a masterful job of interweaving the fates of her main characters who oppose the coal industry, revealing their highly personal motivations for fighting against such powerful interests. These characters work to transcend the oppression of the coal companies, risking personal tragedy and even their lives to do so. Giardina establishes how politics becomes personal for these characters, all of whom become motivated for their own individual reasons. For C. J. Marcum, it was the murder of his grandfather and the taking of his land that made him resent the coal companies. For Rondal Lloyd, it was first-hand experience in the mines at the age of ten and C. J.'s influence on him to fight against the corruption. For Carrie Bishop, it was seeing the effects of the unsanitary living conditions in the coal camps and her relationship with Rondal. For Albion Freeman, it was his conviction that God wanted him to take his ministry to the mining community. Playing against negative stereotypes about the state, Giardina presents West Virginians who are intelligent, diligent, independent, and courageous. These characters love the state and its people, and they embody a range of political and spiritual beliefs. Many of the characters in *Storming Heaven* share Giardina's feeling that they are called to protest the injustices brought on by the rise of the coal industry. The resistance of these diverse characters to the corruption of the coal companies suggests that protest movements rely upon dissimilar individuals finding a way to unite in spite of their disparate worldviews.

C. J. Marcum's hatred of the coal companies is developed from the beginning of the novel, as he describes how his grandfather had tried to resist the railroad men taking over his land. While most of his neighbors sign over the mineral rights to railroad men who claimed a "senior patent," which took precedent over the average citizens' deeds to their land, C. J.'s grandfather refuses to sign. Later, he is relieved when the American Coal company takes the land over from the railroad and from the rightful landowners. Then one day the old man is shot and killed. C. J. relates the story of how three days later Sheriff Omar Kane tells the widow that American Coal now owns the land:

> "What gives you the right, Omar?" Mamaw said.
> Sheriff wouldn't look at her. "Henry set his mark to a paper, didn't he?"
> "His mark?" I said scornfully. "He didn't have no call to make no mark. He could read and write."
> "I don't know about that," Sheriff muttered.
> I wanted to kill him. He was the same man I had known all my young life, Omar Kane from Justice town, who give me a molasses candy when Papaw went to the polls to vote. I wanted to get my squirrel rifle and shoot him. When he rode away and I had not done it, I despised myself for a coward.[7]

At first, C. J. would try to tell himself that the coal companies taking over the land would not completely alter the life of the community: "But when I would pause in the field, lean against my hoe, and the wind would strike and bear a shriek, thin and ghostlike, from up Pliny—the death cry of some huge tree, fallen to make mine timbers and houses for American Coal—then my dream of sanctuary on the farm seemed a mockery and a reproach."[8] The murder of his grandfather and the loss of the life he knew as a child inspire C. J. to try to recover the land and to expose the abuse of the mining interests.

Rondal Lloyd also gains first-hand knowledge of the mistreatment of the coal companies as a child. His first memories involves his father coming home from the mines, filthy and battered, throwing his pay envelope on the table. "'Snake again,' was all he would say, meaning he hadn't been able to mine enough coal to pay off the bills at the company store, that he still owed for food and doctoring and his work tools and blasting powder, that his paycheck had a single wavy line where the money figures should have been."[9] In order to eke out a living, Rondal's father pressures him to go into the mines. C. J. argues for educating the intelligent Rondal, telling him, "'I fret about you growing up here,' he said. We sat on our porch swing. 'Company runs everything, makes all your daddy's decisions for him, even gits his mail. Hit's like Russia with that there Czar. Your daddy ain't a free man. He's like a slave.'"[10] After a coworker dies in a mining accident, Rondal agrees to go live with C. J., and the father makes Rondal's eight-year-old brother work in the mine. C. J. educates Rondal about the exploitation of the coal companies and offers to pay for Rondal's medical education. However, Rondal has decided that he wants to try to bring change to the mines. He tells C. J., "You got so many standards and ideals. Well, maybe I picked up some of them. Maybe I picked 'em up because I love and admire you. And maybe I decided I want to help bring the union in here. Ain't no doctor going to bring in no union."[11] This statement indicates that Rondal's decision to become a union organizer is indeed influenced by C. J.'s idealism.

Carrie Bishop obtains a job as a nurse for the mining families because her brother Miles is an executive for one of the coal companies. As a health professional, she becomes appalled by the living conditions in the coal camps and urges Miles to do something about it. "The privies is built over the creek and that's where most folks get their water. With this many folks living cramped together, you got to build new privies, deep ones, and treat them with chemicals. That, or bring water into the houses. If you don't, you'll keep right on gitting typhoid."[12] Miles writes the company executives, and when they reject the request, he refuses to fight them. When Carrie meets Lloyd Justice (Rondal's alias while he is secretly organizing the miners) after he has broken his foot and he confides that he is fighting against the coal companies, she begins to fall in love with him and to sympathize with his cause. Soon, Carrie says, Lloyd "had taken up residence in my daydreams." She talks Miles into giving Lloyd a job picking slate. She says of Lloyd, "He was so vulnerable, his potential so precious, I would have loved him for that alone."[13] When Miles warns Lloyd to leave, Carrie becomes outraged, but she also commits to improving the living conditions of the workers.

Albion Freeman joins the union cause because he believes it is God's will to work in the coal camps and because he is in love with his childhood friend

Carrie. Still emotionally attached to Rondal, Carrie is reluctant to become involved with Albion, but he eventually wins her over. After Carrie marries him, they move to the coalfield at Felco. Upon first seeing the coal tipple, Albion says, "That there is my church."[14] Albion's Wednesday night prayer meeting provides a venue for discussion of the union, and he proves to be an effective organizer. Carrie tries to treat the sick, but a doctor complains and the superintendent tells her to stop. She ends up working as a nurse for Doc Booker, who pays her two dollars a day. They feel like they are part of an important movement. After Carrie gets hired as Doc Booker's nurse, she considers how hard they had to work to make it on Albion's miner's wages. Through his love for Carrie and his Christian compassion for the struggling miners, Albion becomes a committed worker for the union cause, sacrificing his life when he is brutally murdered on the courthouse steps in Justice.

Although *Storming Heaven* is a work of fiction, Giardina accurately depicts historical events. The timelines of the novel—from the time of the seizing of land and mineral rights in 1890s to the Battle of Blair Mountain in 1921—faithfully reflect historical fact. The three most important events depicted in the novel—the Matewan Massacre, the murders of labor supporters on the courthouse steps, and the Battle of Blair Mountain—all remain true to historical accounts. However, names of places and individuals are changed. Notably, Mingo County becomes Justice County (and the shooting on the courthouse steps occurs in the town of Justice rather than Welch). The murder victims on the steps of the courthouse are Albion Freeman and Isom Justice, rather than Ed Chambers and Sid Hatfield. While Isom possesses many of the key character traits of "Smiling Sid"—legendary marksmanship, heavy drinking, and notorious womanizing—one potential flaw of the novel is that Isom fails to become larger than life like Hatfield, whom, according to Robert Shogan, the miners viewed "as their champion, a man who could be counted on to stand up for their side, even against the odds, in confronting the hired guns of the mine owners."[15] Still, Giardina's work reflects that of an accomplished historical novelist: historical accuracy and engaging storytelling.

Arguably, the most important place in the novel is the town of Annadel, an oasis of liberty in the desert of oppression. Annadel defies the stereotypes about the backwardness of West Virginians. The town is a place of racial integration, where African-Americans like Doc Booker hold important political offices. The unusual enjoyment of liberty in Annadel extends to the operation of brothels and the sale of moonshine whiskey. C. J. Marcum describes the level of freedom and independence in the town of Annadel:

> We got four Negroes on the council now and Doc Booker was mayor twicet before me. We got Negroes on the police force, and colored and white mix in the hotel and in the whorehouses. The *Justice Clarion* claimed Annadel is like "Sodom and Gomorrah, a den of violence, drunkenness, depravity, and miscegenation." Last couple of years they added "radicalism" to their list. What they don't like is that this here is the one place in all these coalfields where a man can be free, speak his mind, do like he pleases.[16]

C. J. and Doc Booker operate a newspaper that prints articles designed to tell the workers' version of events, and they are also members of the Annadel Political and Social Club, a group that gets together on Sunday afternoons to drink and discuss political issues of the day. The group discusses the Paint Creek strikes of 1912 and a coal strike in Colorado that Rondal helps organize. Eventually, the Baldwin guards arrest some of the Annadel citizens for sedition, segregating the black and white prisoners. The blacks start singing "The Star Spangled Banner, and the whites join in. They sing for seven or eight hours until they annoy the sheriff so much that he releases them. The men return home to find the press has been smashed. Isom gets them to make him Chief of Police of Annadel, so they can never be treated like that again, and the men begin to stockpile weapons. Clearly, the coal operators see the leading citizens of Annadel as a threat to their attempts to control the workers in the area. The leaders of Annadel desire to transcend the area's political and class inequities.

In addition to portraying the economic inequities of the time, Giardina also explores gender issues in the novel. Again, a desire for transcendence is key, as many of the characters refuse to abide by the expectations of traditional gender roles. The most important character to a discussion of gender in the novel is Carrie Bishop. As a child, she developed an interest in hunting, but her father told her "aint fitting for a girl."[17] He also did not approve of the way Carrie behaved around men, speaking her mind and doing what she pleased. At one point, Carrie's father tells her she will never marry. "He told me he didn't expect me to find a husband. I was not 'deferrin' enough, my tongue was too sharp and I was too forward in my ways."[18] As Cecelia Conway points out, "Carrie and her brother Miles reverse gender roles."[19] Miles enjoys neither hunting nor the physical labor his father expects of him. As a child, Carrie contrasts not only with her brother Miles, but also with her friend Albion, who appears weak and sickly when she first meets him. Albion even apologizes to the fish he catches. One day a fish swallows a hook, he becomes afraid and Carrie takes the hook out and throws the fish back in the water. Albion tells her that she is "brave enough for ten men."[20] By the time she chooses to train for a career in nursing, the reader understands that Carrie possesses the toughness and the self-reliance of an independent woman.

However, Carrie is also a romantic. Her favorite book as a child was *Wuthering Heights*. Giardina herself has praised this novel, "with its rugged landscapes and tales of women 'who have this passion for a difficult man.'"[21] As Carrie's interactions with Rondal reveal, she clearly expects romance from her relationships, even one with "a difficult man." The love affair of Carrie and Rondal enhances the novel's ability to captivate the reader by making the individuals involved with the labor struggle living, breathing human beings. Having frequently indulged in casual sex as a teenager, Rondal resists any attempts to over-romanticize desire. He describes his first relationship, with Ruby Day, the daughter of a brothel owner, by saying, "I settled into an affair with Ruby Day, Everett's daughter. She wasn't a whore but her daddy's business had certainly made an impression on her. She made few demands on me, and I liked that."[22] Carrie treats him after he breaks his foot in a work-related accident in the mines, and she falls in love with him almost immediately.

Rondal appreciates Carrie's self-reliant spirit, but he clearly possesses intimacy issues, perhaps as a result of his parents' disapproval of his refusing to go into the mines as a child. He projects his own fear of intimacy onto her when he offers her an explanation for why she is single. "You look to me like you're too independent," he said. "You wouldn't take to a man bossing you around." Carrie tells us that "the way he said it didn't sound like a reproach."[23] On the morning after Carrie and Rondal make love, she realizes that Rondal possesses commitment issues. He tells her that they should not become seriously involved:

> "I don't want you to take this too serious," he said.
> I felt as though a cold hand grasped my throat. "What do you mean?"
> "Just what I said. I ain't the kind of man to fall in love with a woman. Don't know why, but that's the way it is."
> "But I thought—"

"I never said I loved you, did I?"

I didn't want to answer him. "No. You didnt say that."

"What happened last night was nice. But dont expect nothin more from me. My life is crazy. Hit aint no kind of life to drag a woman into. And I aint no kind of man for you. You deserve more, somebody to pay you lots of attention. You'll find somebody like that, I know it."

"Dont you dare tell me what I deserve and dont deserve. I dont want nobody mooning over me, nor no rich man throwing money at me. I just want somebody to love, somebody I can love."[24]

Rondal's unwillingness to commit to Carrie and her insistence upon love on her own terms prove impediments to an ongoing relationship.

Since Carrie falls deeply in love with Rondal, it at first seems surprising that she marries Albion Freeman, who returns to the area as a preacher, hoping to settle down with her. However, Albion also appreciates Carrie's independent spirit and offers her the possibility of a marriage with a man who allows her freedom and autonomy over her own life. For example, he does not judge her when she confides that she and Rondal had a sexual relationship. Albion seems content to allow Carrie to discover whether she could ever be in a relationship with him. To her surprise, she finds herself becoming attached to the unorthodox preacher, and she gradually allows Albion into her life. "After three months of his kindness and patience, I let him kiss me, and to my surprise I enjoyed it. By Christmas I began to think that I might want to love him after all. I looked forward to his visits and came to acknowledge the quiet contentment I felt when I was with him."[25] While she may occasionally long for the passion she felt for Rondal, Carrie grows to appreciate Albion's goodness and his strength. Living with Albion gives her life a sense of purpose as she treats the miners' families as Doc Booker's nurse. At one point, she takes pride in how she was able to manage life on her husband's miner's pay. "I looked back with a certain pride on the six months we lived on Albion's seventy-five cents a day. I had accounted for every penny and every piece of scrip, and spent nary a one without thinking of ten things it might be used for and pledging to do without the nine least important."[26] Clearly, Carrie and Albion's marriage offers a model of an equal partnership—in other words, marriage on Carrie's terms.

Not only is Carrie's independence apparent in her insistence upon her individualistic choices in life and love, she also participates in the union cause in a way that was almost unprecedented for a woman. She revels in the possibilities for the miners, saying at one point, "It was a golden summer [1920]. We lived in tents, but the weather was warm and the union sent us food . . . . And whenever we walked to town we were greeted with a sign proclaiming FREE ANNADEL . . . . On every corner, an armed miner stood sentinel with his red bandana knotted around his neck. The gun thugs called us rednecks. It was a name we accepted with pride."[27] These moments of transcendence over her challenging situation is one in which the possibilities for a better future become apparent. She continued, "There was no feeling like it in the world. I believed we could beat any coal company, any sheriff, any governor. So did everyone else. You could see it in the way people swaggered, hear it in the high-pitched laughter when they gathered over the cook-fires."[28] However, when summer turns to winter, Carrie is forced to withstand brutal cold and the harassment of the Baldwin detectives. She demonstrates her physical toughness many times in the novel. She is fearless when the state police attack the tent camps. When the gun thugs kick a pregnant Italian woman repeatedly in the stomach, Carrie throws a rock at them.[29] After women raid a store for provisions for their starving families, Carrie fires a machine gun at the state police, driving away the officers who had planned to thwart the women's efforts. Later in the novel, Carrie marches with the men toward Blair Mountain, even though she suffers from morning sickness, pregnant with Rondal's child. When the fighting starts, she bravely assists Doc Booker in treating the wounded, maintaining her courage even when ruthless Logan County Sheriff Don Chafin sets off a bomb nearby. Throughout the novel, Carrie represents a rejection of traditional women's roles, or at least a refusal to become defined by gender.

Giardina explores masculinity and calls traditional masculinity into question through the characters of Rondal and Albion. In many ways, Rondal projects the courage, physical toughness, emotional detachment, and sexual conquests associated with masculinity. However, what appears to be strength sometimes masks deep insecurities. Most importantly, he insists that Carrie is romanticizing desire, suggesting that he sees it for what it is, a human need. Just after Albion moves back to the area, Carrie talks with Rondal at a dance. They walk outside and kiss. Carrie decides to make a declaration:

> I gathered all my courage. "I love you. I allays have. I'd a married you in a minute ifn you'd asked me."

"I never asked you," he said proudly.

I pulled away.

"Hit's been four year," he said. Cant you forgit? We was just two people that wanted to be together that night."

"Dont speak for me! I made a choice and I won't have it made light of![30]

Rondal continually claims that he does not love Carrie, but he admits that he likes seeing her after she is married to Albion, especially when she tells him to be careful. At one point, Rondal mocks Albion's accomplishments in getting men to join the union through his preaching. When Rondal wonders whether he does it "for the love of God or the love of Carrie Bishop," she replies, "You got not right to talk about love. You told me oncet you couldnt love nobody. Dont make fun of them that do."[31] Rondal's apparent jealousy of Albion becomes clearer when the organizers tell Rondal that he needs to leave in order to save his life. Rondal hints that Albion wants to take over the union and get rid of him because Carrie has always had feelings for him: "You'd like that, wouldn't you, preacher? You'd like to stop the shooting; hit scares you. Besides, you got other reasons you want to get shut of me." Doc Booker and the others point out the facts: Rondal has been betrayed by his lover, Ruby, and the union wants him out of there because he is in danger. Rondal asks Carrie what he should do, and she responds, "I dont care what you do."[32] At this point, Rondal's assumption that Carrie will always be there for him has been undercut by his own masculine posturing.

Later in the novel, after Albion's death, Rondal makes it clear that he is in love with Carrie, but he reveals his continued traditional masculinity by still not being able to bring himself to discuss his feelings. When Carrie tells Rondal, "I never stopped loving you," he admits that scared him at one point. When she points out that he still has not said he loves her, he says, "I aint sure I do. And I aint one to say things I dont mean. But I need you."[33] His intimacy issues are revealed in another passage after Carrie has agreed to join him in the march to Blair Mountain. She tells him, "I love you like my own kin." But Rondal says their relationship is more "like water running and cant nobody hold it back. But when it's gone, it's gone. That aint like kin." He knows that he has hurt her feelings and says, "I can come close to loving Carrie then, after I've hurt her."[34] Time and time again, Carrie expresses her love for Rondal, but he finds himself incapable of saying he loves her. It is a credit to Carrie's patience and wisdom that she understands him well enough not to insist upon a commitment from him late in the novel, seemingly aware of the true nature of his feelings. Rondal describes what transpires when they part as he leaves for battle:

> She kissed me. "I love you," she said.
> The response leaped to my lips and died there. I turned my head away, shamed.
> Her thin arms around my chest never loosened their hold.
> "You don't have to say. I know as much as I need to."[35]

For the first time in the novel, Rondal admits that he wishes he could be more expressive of his love for Carrie.

Several explanations for Rondal's fear of intimacy are plausible. First of all, the danger in his role as a union organizer makes it difficult to sustain a long-term relationship. As we have already seen, he tells Carrie, "My life is crazy. Hit aint no kind of life to drag a woman into."[36] While this might seem like masculine condescension, most members of Rondal's society would agree that a life of danger and travel would place a strain on a relationship. Secondly, Rondal's parents are sparing in demonstrating their affection for him, and in fact, his mother resents him for placing his younger brother in danger by leaving the mines to go live with C. J. Early in the novel, Rondal describes how he enjoyed his father's approval while they worked together in the mines:

> For the first time in memory, I spent time with my daddy. I came to realize he was glad to have me with him. He had few ways of showing it. We seldom spoke underground. We were too busy with our picks and shovels, straining to load as many tons as we could, for the more we loaded, the more we were supposed to earn. But when we left the mine, Daddy sometimes pulled off my cap and gently rubbed his knuckles back and forth across the top of my head. He could never bring himself to touch me with the fleshy palms of his hands. But I knew he loved me.[37]

Clearly, Rondal's father did not often provide his son with affection or approval. A third reason for Rondal's fear of intimacy relates to his experience of sexuality. Rondal came of age as a friend of the sexually loose Isom Justice, hanging around brothels and developing a view of sexuality as a fulfillment of a human need, rather than an act of love. His relationship with Ruby, who places no demands on him, allows him sexual experience without any emotional attachment. By the time he meets Carrie, his sexual attitudes have been formed.

Giardina further develops her exploration of gender through the character of Albion Freeman, showing that a man who is not masculine in a traditional sense can exhibit strengths that defy gender stereotypes. As mentioned earlier, teenage Carrie had developed romantic notions of love from books like *Wuthering Heights*. Carrie describes her first impressions of Albion as a fourteen-year-old boy. "Albion cried when his father left. I was disappointed, because it did not seem brave of him. Heathcliff would not have cried."[38] Indeed, Albion at times seems not particularly masculine because of his peaceful nature. He refuses to shoot at the Baldwin guards or at the scab workers. However, he demonstrates considerable strength working in the mines. Carrie wonders about the practicality of Albion's preaching in the mines, given his lack of traditional masculine strength, "And sometimes he spoke of God calling him to preach in the coal camps of Justice County, his father's home. I could not imagine him in such a place. He would preach Jesus dragging the coal operators out of Hell and die of broken down lungs before he reached the age of forty."[39] However, Albion impresses everyone with his abilities and his toughness, even though he practices a kind of non-violence. When he battles consumption, he insists upon staying with the rest of the union miners. Carrie says, "Doc Booker offered to let us move into his house, but Albion wouldn't hear of it. We must suffer what everyone else suffered. We were all in this together."[40] In one way, Albion exhibits strength that Rondal does not possess, for Albion never displays jealousy of Carrie's first love, even when Rondal incorrectly suggests that Albion wants him out of the way. By showing the kind of security that Rondal lacks, Albion reveals himself to be stronger than Rondal, in that one way at least.

Cecelia Conway has pointed out how Giardina's interest in deconstructing traditional gender roles is apparent from the opening of the novel, in which Dillon Lloyd serves as "a regendered midwife"[41] at Rondal's birth. A man taking on a role that has traditionally been performed by women constitutes our first hint at what becomes a major theme in the novel—that society's tendency to link masculinity with physical strength and physical endeavor and to link femininity with domestic tasks and comparative physical weakness represents an attempt to shape human identity. Carrie's embrace of the masculine tasks of hunting and fishing, contrasted with Albion's and her brother Miles's rejection of them, suggests that strong individuals never allow themselves to be defined by gender constructions.

In fact, Miles unites the themes of gender and class. We are told early in the novel that "Miles hated to hunt, was uncomfortable with guns even though he was a fairly good shot. He didn't mind killing things so much, but would rather be curled up with a book."[42] Of course, he rejects his father's version of masculinity but replaces it with a version of the Horatio Alger dream of moving from poverty to wealth. When he becomes an executive of a coal company, he becomes so driven by his dream of affluence that he ignores the company's abuses and immoral tactics. As mentioned earlier, when she first starts working as a nurse, Carrie confronts Miles about a sanitation issue. The outhouses are built over the creek that supplies the community with its water. After a meek attempt to rectify the problem, Miles accepts that nothing can be done. Later, Carrie taunts him for not standing up to mine owners in Boston. "You aint no man, Miles. You aint got no backbone nor principles."[43] It's interesting that Carrie makes the issue one of masculinity because she could easily accuse him of classism. True, Miles obviously does not stand up for what is right out of fear, but he is constantly focused on creating an image of success. He decides not to court the uneducated Clary Leach, instead marrying "the daughter of the bank president in Justice."[44] Miles is a character who makes the reader aware of the novel's critique of the capitalist ideology, in which greed often takes precedence over principle.

This critique includes an exploration of the American dream. Miles obviously believes that his education has led to a higher paying job. He would argue that if one works hard, then prosperity will follow. However, many of the miners in the novel work hard in pursuit of economic gain, but find it elusive. Based on the experience of immigrant Rosa Angelelli, it would be hard to argue that the Italians who came to this country to make a fortune in the coalfields prosper in the novel. Indeed, Rondal's father works hard, only to have the company charge him so much for equipment and supplies that he ends up making nothing, becoming so desperate to improve his financial situation that he forces his sons to work with him in the mines. However, he does not question the capitalist ideology like C. J. and Rondal do. As Cecelia Conway points out, "The father may be selling his soul 'for the almighty dollar,' but he believes he is providing for his family. Individually incapable of ensuring their economic survival or overcoming the exploitative system, many coal miners reproduce the abuse upon their own sons and wives."[45] Clearly, the novel suggests that no matter how hard an individual works, the powerful are privileged in the American system, while the powerless are exploited for cheap labor.

The novel resists easy answers on the question of whether the characters experience more tragedy or transcendence. Many of the important characters lose their lives in the conflict with the coal companies and the Baldwin guards. Johnson, the African-American union organizer, is brutally killed early in the novel. C.J. Marcum dies in the Annadel shootout with the Baldwin guards, Albion Freeman and Isom Justice are killed on the courthouse steps, and Rondal becomes paralyzed at Blair Mountain. While these are all tragic outcomes in one sense, each of these characters imagines a more equitable world, lives their dreams at least fleetingly, and makes possible the eventual improvements in living and working conditions and the expansion of individual liberty and human rights that come into being during the 1930s. While Giardina portrays these characters' accomplishments as partial victories in the novel's Afterword, the characters make it possible for the union to be given the freedom to organize and the mine guard system employed by the coal companies was outlawed. In the creation of Annadel, the characters imagine a world in which blacks and whites live together equally, citizens exercise power over their own destinies, and residents enjoy the possibilities inherent in the American dream: life, liberty, and the pursuit of happiness. While the transcendence the characters in the novel enjoy is fleeting, it does include a promise of what society could become.

In *The Unquiet Earth*, the sequel to *Storming Heaven*, Giardina continues to explore similar themes, by following the lives of descendants of the first novel. The novel focuses on Carrie and Rondal's son, Dillon Lloyd, and on Carrie's niece, Rachel Honaker. The coal company continues to exploit and intimidate, devoting its energies to strip mining and mountaintop removal. The novel builds to an apocalyptic conclusion, with a flood that is reminiscent of the Buffalo Creek disaster of 1972. *The Unquiet Earth* attacks the exploitation of the coal company at every turn. It criticizes the seizing control of land, the destruction of natural beauty, the under-compensation of workers, the reduction and elimination of benefits, and the attempts to destroy the miners' union. Dillon Lloyd proves to be as determined as his father to fight against the coal industry's oppression of its workers. He convinces the union to strike, and the FBI puts him under surveillance. When scab workers replace the union miners, he plots to limit the transportation of the coal out of the area. At one point, he blows up a railroad bridge to halt the distribution of the coal, an action that lands him in federal prison. Eventually, a new group of thugs, aided by high-tech surveillance equipment, works to intimidate Dillon and those who assist him. However, like his father Rondal, Dillon refuses to relinquish his fight against the powerful coal interests.

Gender issues in *The Unquiet Earth* center on Dillon's first cousin, Rachel Honaker. Raised to be a proper young lady, Rachel seems torn between the example of her mother and that of her Aunt Carrie. She becomes a nurse, but twice marries men who can provide economic security for her. Her need for the appearance of respectability leads her away from Dillon, whose methods she finds extreme, to Arthur Lee Sizemore, the coal company official who controls much of the community's business operation. At times, Rachel can be a maddening character. The reader wonders how she could not know of the unethical behavior of Arthur Lee. Why would she marry the man who is the enemy of Dillon, the cousin she loves? The answer is that Rachel can never free herself from the values her mother instilled in her. Rachel's inability to shake free of her dependence upon men disappoints the reader, given the novel's two prominent examples of independent women: Carrie Bishop Freeman, who figures more prominently in *Storming Heaven*, and Tommie Justice, an independent woman who enjoys a level of sexual freedom that Rachel can never allow herself. Like Rachel, Tommie is a nurse who bravely serves in World War II but who refuses to defer to men. Another important character to the theme of gender is Rachel's daughter, Jackie, who becomes a journalist who reports on the coal company's mistreatment of the mining community. Jackie develops a level of independence her mother never fully reaches, refusing to settle in relationships after falling in love with a priest who devotes himself to God and, of course, can never marry Jackie. Still, Jackie reveals herself to be a courageous independent journalist, who believes that a relationship should be based on passion, not respectability. All in all, *The Unquiet Earth* impresses—it won the American Book Award—but it occasionally lapses into melodrama in ways that *Storming Heaven* does not.

Giardina's *Storming Heaven* succeeds on several levels. In its critique of the excesses of capitalist greed, it raises awareness of the abuses faced by organized labor in the early twentieth century. Giardina shows that the powerful mining interests could even rely on the firepower of the U. S. military against the striking miners. As historical fiction, *Storming Heaven* dramatizes the Battle of Blair Mountain, a part of West Virginia history that has long been overlooked, a conflict that Shogan calls "an afterthought in our historical consciousness."[46] Giardina says that as a child she had "never heard of the battle."[47] *Storming Heaven*, with its focus on the life and relationships of Carrie Bishop, explores gender issues and offers an example of a truly independent Appalachian woman, one who defines herself and her relationships on her own terms. Giardina's work also examines societal constructs of masculinity in its portrayals of Rondal Lloyd, Albion Freeman, and Miles Bishop, showing how traditional gender roles limit and distort human experience. In its multiple dimensions, the novel thrills and captivates, impresses and instructs. In its expose of exploitation, its excavation of a buried history, its examination of gender roles, and its exploration of the possibility for transcendence over oppressive conditions, *Storming Heaven* is an important Appalachian novel, which deserves a wider audience.

CHAPTER 5

Irene McKinney's
Vivid Companion

In 1994, Irene McKinney was named Poet Laureate of West Virginia, a richly deserved honor for the writer that Jayne Anne Phillips has called "a major American poet."[1] McKinney's reputation rests on the quality of her five books of poetry, including her 2009 volume of selected poems, *Unthinkable*. She was a friend and advocate of fellow Appalachian and West Virginia writers. In 2002, she edited a collection of literature entitled *Backcountry: Contemporary Writing in West Virginia*, featuring work by some of the Mountain State's finest writers. Late in her life, McKinney's essays were featured monthly on National Public Radio. Her poetry was published in *The Georgia Review*, *The Kenyon Review*, *Poetry, and Southern Poetry Review*, among others. She received a National Endowment for the Arts Award in poetry and a scholarship to the Breadloaf Writers' Conference. She provided the epigraph for *Listen Here*, an anthology of Appalachian women's writing: "I'm a hillbilly, a woman, and a poet, and I understood early on that nobody was going to listen to anything I had to say anyway, so I might as well just say what I want to."[2] In her role as Poet Laureate, McKinney continually championed the worth of literature. She described how she saw the role in an interview with Jeff Mann:

> It seemed to me that the position was a wonderful opportunity to talk to people about the value of poetry in their lives. It's not that I'm a zealot and want to go out and convert the world; it's that I feel that people need poetry and can't always find it. Once they find it and realize what a lot of crucial things it answers for them, then they'll keep reading it, they'll seek it out. . . . And I finally decided it was something like this: everybody instinctively knows that poetry is the place you go to tell the truth. [3]

With such a passionate view of the role of poetry, McKinney displayed in her work an uncompromising search for truth.

Raised on a farm near Belington, West Virginia, McKinney learned early in her life about the challenges of poverty and the limitations placed on women. After marrying at the age of seventeen and having two children, she decided to pursue a degree at West Virginia Wesleyan College, earning a B.A. in 1968. Two years later, she earned an M.A. in English at West Virginia University, writing a creative thesis. By the time of her divorce in 1974, she had fully committed herself to becoming a writer, having read widely in poetry and other works. Influenced by Emily Dickinson and Sylvia Plath, McKinney published her first book, *The Girl with the Stone in Her Lap*, in 1976. After earning a doctorate in creative writing at the University of Utah in 1980, McKinney went on to publish two more books of poetry—*Quick Fire and Slow Fire* (1988) and *Six O'Clock Mine Report* (1989)—before joining the faculty at West Virginia Wesleyan College in 1990. The poet laureate position followed in 1994, and by that time, McKinney's place in West Virginia literature, and among West Virginia writers, was secure. She spent most of the nineties teaching at Wesleyan, guiding young poets to publication, and giving scores of public readings, demonstrating to listeners all over the state the true power of poetry.

Since McKinney's contribution to the Mountain State's literature included both her own poetry and her advocacy of the state's finest writers, I am tempted to call her West Virginia literature's player coach. In conversations about literature, McKinney was generous, recognizing the writers who helped her find her own voice, even younger writers. For example, in an interview, she praised Maureen Seaton's *Furious Cooking*, saying the book "really set me off again. It was like I went back and started over." In conversation, she offered a quick history of West Virginia's last half century of literature:

> The generation ahead of me had a real battle within themselves about "how much am I going to give up of my culture to fit in?" My generation was the one that was emerging. Breece Pancake, who went to the University of Virginia, was struggling with that same question. He tried very hard to get the two cultures [Virginia and West Virginia] to pull together. He was always asking colleagues to go hunting with him or go hang out in some bar or go fishing or take drives up in the mountains. It's clear to me that what he was trying to do was make some kind of connection between mainstream culture

and his own culture. And then the generation after me—Pinckney Benedict, Jayne Anne Phillips, Ann Pancake—they found it much easier because they had some models to look back to, whereas that earlier generation was inventing West Virginia [from a literary standpoint].[4]

In her role as advocate and historian, McKinney offered ample evidence of the state's impressive literary output.

Adding to that literary heritage, McKinney published perhaps her finest collection of original poetry in 2004. *Vivid Companion* displays the impressive range of her work. The collection contains forty-four poems, a remarkable forty of which had been previously published in literary magazines. Alternately comic and poignant, the collection features autobiographical poems chronicling different stages of the poet's life, including her bout with multiple myeloma and the loss of her father. It features poems about coming of age, escaping the societal demands placed on young females, the struggle to become an artist, and the culture's dismissive attitudes toward maturing women. However, the collection also includes a number of persona poems, in which McKinney assumes the voice of a real or imagined person. For example, she explores sexual politics in the poems about the nineteenth-century Oneida community, the members of which, according to McKinney's note in the work, "tried with intense generosity and thoughtful goodwill to eliminate all selfishness and violence from their lives."[5]Another focus in the collection—in poems like "Homage to Baroness Elsa von Freytag Loringhoven," for example—is the celebration of women who dare to break from societal dictates and indulge their artistic ambitions and their individuality. Finally, to an extent not seen before in her work, the poet writes about the body in ways that are fresh and astonishing. In *Vivid Companion*, McKinney celebrates the human body and rejects cultural restrictions on pleasure. She explores how it connects us to both the natural and the spiritual world. However, she also reveals the ways in which our bodies can fail us, break down, and force us to grapple with issues of mortality—to confront what she referred to in her earlier poem "Visiting My Gravesite" as "this unknown buried in the known."[6]

In *Vivid Companion*, McKinney also writes about class, mainly as it relates to place. In a work with so many universal themes, McKinney writes eloquently about her specific locale—in particular, West Virginia and how American society perceives the Mountain State. She tends to discount both the romanticizing and stereotyping of Appalachians as distorted or downright false, while combating the kind of classism directed toward the region. In "Home," the speaker of the poem has returned to West Virginia, but does not feel the connection with the land and the people she once felt. She mocks the sentimentality of the tourist slogan, "Come on Home to West Virginia," lamenting the way new roads and developments have endangered the land and the wildlife around them. Sprinkling in lines from traditional songs, she particularly criticizes the apathy of the people toward the devastation—in the poem's powerful conclusion:

> The roads are looping and winding
> through the Appalachians in
> switchbacks, plunges, broken pavement.
>
> You Got Your Dead Skunk in the Middle
> Of the Road. You got your slaughter.
> You got your songs, and your Mack trucks
>
> and your foxes and bears, and they don't care.
> You got your rivers: The Gauley, The New,
> The Greenbrier, the Gandy and the Sinks of Gandy.
>
> You got your dealers in quilts
> and your dealers in coal.
> You got your people trying to work
>
> and your people trying to eat,
> and they don't care. Come on Home.
> Dance, if you can, Little Fawn.[7]

The rejection of the idea that all is "almost heaven" in West Virginia reveals how the speaker resents overly romanticized perceptions of the region. In this poem, instead, nature is exploited for the sake of profit, and most of the people are either unwilling to notice the destruction, or simply do not care.

In "Monkey Heart" McKinney satirizes the arrogance in some people's perceptions of West Virginians, while also reminding us that we are not as superior to the other animal forms as we sometimes imagine. She extends the criticism to all of us when she writes, "The species we look down on/are not looking up at us."[8] The animal references set up a powerful payoff as McKinney attacks the kind of classism that is routinely directed at people from the Mountain State:

A woman in Charlottesville told me a joke
about West Virginians, involving mobile
homes and incest. When I didn't laugh she said
she'd meant no harm, that some of her best
friends were hillbillies. I didn't tell her
to stop monkeying around or that she
reminded me of an ocelot, albeit one
who had gone to Sweetbriar.[9]

In that powerful passage, McKinney strikes back on behalf of all West Virginians against the stereotypes that diminish the state in the eyes of the rest of the nation. The fact that the woman in the poem is college-educated, yet still indulges in those stereotypes makes McKinney's response even more necessary and pointed. Furthermore, the poems reveal that many of the attitudes that outsiders express toward West Virginia involve socio-economic class.

In an earlier interview with Emily Corio, McKinney discussed her upbringing and her connection with the land. "Having grown up on a farm in a pretty isolated place, I was really tuned in to everything that was going on in the natural world, in the animal world, in the vegetable world. We were very close to all those processes. It was just inevitable."[10] With her strong connection to the land and its people, McKinney remained committed to combating the distortions about the region—both the mean spirited and the overly romanticized.

However, even though some of the poems focus on class and place, gender is the prevalent topic in *Vivid Companion*. She writes about masculinity in the poems about her father's illness and death and in "Woods Burning," in which she assumes the persona of an arsonist. In the poems about her father, McKinney focuses on the tragedy of death and the mystery of life. Cognizant of the reversal of the child taking care of the parent, she focuses on the inability to understand or communicate with her dying father. In "Three Three Three" McKinney writes of her father's stroke and how it damaged his ability to speak. The speaker recounts how he repeats "three three three," which she describes as "an unhinged number / that he'll never reconnect."[11] In an interview McKinney described the fears brought on by seeing her once vital father reduced to a shell of his former self:

In "Three Three Three" I was aware that we all need to be reminded of the stark truth of not only our mortality, but the terrible circumstances leading up to death. Often, people will say that they aren't afraid of dying, but of the pain and chaos leading up to it. I address that question first, both for myself and others, by asking blunt questions that force us into humility. I want to shock us into understanding that the present level of comfort we have is subject to sudden reversal. Then I can progress to the particular circumstances of my own life and my father's confusion and suffering. As a poet, a person who lives by words, there is nothing more terrifying than the idea of losing the capacity to speak, of being reduced to single syllables, as the aphasia victim is, and as my father was. I wanted to convey the raw truth of this, but also I wanted to convey that the basic emotional life of the heart persists even in this, so that finally that is all we hear.[12]

In conveying the "raw truth" of her father's loss of language, the poet found in "his raw heart's voice," something that spoke to her beyond language.

In "Full Moon: Sitting Up Late At My Father's Bedside," McKinney further explores her father's declining health and the breakdown in verbal communication. The poem begins with an image of the full moon and suggests that even it feels transitory. "But we are going to touch it, / and then it will go away."[13] The speaker feels powerless, even to find the words to describe how she feels:

What can I say when my father is dying,

with his new eyes and his new heart.
His mind is like a flapping line of laundry,

clothing full of wind. How can I speak
about the babble of his speech? His saying

does not go from here to there, it's only here.[14]

As the speaker observes her father, she looks for meaning in the inscrutable. She states, "I see intensity in all / he misconstrues,—I think he misconstrues. / The night is brilliant, and the moon's too close. / It calls him out: to where, I cannot say."[15] In these closing lines, we see the poet still dignifying the humanity of the father, while recognizing the growing distance between them. The father's loss of vitality is deeply felt by the daughter.

Another poem that explores masculinity and relationships with one's father is "Woods Burning," in which the speaker is a troubled man who has started a forest fire. It begins with the epigraph from a news story, "The arsonist returned to aid the firefighters."[16] In creating a persona based on a factual event, McKinney explores why a person might set a fire and why he would return to help extinguish it. The speaker talks a great deal about his father, a strong, self-reliant man who could butcher a pig and fill the smokehouse with provisions. Throughout the poem, the speaker associates his father with smoke, that of the smokehouse, the burning of brush while logging, the "fire in the hole" in the mines, and the fireplace the father tended on winter mornings. Desperately trying to think of himself as self-sufficient like his father and not "dilatory" like his wife, Molly, the arsonist sets a fire that he will later help fight:

Like my daddy
before me I can make things happen.
When the fire trucks come screaming
up the river I'll be there
with the rest of them, fighting
the flames, not afraid
to put my hands in the fire.[17]

In a case of failing to live up to his own code of masculinity, as suggested by his unfavorable comparison with his father and his projection of the charge of laziness onto his wife, the speaker longs to think of himself as a man "who can make things happen," but ends up indulging in a misguided and destructive act of male bravado.

In addition to its well-crafted explorations of masculinity, *Vivid Companion*, of course, focuses most directly on the nature of femininity. In her more autobiographical poems, McKinney attacks the way society has traditionally conditioned women to be subservient to men and deny their individuality. As Casie Fedukovich writes in her review of the collection, "*Vivid Companion*'s 44 poems defy the tendency toward self-deprecation, and McKinney forcefully embraces her body and history as relevant, positive, and spiritual."[18] In many ways, the collection is an unapologetic portrait of the artist as a mature woman. In poem after poem, McKinney makes the following points on gender. Conventional society tells young women that the body is not a proper topic of discussion and places restrictions on them indulging in the pleasures of the body. In a patriarchal society, women who aspire to self-expression or self-creation in their lives will encounter disapproval and discouragement.

After women reach a certain age, the culture marginalizes them. Finally, in spite of this stigmatization and marginalization, a mature woman can reach a level of peace and insight that may provide the greatest sense of fulfillment she has ever known.

A poem that comically treats society's restrictions on the female body is "Covering Up," in which the speaker recalls how at age eleven she began to develop breasts and would walk around without a shirt. The adults' disapproval and the speaker's rebelliousness are revealed in the poem's opening stanza:

> When I saw that I would have breasts
> and that they wanted me to cover them up,
> I took my shirt off and tied it around my waist
> and stomped out into the yard.[19]

After everyone dismisses her for "acting crazy," the speaker marches around for three days, "refusing to wear a shirt." Outraged at the adults' insistence that she "cover up," she says about her breasts, "They were two badges on my chest, / each of them saying 'This is me.'"[20] She beats a hoe to splinters and recognizes that she has just fought the first battle in what will be a long struggle:

> I knew it wasn't over,
> but I was exhausted. I would have to enjoy
> not covering up in secret. That's when
> I began to speak in my head as the naked one,
>
> and the other went clothed into the world.[21]

The speaker sees the command to cover up as a restriction on her self-expression and realizes that she will have a public and private self from this day forward. In "Covering Up," McKinney turns a somewhat comic situation into one of poignancy, with the speaker recognizing that as a female she will be expected to defer to the wishes of patriarchal society, where the feminine will be marginalized. She has been asked to ignore and hide her body, or at least relegate it to something one acknowledges only "in secret." As Patti Capel Schwartz states in her review of *Vivid Companion*, McKinney writes as if "the body and sexuality are inseparable from the mind."[22]

In "Covering Up" the speaker is developing her own identity, beginning to speak in her head, finding her own voice. Developing "the bud of
a voice" is also the theme in "Constant Companion," a poem whose title
echoes that of the collection. Fedukovich describes the importance of this
poem to the book as a whole. "Though McKinney features no title piece,
'Constant Companion' emerges as the heart of the collection. Her speaker
deftly navigates culturally constructed femininity. . . . The speaker's poetic
expression evolves into her 'constant companion' and the 'bud of . . . voice'
that, after arbitrary definitions of 'beauty' are thrown aside, can swell to a
crescendo as the book progresses."[23] With its connection to "Constant Companion," "Covering Up" is one of the pivotal poems in the collection, as it
introduces the idea of a female beginning to discover her voice, independent
of societal demands.

McKinney writes again of the body in "Clitoral," a poem that appropriates thematic and lyrical ideas from Thomas Hardy's "During Wind and Rain."
In his poem, Hardy writes about the passage of time and the kinds of daily
rituals that consume our lives and punctuates each stanza with the phrase
"Ah, no; the years," thus contrasting the impermanence of human activity
with the seemingly perpetual natural elements. In "Clitoral," McKinney takes
Hardy's idea and equates the passage of time with the decline in sexual activity as one ages. Instead of the refrain "Ah, no; the years," McKinney offers wry observations like "Ah God, we're getting old" and "Lord, my body is
lonely." Instead of singing "their dearest songs" as in Hardy, the individuals in McKinney's poem "sing their aching song."[24] Thus, in the poem's final
lines, McKinney presents growing older as the gradual decrease in the sexual
as "the sweet flesh shrinks" and time marches on relentlessly:

> We leave the gathering-place
> and go to our chosen homes—all of us go,
> back to our couches and kitchen curtains and dogs
>   but we go with the clitoris,
> beaten, happy, sore, ignored . . . .
>   clitoris the nerve of the mind,
> and the cold rain sluices down my skin.[25]

Once again, McKinney grapples with the essence of femininity and growing
older, linking them to the temporality of the body and the ache of desire,

which she juxtaposes with the persistence of natural elements, represented here by "the cold rain."

In contrast with some of the autobiographical work, the Oneida poems in Section II of the collection offer McKinney the opportunity to address sexual issues through personae. As she states in a note, members of the Oneida Community "practiced 'Complex Marriage,' where each was married to all."[26] Older women sexually initiated young men, while older men did the same for young women. In an interview, McKinney described how she became fascinated with the Oneida Community:

> When I was teaching at Hamilton College in upstate New York, I was only a few miles away from the Oneida Community, and the college had a lot of material and manuscripts from Oneida. I became utterly fascinated and really obsessed with the social experiment they had undertaken there, and I did research on it for a year or so, and finally had so much information and so many voices in my head I had to start writing about it. The engine that drove all this was the fact that I was newly in love with a colleague there who was married, and I naturally began to be drawn to Oneida's exploration of the questions of marriage, community, and sexuality. He suggested that we go and visit the old community, which we did, and interviewed an elderly woman, Imogene Stone, who had been an original member of the community. Walking through the old mansion with her, where she still lived along with other elderly members, I felt transported back into that life and those hopes and aspirations for human possibility.[27]

By abolishing double standards and the stigmatization of sexuality, the members of the community tried to create a society of gender equality. In "Mary Cragin: The Honeymoon, 1834," Mary thus describes desire: "None of us can do it alone. Congress, / the bridge from one to the other."[28] The Oneida Community believed that by treating sexuality as something fundamentally human, they were eliminating selfishness and encouraging spiritual growth. McKinney clearly is intrigued with the possibility of removing the selfish and the judgmental from the sexual side of human nature.

In addition to poems about sexuality, McKinney writes autobiographical poems about her own rejection of the patriarchal construction of gender roles. In the brilliant "At 24," McKinney offers a portrait of herself as a young woman struggling with the demands of motherhood while dreaming of the life of a creative artist. She begins the poem by describing how she "had written and read until [her] eyes were bloodshot," working "while the baby slept." Then comes the powerful statement of purpose as a 24-year-old. "I was writing to save my life as I knew it / could be. I was writing to inscribe my body / on a stone tablet, writing in defiance and silence."[29] McKinney tells us how she avoided anything that would tear her away from her work, saying no to "impossible / jobs and prissy motherhood."[30] Clearly, the speaker longs to stop being defined by the conventional roles of wife and mother—a kind of slavery, in her mind—and dreams of pursuing the life of the mind. As the poem progresses, interestingly, the speaker describes reading books about artists, like Van Gogh and Toulouse-Lautrec, sensing in the power of art a possible calling for herself. At the end of the poem, she declares her independence from male authority figures:

> That was a long time ago and now I know that
> I knew nothing then, and if I had I wouldn't
> have gone on. Dear Mr. President, I said, Dear Dean
> Dear Husband, Dear Our Father, Dear Tax Collector,
> you don't know me. I don't know what I am,
> but whatever it is, you can't have me.[31]

Through this poem, McKinney shows how difficult it can be for women in a patriarchy to chart their own courses in their lives, and how they may be considered freaks for doing so. In fact, nowhere does McKinney suggest that the life of a poet is not lonely or not without sacrifice, but she does show that it can be done through force of will.

A recurring theme in *Vivid Companion* involves the marginalization of women who are past their youth. In "Constant Companion," the speaker dances naked and alone. In "Clitoral," the speaker says, "Lord, my body is lonely."[32] Many of these poems suggest that by choosing to pursue the life of an artist, the poet has guaranteed herself many solitary moments. Another poem that treats this theme is "Stained," in which the speaker describes an experience when she had quit smoking and was working a thankless position as a substitute teacher, a job she describes as "something that couldn't / possibly matter."[33] She pulls off the road, stands in the freezing weather, and sees a squirrel. The squirrel's indifference to her turns out to be an appropriate symbol of her situation, one in which she feels cut off from the rest of the world:

There was a squirrel there, not
afraid at all, turning a hickory nut in its
hands and ignoring me. I must've looked
like what I was, a woman who had lost her
bearings and refused to admit it. It was
another day in my history of posthumous
days, another day when nobody touched my body.[34]

Once again, McKinney presents the isolation of the poet who has chosen the writer's life and the marginalization of a mature woman in a society where youth is privileged over experience. However, the connection with nature, in this poem, also suggests a way for the speaker to recalibrate her perceptions of her place in the world. As McKinney said in an interview, "The fact that the natural world goes on without us is a source of great joy, because it puts our ego and self-centeredness in its place. Then it might be possible for us to feel genuine tenderness toward ourselves and our little pains, without whining or self-pity. I feel deeply compelled to acknowledge our 'human stain,' the imperfection of being alive, because this can counteract hubris and destructive abstraction."[35] Clearly, the speaker in the poem is on the brink of a realization that her problems are not as consequential as she had believed. She seems to be having a moment of grace, or what McKinney calls "genuine tenderness toward ourselves."[36]

Throughout the collection, McKinney celebrates women who are true to themselves, unwilling to let society control their behavior. The best example of the poet's attitude on this topic is found in the poem "Homage to Baroness Elsa Von Freytag Loringhoven." A Dadaist artist and poet, the baroness was known for her unique life and art. The opening of the poem provides a suitable introduction:

To hang teaballs from your ears and a caged canary
inside your cloak over your pubis is to inscribe on the outside air
your lobes and singing, and to paste pink postage stamps

on your cheeks is to say kiss me quick on my beauty-mark
and lick my sticky skin.[37]

And while McKinney salutes the outlandish behavior, she acknowledges the price: loneliness and the company of men who do not understand: "When all of Dada thrived, you panted after, / and the dirty little dogs were your only companions / at night in your cold one-room walk-up."[38] McKinney mocks the caddish audacity of one famous poet:

William Carlos Williams gave her peaches

and money, but later punched her in the face, just
because he wanted her. He said he was "crazy
about the woman." Why do we think our great poets

are enlightened?[39]

The speaker praises Elsa for her integrity ("She knew what she knew and she wouldn't lie, / not even for love"), but mostly for her ambition (". . . she wanted a lot, and believed she deserved it"). At the end of the poem, McKinney claims a kind of kinship, declaring "this is not over" and drawing inspiration from Elsa's example: "and tomorrow I could appear in a coal-scuttle hat, / pasted with postage stamps, mailing myself to the world."[40]

In poems like "Homage to Baroness Elsa Von Freytag Loringhoven," McKinney makes it clear that she admires women who age gracefully, unafraid to risk criticism in order to explore life's possibilities. In my interview with McKinney, she talked about what drew her to outlandish artists and women like the baroness. "Well, I just love that kind of defiance, and also it's not just about being an artist, I don't think. It's about feeling the freedom to be as odd and eccentric as you want to be. People who are able, both men and women, to plunge into the unknown, I mean, they don't know what's going to happen, it's might be a total failure, an enormous mistake— and in many ways the Baroness Elsa did make some huge mistakes in her life—I just want to celebrate that kind of either bravery or desperation, or maybe it's a combination of the two."[41] McKinney clearly admires the risk taking of artists in general and particularly women artists, suggesting that risking mistakes makes us stronger and creates the possibility for unlikely achievements. However, she makes it clear that the life of a creative woman can be very lonely, as it was at times for the baroness.

In spite of the many ways a creative woman can feel isolated as she grows older, McKinney also reveals the ways in which with age can come wisdom and inner peace. Three poems from the final section of *Vivid Companion*, in particular, demonstrate how surviving adversity and seeking for answers can lead a person to a sense of transcending the troubles of one phase of life and greeting the next with a sense of wonder: "Face," "Viridian Days," and "Ready." "Face" is constructed around an "if/then" formulation. The poem begins, "If you can continue to consider yourself beautiful / although you never were . . . ,"[42] and goes on to present a number of scenarios in which a woman has come to terms with life's series of sensations. In the first half of the poem, the speaker presents the possibility that one could find comfort from a passing train, become fascinated with the different shades and shapes of leaves in a grove "to enter with gratitude," and come to terms with the fact that the face "has become a repository of thousands / of smoothed-out thoughts and blended miseries."[43] After a page of the "if" construct, the speaker presents the "then" conclusion: days in which one finds serenity in mirrors and comfort from daily routines until one's face leads her to the garden. Then the speaker delivers the resolution with its resounding presentation of a vital woman who is comfortable in her own skin:

> Your face like the philosopher's lamp held up before
> the mind, looking and yearning forward with each step,
>
> uncovered and soaking up the rain, peering into
> the darkness, where a scarlet hollyhock leans out
>
> to touch it, while the rain sluices down it—no,
> it's not like tears—and your face is no longer what it was.[44]

In the final lines, McKinney guides the reader to the meaning, that experiencing life deeply and reveling in natural beauty do not lead to sorrow ("no, it's not like tears"), but to deeper self-awareness.

Another poem that develops the theme of connection with nature is "Viridian Days." In fact, this poem synthesizes many of McKinney's themes: the rejection of traditional gender roles, women's struggles for autonomy, and the sometimes lonely pursuit of the life of the mind. The poem starts with a declaration: "I was an ordinary woman, and so / I appeared eccentric . . ."[45] The speaker describes herself as "unhooked / from matrimony" and lands in "disheveled / West Virginia, where the hills are flung / around like old green handkerchiefs / and the Chessie rumbles along, shaking / the smooth clean skin of the river."[46] With "no small children to be humiliated / by [her] defection," the speaker justifies her eccentric, solitary lifestyle of gluing magazine pictures to the wall and walking around without clothes on: "Why not. That was / my motto." She describes reading books "down to the finest print,"[47] pointing out that "since no one / was there, nobody stopped me." The poem's multiple references to the color green develop the connection with nature that she expresses in the conclusion:

> I climb over the fence
> at the edge of the woods, back and forth
> over it several times a day, gathering ferns,
> then digging in the parsley,—shaggy, pungent, green.[48]

We see in this poem a speaker who is at peace with nature, comfortable with her choice of the creative life, and more at home in West Virginia than ever before. Her connection with nature links her with the elemental rather than with the temporal. The speaker has given herself permission to ignore societal claims on her, and now she does what she wants and says, "Why not?" It is as if the passage of time had taught McKinney that it is possible to take on many different personae before discovering the role that is most authentic.

McKinney explored this idea of living several lives within one lifetime more fully in the collection's final poem "Ready." The poem begins with a reminiscence from childhood, a Sunday of churchgoing and home-cooked meals. The speaker presents an image of her sister and her girlfriends and confirms the truth of the memory. "The sun was bright and / their clean cotton dresses swirled as they turned. / I was a witness to it, and I assure you that it's true."[49] Then the poem moves to thirty years later when the speaker is in the hospital recovering from surgery. Accepting the limitations of her life ("I would never chair the Department of Importance"), she walks down the hallway with an IV, pushing a cart of "vital fluids." In this moment of survival, the speaker dedicates herself to writing a new chapter of her life:

> Nevertheless,
> I was about to embark on a third life, having
> used up the first two, as I would this one,
> but I shoved the IV with its sugars and tubes
> steadily ahead of me, passing a frail man in a hospital
> gown pushing his cart from the other direction.
> Because I was determined to pull this together,
> Hooking this lifeline into the next one.[50]

In her interview with the Wick Poetry Center, McKinney commented on the meaning of the phrase "a third life": ". . . I'm also thinking of the infinite riches of a single human life, which contains a great many lives within it, and I want to eagerly consume each one of them, even if they are painful. And of course the writing life, not to mention the reading life, encompasses many lives. And there's the edge of a hope that maybe this great richness might go on to a fourth, or a fifth, after death."[51] As a cancer survivor and a housewife turned poet, McKinney delivers in "Ready" an inspirational poem that celebrates her dignity and determination to continue to affirm life with all of its disappointments and challenges.

In rejecting traditional gender roles, pursuing her dream of a creative life, finding a voice for her poetic imagination, and recognizing her ability to create multiple lives within one lifetime, Irene McKinney offered readers an impressive body of work. It's no wonder that her fellow West Virginia writers wonder why her work is not more widely read. Pinckney Benedict said it best. "This woman should be internationally famous."[52] Her poetry has that rare ability to make the personal seem universal, even mythic. What woman cannot relate to "saying no" to patriarchal demands and setting her own priorities? What woman cannot relate to the rejection of a body image manufactured by the fashion industry? Coming of age in a more traditional society, McKinney reconstructed gender in a way that liberates the mind and the body. She presented women and men with the possibility of moving past restrictions, of celebrating their inner freak, of not fearing the pursuit of the personal, no matter how much that pursuit might be misunderstood. In doing so, she offered an affirmation of integrity, a promise of transcendence, a hope of rising above the external constraints that would subdue our individuality and our humanity. She revealed how poetry is "the place you go to tell the truth."

CHAPTER 6

Ann Pancake's
Strange as This Weather Has Been

Ann Pancake's *Strange as This Weather Has Been* (2007) tells the modern-day story of conflict between the coal industry and private citizens concerned with the devastation of mountaintop removal. The novel prompted Jayne Anne Phillips to call Pancake "Appalachia's Steinbeck," adding, "Not since Harriet Arnow's *The Dollmaker* has a writer so truly envisioned rural poverty, rural art, rural grace, but Pancake's book is utterly contemporary."[1] Indeed, the book focuses not only on important historical events like the Buffalo Creek tragedy of 1972, but also alludes to recent incidents like the 2000 slurry impoundment disaster in Martin County, Kentucky. *Strange as This Weather Has Been* portrays the sense of powerlessness that many Appalachians feel when voicing their disapproval of the latest methods of producing coal. Like Giardina's *Storming Heaven*, the novel won the Weatherford Award, a prize honoring books that "best illuminate the challenges, personalities, and unique qualities of the Appalachian South."[2] It made *Booklist*'s Top Ten First Novels of 2007, and *Kirkus Review* named the novel one of the Top Ten Works of Fiction of 2007. It also garnered some very positive reviews. In *The New York Times Book Review*, Jack Pendarvis calls Pancake's technique "powerful, sure-footed, and haunting," while Laura Longsong, writing in *Appalachian Heritage*, praises the novel's "bold and gritty realism" and calls it "the most enchanting novel you'll ever read that will also leave you with outrage and grief."[3] The *Seattle Post-Intelligencer* writes that the novel "heralds the emergence of a major literary talent." On *Oprah.com*, Pam Houston commends the way Pancake's narrators "speak a language both lyrical and fierce, full of honesty and urgency . . . ."[4]

A distant relative of Breece Pancake, Ann Pancake grew up in Romney and Summersville, West Virginia. Pancake has addressed how her childhood experiences inform the novel. "I lived in a coal-mining part of West Virginia until I was eight years old, so I was introduced to strip mining as a little kid . . . . Then I moved to Hampshire County, where I lived until I was eighteen, and there's no coal there at all."[5] Pancake has said that as an adult she did not think much about environmental issues involving the coal industry until graduate school. After earning a bachelor's degree from West Virginia University, Pancake earned a Master's at the University of North Carolina. She has spent much of her adult life in Washington state, earning a Ph.D. from the University of Washington and teaching creative writing at Pacific Lutheran University. In 2000 she published her first book, *Given Ground*, a collection of stories that won the Bakeless Award, presented by Middlebury College to new authors of literary works. Her stories have appeared in literary magazines and journals such as *Glimmer Train*, *Shenandoah*, and *Mid-American Review* and have been anthologized in *New Stories from the South*. After success as a short story writer, she developed the idea for her first novel from interviews she conducted while working with her sister Catherine on a documentary entitled *Black Diamonds*. The promise of her early short fiction was fulfilled in *Strange as This Weather Has Been*.

An issue novel like *Strange as This Weather Has Been* runs the risk of allowing the political perspective to undercut the aesthetic quality of the work. In his generally positive review of the novel, Jack Pendarvis alludes to "a few slips into frank didacticism."[6] In an interview, Pancake indicated that she is well aware of the risk of writing a book with a political message. "When I [was] working on my dissertation, I did research on political novels, especially those written in the 1930s, and I learned that many of them failed as art because their politics was the driving force, which made them polemical. When I went into this novel, I was really invested in the art. I knew that for the novel to be successful politically, it would first have to be successful aesthetically."[7]

Pancake works to maintain factual accuracy, while giving her characters inner lives that possess many dimensions, some of which are not political at all. Like *Storming Heaven*, the novel relies upon multiple points of view to provide more objectivity in the narration of the story. The reader sees the action from the perspectives of five characters: Lace; her children Bant, Dane, and Corey; her uncle Mogey; and Avery, a survivor of the Buffalo Creek disaster who has moved to Cleveland. Pancake not only incorporates shifts in points of view, but also shifts in time, with Lace, Mogey, and Avery relating their histories in the area. And just as Denise Giardina did in *Storming Heaven*, Ann Pancake uses gender issues to add complexity to her characters. However, in *Strange as This Weather Has Been*, gender and class are interrelated. Like many women of the region, Lace enters the work force when her husband, Jimmy Make, cannot find a job in the mining industry. As was the case in *Storming Heaven*, class issues are the focus from the opening pages of the novel.

The theme of socio-economic class is dominant throughout the novel. Lace drops out of college after becoming pregnant, and she eventually tries to make a life for herself and her family in southern West Virginia. Jimmy Make's dream of a higher-paying job takes the family to Raleigh, North Carolina, for a time, but Lace feels a connection to the land that brings them back to West Virginia. As Pancake points out in an interview with Nicholas Arnold and Michael Baccam, many Appalachians feels such a connection. "I was raised on a farm, the seventh generation to have that land. My family had been there ever since the 1770s, and we were indoctrinated not to ever sell it. I think a lot of people in West Virginia are indoctrinated with the idea of holding onto land."[7] Lace develops a connection to the land while she is pregnant, though she did not always feel such a close bond with her home. She recalls how when she first returned home from WVU, she had resented her humble origins. "And glaring down at the house, I saw it again how I'd seen it before I left. Grubby, grim, gritty, covered with that asphalt shingle stuff with fake brick shapes pressed into it. The bubbled greasy place where the coal-stove pipe came out of the wall. The old outhouse still tilted in the corner of the yard, we hadn't got an inside bathroom until I was two, and even now Daddy sometimes used the outside one."[8] A main focus of the novel becomes Lace's ability to discard others' views of herself and her home and to develop a stronger sense of pride in her identity and her family heritage.

After the first section, narrated by Lace, the novel shifts its focus to the present, in which Lace is married with four children. In the sections narrated by Lace's daughter Bant, the reader becomes acquainted with the modern-day threat posed by mountaintop removal. Having heard her mother talk about the danger to the area, Bant satisfied her curiosity by exploring the site for herself on a number of occasions. Early in the novel, she describes how the mountains have been altered. When she and Jimmy Make gaze upon the fill, Bant realizes the full extent of the destruction of the mountaintop. "The closest thing I'd ever seen to it was the Summersville Dam, but this was bigger, darker, and looser. I hauled back my head and looked up its whole height, and it seemed to me it must be as tall as the highest buildings in Charleston, but who knew for sure. There was simply no way to gauge how tall the thing was because there was nothing natural about it, nothing you could compare it to, and then it dawned on me what exactly I was standing under—Yellow-root Mountain, dead."[9] Bant's interest in the mountaintop mining increases when she gets a job painting at a local motel where the non-union miners stay. She discusses the company's treatment of the mostly out-of-state work-ers. "The miners drove nice trucks with out-of-state tags—Illinois, Wyoming, Indiana, Kentucky—and I learned they worked twelve-hour shifts running heavy equipment unless the company wanted them to work longer, and then they did. Few were union, so they had no choice."[10] While Bant doubts the extent of the company's exploitation in the beginning, her first-hand expe-riences provide important evidence of the destruction of the mountain and the disregard for the welfare of the local community. The coal company has tried to convince the West Virginians that mountaintop removal is essential for jobs, but the technology requires fewer workers than underground min-ing and many of the available jobs go to out-of-state workers.

As the novel progresses, Lace's children become increasingly aware of the ways in which mountaintop removal damages the area. Ten-year-old Corey notices how the creek "used to be too deep to wade, but every year it gets more shallow, and the water with a bad odor to it, even though it was two years ago all the fish and crawdads died."[11] One day, Lace becomes upset when six-year-old Tommy finds dead fish in the creek, yelling at him to put them down.[12] Twelve-year-old Dane works as a caregiver for an older woman named Mrs. Taylor, whose fatalism about the inevitability of the destruction frightens the boy. She is a survivor of the Buffalo Creek incident and now feels that it is her lot in life to feel endangered by a coal company. "Thirty years later, and I'm right back in it. That was Pittston, this is Lyon. But one company or another's bound to drown me before I did a natural death."[13] One day when a blast goes off at the worksite, Mrs. Taylor asks Dane to check whether "any more plaster come down in that bedroom."[14] However, it is fifteen-year-old Bant who becomes most interested in her mother's preoccupation with the damage the mining is doing:

> She'd tell me about the latest blackwater, the latest fish kills—"Maureen said
> up there at Rock Branch she can't even walk into her back bedroom, stink's

so bad"—tell me who was selling out now. At first, I'd roll towards her as she told me, I'd raise up a little so I could see her, while she told of overloaded coal truck wrecks—"they couldn't even tell them three kids apart, mangled up bad as they were"—fly rock crashing into people's houses, chemical leaks in sediment ponds. Drownings in flash floods, people breathing cancer-causing dust."[15]

As these examples show, Lace and her family learn about the adverse effects of mountaintop removal as the novel progresses.

Pancake dramatizes the issue in Lace's family dynamics. While Lace becomes increasingly interested in raising awareness about the questionable practices of the coal companies and the adverse effects of the mining, her husband just wants a job. Jimmy Make does not consider surface mining as true coal mining. As a one-time union underground miner, he argues that the mountaintop workers are "nothing but ditch diggers."[16] Worried that the industry may have passed him by, he wants to return to North Carolina where jobs are more prevalent. Having once enjoyed a well-paying job in mining, he feels that the lack of good jobs has diminished his ability to provide for his family. In summing up his situation, Lace says, "Jimmy Make'd spent the winter of '98-'99 looking for any deep mine or construction outfit that might be hiring, but nobody was. He acted like he wouldn't work for a mountaintop job, but truth was, even if he'd wanted to, he couldn't have gotten on, most of them passed over workers with union experience, and, besides, the skills you needed on those operations were different from what you learned underground."[17] Still, Jimmy Make refuses to take a job in the service industry, perhaps seeing such employment as not real work, or work not fitting for a man. Jimmy Make's situation is complicated by the fact that he once suffered an on-the-job back injury that required surgery. Still, Lace wishes he would put aside his pride. "He still wouldn't apply for what few minimum wage jobs there were, even though that would have doubled our income and been easier on his back. We were in a terrible tight for money, I worried about it just all the time, and going into that fall, I couldn't even get the kids school clothes, it was all we could do to eat, and a lot of that we did on credit."[18] Jimmy Make's desperation for what he sees as meaningful work reveals how demeaning unemployment can be to a person who has once enjoyed gainful employment and how West Virginians have often been at the mercy of changes in the economic fortunes of the coal industry.

The novel eloquently explores the harsh effects of poverty on the self-esteem of West Virginians. On the basis of family income, Corey feels inferior to his friend Seth, who possesses many video games and DVDs and whose father owns a four-wheeler that Corey covets. Corey feels ashamed of his home and thinks about how unattractive the hollow looks, "plugged with little houses and little trailers and their little chain link fences. At times Corey torments himself by thinking what if Paul Franz and them from school came up this hollow and saw where Corey lives."[19] When Jimmy Make and Lace lived in North Carolina, she recalls how "somehow people knew we were different from them, even before we opened our mouths, although I couldn't for the life of me see how we looked much different from anybody else."[20] Later in the novel, Avery Taylor remembers attending public school in West Virginia and describes how when he was in eighth grade, he could sense the cautionary tale implied in the lives of the most economically deprived children. "And, always, again, the poorest kids, their warning: look what will happen to you if you don't work hard, do as your told, expect little, American poverty Appalachian style: the shanties and decaying trailers, the retarded and the crazy, those without plumbing reeking on the school buses, the ringworm and scabies and the lice, your daily meal the free one at school, your clothes somebody else's first and everyone can tell . . . ."[21] In passages like these, the novel shows how devastating poverty can be when society equates self-worth with financial worth.

Members of the struggling working class, like Lace and her family, become victims of bias, or classism, which Lois Tyson defines as "an ideology that equates one's value as a human being with the social class to which one belongs."[22] Clearly, Corey is a victim of classism when he feels inferior to Seth just because Seth's family can afford to buy more material things. Tyson adds, "From a classist perspective, people at the top of the social scale are naturally superior to those below them: more intelligent, more responsible, more trustworthy, more ethical, and so on. People at the bottom of the social scale, it follows, are naturally shiftless, lazy, and irresponsible."[23] Of course, the classist ideology distorts reality: Lace is not lazy, just disadvantaged, and Jimmy Make sincerely wants to work in the mining industry. However, because it distorts the worth of individuals, classism makes poor children, like the ones Avery remembers, feel diminished. Their sense of self-worth is damaged in a culture that places too much emphasis on material wealth.

Strange as This Weather Has Been portrays how powerless many West Virginians feel about their poverty and also depicts how powerless they feel in confronting coal companies that exploit the land. The major tension in Lace and Jimmy Make's marriage stems from the fact that she thinks they should try to fight against the coal company and he believes that such a fight would be futile and dangerous. Lace describes one of their many arguments:

> "This is my homeplace, Jimmy Make," I said. "What about the kids? What do they got to look forward to if we don't fight?"
> "Fight?" he snorted, and then he turned from the screen to fame me this know-it-all-how-stupid-can-you-be look. "Honey, you won't never beat coal. It's who has the money, the rich people always win, that how it's always been, especially in the state of West Virginia. That's why the smart people get out."[24]

Jimmy Make touches on a perception shared by many West Virginians—that the state's residents must accept the dynamic of the powerful and the powerless.

At another point in the novel, Jimmy Make warns Lace about the dangers of becoming involved with environmentalists. "I've told you a hundred times. You stay clear of the shit-stirrers. You get too close to shit-stirrers and we really will get killed."[25] However, Lace is well aware of the risks of activism. In fact, she refuses to become an official member of an environmental group out of her knowledge of "the real reasons to be scared. Like how a year or two before, over in Logan, they hung effigies of environmentalists. How just that past summer, '99, the Logan County Commission hired school bus drivers and other county employees to attack people reenacting the historic unionizing march on Blair, and they even beat up Secretary of State Ken Hechler, eighty-five years old, they bloodied him good."[26] Pancake uses these real-life incidents to grant more credibility to the fictional narrative.

Nowhere is this tendency to incorporate historical fact to keep the novel from seeming contrived and thus too polemical more prominent than in Avery's childhood memory of surviving the Buffalo Creek tragedy. One of Pancake's sources for the novel is Kai T. Erikson's book *Everything in Its Path*, which presents eyewitness accounts of the tragedy. Erikson describes how the Pittston coal company had constructed an impoundment that "was composed not only of slag but whatever fragments of metal or timber—mine posts, crib blocks, roof bolts, wedges—that had been thrown aside into the refuse pile."[27] The impoundment "trapped 132 million gallons of black water—a lake of some twenty acres in size and forty feet deep at the edge of the impoundment."[28] On February 26, 1972, at 8:00 in the morning, the dam collapsed. The deluge destroyed the town of Saunders completely and, according to Erikson, "scraped the ground as completely as if a thousand bulldozers had been at work."[29] One eyewitness said that the water, which was twenty feet high at one point, "just looked like a black mountain going down that hollow, and there were houses on top of it."[30] According to the West Virginia Division of Culture and History, 118 people were killed, with seven more missing. Over 4,000 were left without a home. "The flood demolished 502 houses and 44 mobiles homes and damaged 943 houses and mobile homes. Property damage was estimated at $50 million."[31] In the novel, Avery remembers how the flood "peeled the railroad right off the ground, scattered ties everywhere, then coiled up the rails into lassoes."[32] He recalls encountering a man looking for his mother and another man who mistakes Avery for his son. Most importantly, he must come to terms with seeing his friend Tad perish in the flood waters.

Avery is a character who decided to leave West Virginia because he accepts the dominance of the corporations. He studied the tragedy while a student at Marshall University. A sociology professor interviewed him about his Buffalo Creek experience and gave him books to read on the subject. Avery describes how from that point on, he became obsessed with knowing more. "He learned who could get away with what—where, when, and on whom. He learned the February 26, 1972, dam bust was not Pittston's first, wasn't even the first one they'd had on Buffalo Creek . . . . He learned that over 100,000 people were killed in U. S. mines between 1906 and 1977, learned that 1.6 million were injured from 1930 to 1976. That a U. S. miner dies of black lung every six hours."[33] Avery also recalls how his research revealed that the lives of the residents of the Buffalo Creek area were not valued very highly by a government under the influence of the powerful. "He learned that a body in some states can cost a killer millions of dollars. In other states, a person is beyond price. He learned that in the state of West Virginia, at the time of Buffalo Creek, a body's value was capped at $110,000. He learned that some Buffalo Creek family members got for their dead no more than a couple thousand bucks."[34] Avery must also come to terms with how the experience has affected him. Years later, he recognizes the impact. "He keeps to himself, doesn't get close to anyone much, drove his first wife crazy that way, found a second one who doesn't mind it too bad."[35] It is a telling moment in the novel when the adult Avery sees the damage mountaintop mining is causing, and he oddly feels "a kind of satisfaction," as if he knows what's coming. "Because if the entire truth be told, the slaughter also fulfills a secret unspoken urge Avery carries always. This itchy voice, this desperate chant that begs: Okay. Let's just get it over with."[36] Like Jimmy Make, Avery has resigned himself to the power of the coal interests.

However, the novel presents a number of seemingly ordinary individuals who protest against the environmental and property damage. At the Dairy Queen where she works, Lace meets Loretta Hughes and Charlie Blizzard, who have been educating themselves about the threats and legal issues posed by the mountaintop mining. Pancake makes a point of highlighting their lack of postsecondary education: "It was amazing what all they'd taught themselves, Loretta with nothing but a high school diploma and Charlie without even that, but when I mentioned it once to Charlie, he just grunted, 'You'd be surprised how quick you can learn about something that's on the verge of killing you.'"[37] Lace finds a role model in Loretta, a woman who is unafraid to speak her mind and willing to try to effect change. Convinced that very little good can come from mountaintop mining, Loretta scoffs at how local residents tolerate the destruction out of fear of losing jobs, asking, "Why should a few people, most of em from out of state, get $60,000 a year while the rest of us got nothing but dust and floods and stress and poison and never knowing when that water's gonna take your house with it?"[38] At one point, Lace accompanies Loretta to her home to see the damage the mining has done to her property. What Lace sees is stunning. "Between the white house and the others slashed a clawed-out gulch choked with big rocks, . . . the rocks thrown out all around it even farther, eating up the yard, and at the upper end of the slash, you could see a barn caving down into it."[39] Loretta's attempts to gain compensation for the damages have been ineffectual. When she complained to the DEP about the damage, the agency responded that it was an "an act of God. Normal weather event. Mining didn't contribute at all."[40]

Charlie's experiences with the mining interests have also been ineffectual and disheartening. A former miner, one who for a time even worked in strip mining, he takes a stand against the coal companies not just because they have damaged his land, but because he resents their taking away individuals' liberty. Charlie tells Lace a story about how a coal company tried to buy people's land in Tout in the nineties. In order to sell a house, the seller "had to sign a form that said you'd never protest a mine again and would never move back within twenty-five miles of Tout."[41] What angers Charlie is the presumption of such a request and the acquiescence of some of his neighbors who signed this form. "But I refused to sign, not necessarily because I wanted to stay within twenty-five miles. Not even because, at that time, I wanted to protest a mine. But because a coal company wasn't going to tell me where I could live and what I could say."[42] In many ways, Charlie's actions reflect the rugged individualism of many Appalachians. He insists as a matter of principle upon his freedom even when this choice leads to tough consequences.

As Lace becomes more involved with protesting against mountaintop removal, she experiences intimidation first-hand. She joins a group protesting at a Lyon stockholders meeting in Charleston, and the company responds by bringing in some of their workers to lead a counter protest. Lace says, "A couple started antagonizing us, calling us out-of-state agitators. One hollered, 'You're takin food out of my kids' mouths,' and I just hollered right back, 'You're taking the life outta my kids' bodies,' and by the time the WSAZ camera got to me and asked me what I was doing there, I was mad way past stage fright. I had my say."[43] Not long after that, Lace stops at a convenience store, and when she comes out of the restroom, a man blocks her way. At first, she thinks he may be making a sexual advance, "but then he blocked me with his whole leg and pulled out enough of the gun that I could tell what it was. Then he let me go."[44] Still, Lace, Loretta, and Charlie refuse to be intimidated and show how seemingly ordinary people can do extraordinary things. These three characters all are products of the working class, with very few financial resources, and yet they work hard to raise awareness and to thwart the steady march to profitability. They all see their struggle in moral terms. During one of Lace's arguments with Jimmy Make, he claims that the coal companies are not evil, just out to make a profit. Jimmy Make claims, "It's just greed and they-don't-give-a-damn. It's money," and Lace responds, "Greed and money and they-don't-give-a-damn *are* evil."[45]

As stated earlier, Pancake does a wonderful job of interweaving the themes of class and gender, since Jimmy Make feels diminished—and in some ways, Lace feels empowered—by his difficulties in finding a job and Lace providing for the family as well as she can by working at Dairy Queen. In her interview with Arnold and Baccam, Pancake discusses a phenomenon that is not uncommon in West Virginia:

. . . through Jimmy Make and some other characters, I wanted to show how shifts in economics in Appalachia cause a kind of emasculation in some of the men. Now a lot of wives are breadwinners because they do the white collar jobs and the service industry jobs, whereas the men, who traditionally worked in mining and logging and manufacturing and farming, are now more temporarily and seasonally employed. So men have lost some power, control, status, because they've lost work, and I wanted to illustrate this through Jimmy Make.[46]

One can see the power shift in the novel from early in the marriage when Jimmy Make worked a union job and provided for the family while Lace raised the children to later when Lace works and the former breadwinner struggles to find a job.

There is a corresponding physical transformation in Jimmy Make as well. Early in the novel, his physical vitality powerfully attracts Lace, who immediately becomes mesmerized by "the beauty, beauty of that boy. Like what you feel off animals, big cats. Wet horses. It was a beauty could carry you a ways."[47] Even though the pregnancy and Lace's unwillingness to press him to marry her threatens the relationship, the physical attraction sustains it until a second pregnancy leads to marriage. Lace says it is not just desire that drove the relationship, though she sometimes tried to rationalize her feelings for him. "But I can tell myself it was lust, the baby, loneliness, that it was nothing else to look forward to, when, in truth, I know it went beyond all that. I loved him."[48] Landing the union job, doing physical work, and making good money empower Jimmy Make.

In the early days of the marriage Lace recalls how he would come home from work and "swagger in all gruffy and rough," like a "boy wearing a tough man mask."[49] Lace sympathizes with Jimmy Make when he hurts his back at work and develops a limp after surgery. Still, she recognizes that her desire for him has diminished at an early age: ". . . that hot wetness had been dripping away for years, but with the injury, it drained clear gone. Jimmy Make was twenty-five years old."[50] By this time, Lace has been involved with him for ten years, and she has seen him decline from a strong adolescent to an aging man with a pronounced limp. In addition to the diminution of his physical strength, the fact that Lace becomes the primary breadwinner makes him feel like he is a lesser man.

Of the couple's three sons, Corey most resembles his father in linking masculinity with physicality. For Corey, masculinity means fast vehicles and physical toughness. Aware that his father's truck is his "pride and joy," he dreams of riding Seth's four-wheeler. He collects parts from the flood's debris and dreams of enlisting a neighbor's help in building a customized four-wheeler. "He has the parts. He just doesn't know how to put them together. *Like a little low-to-the-ground speedwagon*. That is his plan. It'll make a noise like a lawnmower starting up, with more of a grumble and grunt to it than a four-wheeler, lower pitched than your average four-wheeler, but it'll go over any kind of ground like a four-wheeler can."[51] Corey also links his desire for speed with physical courage. He becomes so obsessed with riding the four-wheeler that he challenges Seth to a "bike contest." In a large drain, the boy who rides his bike the highest up the wall wins. Seth will win ten dollars if he wins the competition, Corey a ride on the four-wheeler. Corey risks a major injury by attempting a 360. "Corey is coming down first, because by this point, Corey is underneath the bike, and Dane springs to his feet in time to see Corey slam into the bad water, the bike close after him, landing partly on his legs. Corey cringes into a crumple, his knees pulled to his chest, his hands cupping his face . . . ."[52] Seth tries to sneak away, but Dane stops him. Seth explains that no one else can ride the four-wheeler because of liability reasons. After Corey hurls obscenities at his rival, Seth replies, "At least I aint got a faggot for a brother."[53] After Seth leaves, all of the other boys, including Corey, begin chanting, "Homo!" at Dane. Afraid of appearing weak and therefore unmasculine, both Corey and Seth try to project their fear onto the more defenseless Dane. Throughout the Corey scenes, the resemblance between the ten-year-old son and his father become more and more striking. The attempt to link masculinity with physicality ends badly for both of them, and in Jimmy Make's case, it makes the demise of his marriage inevitable.

The end of Lace's relationship with Jimmy Make, in some ways, makes the novel's strongest feminist point, for Lace has become an independent woman and no longer needs Jimmy Make physically, financially, or emotionally. Early in the novel, while acknowledging that the marriage is a bad idea, she feels the pressure to marry him anyway. "I was the first Ricker, the first See, to go to college, and now I disappointed my family three ways: first, by getting pregnant; second, by dropping out; and third, by refusing to marry Jimmy Make." She knows that if she had married him at that time, "the marriage would fall too short to soon of the life I'd always seen for myself,"[54] After they marry, Lace's fears gradually become realized, yet she resists the temptation to lower her expectations. When Lace's mom tells her that at least she's lucky that Jimmy Make is not a drinker, Lace thinks about her the state of her marriage:

> The older he got, the less he drank, and I knew I was lucky, I knew where the kind of work he did could push you. Liquor, painkillers, illegal drugs. Take the edge off. A little of the uncertainty. Some of the hurt. But I'd never thought that was the kind of lucky I'd need, and I could tell from the way Mom said it, she'd expected more for me, too. I have to give her that. And I thanked her in my head for not saying what some others did—"and at least he don't beat on you or the kids." I still couldn't be grateful for a bar as low as that.[55]

Given the quality of her relationship and her husband's disapproval of her budding environmental interest, it is not surprising when Jimmy Make leaves for Raleigh, but Lace is still disappointed about the failure of the marriage.

At first, Bant's relationship with R. L., a scab worker at the mountain-top site, seems to resemble that of Lace and Jimmy Make in the possibility that a physical relationship may lead to marriage. However, Bant ultimately rejects R. L., who deceives her about his willingness or ability to take her to the impoundment. And unlike her mother's involvement with Jimmy Make that is motivated by physical attraction, Bant's relationship is driven more by her adolescent insecurities than by her desire. After her friend Sharon has a boyfriend, Bant worries that she is not attractive enough to attract a boy. She describes how she worried about her complexion and "bought every skin treatment Dollar General sold."[56] However, her fears persist. "But it wasn't just my skin, I knew, that was the problem. It was the high jag of my cheekbones, the hollows under them. It was the long bony nose, my eyes too small, my chin too thin. And you couldn't buy nothing for those."[57] As a result of her insecurities, then, she is flattered by R. L.'s attention, and yet she feels self-assured enough to reject him. At one point, Bant recalls what her mother says about men. *They never have to grow up, Lace would say, stay babified. Never have to because the women always take care of them, first their mothers, then their wives, and then they die.*" Lace goes on to talk about how women end up being stronger than men:

> "Everybody around here is raised to take it, Lace would say, to put up with it and take it, that's what makes us tough, but especially the girls, the women, are tougher than the men, because the men just take it from the industry and then the government, and then they take that out on the women. So the

women are tougher because they take it from the industry, the government, and the men, which means the women are stronger . . . ."[58]

Bant's recognition of R. L.'s emotional immaturity allows her to end an unsatisfactory relationship.

However, in spite of her portrayal of traditional males like Jimmy Make and R. L., Pancake takes great care in the novel to avoid the appearance of male bashing by presenting some male characters with more expansive definitions of masculinity. When asked in the Arnold and Baccam interview about whether the women in the novel are strong, while the men are "babified," Pancake responded, "Mogey and Avery *aren't* babified. That's one reason I put them in the novel. I didn't want the reader to assume that Appalachian men are in general 'babified' just because Lace perceives Jimmy Make that way."[59] In fact, Mogey is the most fully evolved male character in the novel because he not only has demonstrated the physical strength traditionally associated with masculinity, but he possesses the spirituality and the wisdom that should come with age. In fact, Mogey supplies the novel's summative statement. Bant has gone once again to look at the mountaintop site and recognizes that more destruction is probably imminent. She draws comfort from what Mogey told her after her grandmother had passed away. "In times like these, you have to grow big enough inside to hold both the loss and the hope."[60] This line provides a sort of answer for the characters who care about the land and want to fight for it against the odds. Mogey's version of masculinity allows for personal growth after a man has reached his physical peak, something that Jimmy Make does not seem to understand, given his tendency to see masculinity in more conventional terms.

In spite of the limitations involving socio-economic class and gender roles, some of the characters experience a kind of transcendence that is based on a connection with the land that borders on the spiritual. As we have seen, Lace feels this bond as a young woman who marvels at the pull the place has for her. "And I asked myself, what is it about this place? What? I pressed my forehead against the oak. Because for a long time, I'd known the tightness of these hills, the way they penned. But now, I also felt their comfort, and worse, I'd learned the smallness of me in the away."[61] However, the character who most strongly experiences the link between spirituality and nature is Lace's uncle Mogey. He describes how as a younger man he worried about whether it was right to feel more spiritual in nature than in the church. "Although I have been a Christian all my life, I have never felt in church a feeling any-place near where I get in the woods . . . . To walk in the woods was a prayer. But I knew it was wrong. Some kind of paganism or idolatry, I didn't know what you'd call it, but I knew it must be sin."[62] He tells of an experience he had when he had gone hunting at age ten and felt a spiritual presence out in nature. "It melted my edges. It blended me, I don't know how else to say it, right on out into the woods. It took me beyond myself and kept going, so I wasn't no longer holed up in my body, hidden, I saw then how before I'd been hidden, how I'd believed myself smaller than I really was. It made me feel bigger in myself, and it made me feel more here even though you might have expected such a thing to make me feel gone. And with it came total sureness. And with the total sureness came peace."[63] Mogey's and the other characters' spiritual connections with the land understandably increase their rage when they see the coal companies' carelessness with nature.

Mogey makes the exploitation of the mining companies clear. He talks about how he has trouble sleeping, and he thinks about the damage the min-ing is doing to his house. "So I lay here feeling around me this house I built with my own hands, falling apart. Blasting's cracked my Sheetrock, cracked the walls in my bathroom, cracked the cinderblocks under my house. Just a few weeks ago, it split my concrete porch in two. In this valley now we are completely surrounded by the mining."[64] He elaborates on his frustration with the powerful industry. "You work all your life to have you a home. And you want your home to be quiet and peaceable. I built this house, I know how well-made it is, and it's the only thing I got to leave my boys. And here they can take it from me without even walking on my land."[65] Mogey's frus-trations extend to the damage the coal companies have done to the animal and plant life of the area. "They've tore up our ramp and ginseng patches, they've run off all the game. And you can't fish. Even if you found you a live fish to catch, I'd be scared to eat it . . . ."[66] Again, Mogey sees the devasta-tion in moral terms. ". . . what we're doing to this land is not only murder. It is suicide."[67]

In *Strange as This Weather Has Been*, Pancake's exploration of gender keeps the novel from becoming overly polemical by adding depth to the human expe-riences that are threatened by the development of new technologies. However, the novel ultimately focuses on class issues more than gender roles because it details the ways in which business interests accumulate enough power to exploit private citizens and natural resources for profit. Lace's father's life is shortened by black lung disease. Jimmy Make suffers an injury that alters the way he walks. Due to environmental damage, traditional mountain people can no longer live off the land. Many Appalachians choose to do what Jimmy Make does: leave the area for better economic opportunities. However, others, like Lace, Bant, Loretta, and Charlie, recognize that while there is little they can do, they refuse to leave and abandon the land to those who would damage it. Rick Bass said of *Strange as This Weather Has Been*, "Ann Pancake has written a novel that crackles with this century's great background white noise of loss, greed, dishonesty—but the honest complexity of both her characters and their sometimes-beloved, sometimes-estranged or forgotten landscape yields a hope which on the surface may seem unjustified, but ends up being as durable as the spark of life itself, and then some."[68] Pancake's account of ordinary people doing extraordinary things etches itself indelibly in the mind of the reader. Pancake dedicates the novel to "the people in the central Appalachian coalfields who struggle against catastrophe every day." She adds, "Nowhere have I seen courage and integrity like theirs."[69]

CHAPTER 7

Jayne Anne Phillips's
Lark and Termite

Jayne Anne Phillips's *Lark and Termite*, published in 2009, develops characters who have endured hardship and misfortune, but who search for ways of transcending suffering and loss, finding a promise of fulfillment and meaning in their lives. The novel shares many themes with 1984's *Machine Dreams*, such as coming of age, desire, war and mortality. However, *Lark and Termite* represents a departure from Phillips's earlier works, in which characters sometimes seem defeated by tragedy, and reveals the redemptive quality of fiction. In an interview with Thomas E. Douglass in the early nineties, Phillips said, "I think the function of fiction is basically religious. It has to do with redemption really. That if you are dealing with the elements of a past . . . you are basically trying to redeem that past, trying to make it live again and save something of it. Save something. Keep something from fading away."[1] In *Lark and Termite*, Phillips explores religious themes of redemption and transcendence.

The novel earned glowing reviews, some of which are captured on Phillips's website. Alice Munro raves, "This novel is cut like a diamond, with such sharp authenticity and bursts of light." Robert Olen Butler writes, "Jayne Anne Phillips has the universal soul of an artist, and she is at the height of her powers in *Lark and Termite* . . . . This is a major novel from one of America's finest writers."[2] The novel's nominations for a National Book Award and for a National Book Critics Circle Award provide further evidence of Phillips' growing stature in contemporary American literature. Of all the writers included in this review of West Virginia writers, Phillips has garnered the most national and international recognition.

Lark and Termite alternates between scenes in South Korea and the fictional Winfield, West Virginia. The sections in Korea depict Corporal Robert

Leavitt's attempts to survive friendly fire during the No Gun Ri incident of 1950, while the West Virginia scenes focus on the same days nine years later in the lives of the two siblings of the novel's title: Lark, Lola's daughter, and Termite, the developmentally challenged child Leavitt conceived with Lola before he departed for military duty in Asia. As in *Machine Dreams*, the younger characters find themselves facing similar situations as those of the preceding generation. However, Michael Dirda points out an important distinction between Phillips's first novel and her most recent. "While *Machine Dreams* closes with a young man's death in wartime, *Lark and Termite* instead traces more fully the aftereffects of such a loss—the unrelievable burden, an ongoing sadness . . . . But by the end of the novel, the old wounds will begin to cauterize."[3] One character learns the truth about her parents, and another learns to let go of the past while embracing the present. At the end of the novel, the characters have found a number of ways of rising above the possible limitations in their lives.

As with the other works analyzed in this book, class, gender, and place play major thematic roles. Male characters work hard to keep their businesses operating and experience complicated relationships with their mothers (Leavitt's father and Charlie). Women break with traditional gender roles (Lola and Nonie). Furthermore, the fictional Winfield, West Virginia, becomes not just a typical small town, but a place of magical happenings. However, in this novel, the limitations the characters must rise above also involve time and place, so the characters experience moments of transcendence in a greater number of ways. At times, they see the truth with greater clarity, reaching an insight about themselves or the nature of reality that is refreshingly new, as when Lark sees the town of Winfield and herself as transformed after the flood. The characters often feel a connection with another human being that far exceeds that of everyday life, as when Lark and Termite feel supernaturally connected with their dead parents. The connectedness can be seen not only in the sibling bond of the title characters but also in the novel's depiction of romantic relationships. Sexuality is depicted as much more than physical gratification. The imagery of Phillips's novel deftly supports the idea that certain types of human experience bond individuals with each other in ways that transcend space and time. As in some of her earlier works, Phillips depicts characters living on in the memories of their loved ones. Finally, *Lark and Termite* includes supernatural events that reinforce the sense that the mind cannot fully understand or explain all facets of human experience.

Through these experiences of heightened awareness, extraordinary connections with other human beings, and instances of the supernatural, Phillips creates a world where rising above life's trials and tragedies becomes possible.

The theme of transcendence is introduced early in the novel. With the Korean War about to begin in earnest, Corporal Leavitt, participating in a project called Language Immersion Seoul, finds himself leading local civilians away from the invading North Koreans. "The South Korean inhabitants of numberless rural villages flee behind whatever resistance American troops can offer . . . . Thatch roofs, saturated by weeks of rain, burn wet and smoky once they're set afire. Smoke veils the air like souls in drifting suspension, declining the war's insistence everyone move on."[4] Phillips develops the idea of "souls in drifting suspension" in a passage that combines the loss of war with intimations of immortality. "The war makes ghosts of them all. Fifty years, a hundred years, they'll still be here: vestige mist moving along a double rail bed near a wobble of a stream, the South Koreans in their white clothes, the GIs in mud-crusted khaki."[5] Through an anecdote told by Tompkins, Leavitt's closest friend in the military, Phillips links the idea of transcendence to a religious belief in Chung Chong Buk-Do, "the most rural province of Korea." The people there "believe that violent death or death afar requires the soul to journey home." In this culture, "the living leave hints for the dead. Ghosts are not feared. . . . The soldiers, Leavitt thinks, the invaders and foreign protectors, become the ghosts, flying through time, across oceans, nothing to guide them but intent and need."[6] Leavitt's own attempts to "fly through time" introduce the theme of transcendence, and the author's presentation of Leavitt's experiences in Korea imbues the novel with a mythic quality. Ultimately, in *Lark and Termite*, Phillips develops the theme of transcendence in three ways: the use of parallel scenes in Korea and West Virginia, the depiction of personal relationships as redemptive, and the inclusion of elements of magical realism.

Phillips heightens the connections between her characters through the creation of parallel scenes. The most important parallels between the sections involving Leavitt (and through his reminiscences, Lola) and the sections involving the title characters include the following points. First of all, in both the Korea and West Virginia scenes, trains and tunnels serve as motifs—as well as sites—for rites of passage. Secondly, in both locales, a girl has to take care of a handicapped younger brother, and, in each case, the young boy possesses heightened senses compared to those of the other characters.

Thirdly, a Korean woman in the tunnel where Leavitt and others have taken refuge kills herself with his gun, a situation eerily similar to Lola's suicide a short time afterward. Finally, Leavitt's reminiscences reveal Lola's fascination with escaping to Florida to renew her life, and later Lark will attempt to flee there with Termite as well, in both cases escaping complications and painful memories in West Virginia. Michiko Kakutani, in her review of the novel, eloquently described the effect of the novel's parallels. "Repeated images and leitmotifs link these people's stories together, lending the novel a haunting musical quality, even as they suggest the unconscious, almost magical bonds shared by people who are connected by blood or love or memory."[7]

The tunnel motif helps develop what Kakutani referred to as the "almost magical bonds" between Leavitt and the two title characters. In both the Korea and West Virginia sections, tunnels create parallel scenes involving life-altering moments and nearly spiritual connections between the characters. The descriptions of the tunnels in Korea and West Virginia are strikingly similar. Early in the novel, as Leavitt casts about for refuge, the tunnels are described as "slightly curved and relatively deep."[8] Later in the novel, Lark discovers Lola's sketch of the West Virginia tunnels and is impressed by its accuracy. "[Lola] remembered it exactly, the way the stones and mortar curve at the top."[9] Since Leavitt saw the sketch before going overseas, it further links Leavitt with Lark and Termite. In Phillips's masterful hands, the tunnel motif adds depth and symmetry to the novel's rites of passage. The following life-altering moments all occur in tunnels: Leavitt is wounded at the tunnel's entrance, as he lies dying he senses when Lola is giving birth to Termite, a Korean woman commits suicide, Lark has a sexual encounter with her longtime friend Solly, and Termite "sees" bodies in the tunnel (presumably the parallel scene in Korea) and a man's shape turning toward him. Each of these events and their reverberations contributes to the novel's magical qualities.

The tunnel motif is established early in the novel. In Korea, as bombs fall from planes flying overhead, Leavitt urges the refugees to flee into a tunnel for safety. A Korean girl approaches and demands his help. Leavitt describes her as "a purely rural girl who has never been to Seoul,"[10] suggesting a similarity with Lark, who has rarely left Winfield. While fleeing the battle scene, the Korean girl convinces Leavitt to assist her in finding refuge for the old woman and young boy in her care. Ignoring his orders—"monitor, do not assist"—Leavitt agrees to help them but immediately feels a sense of foreboding. "Leavitt nods at the girl, *yes*, and dread breaks over him. Something imminent approaches, something to hurt them all, carry them away."[11] As he carries him to the tunnel, Leavitt notices that the boy is blind and perhaps possesses powers of second sight. "The cloudiness in his eyes seems to subtly pulse or dilate; the boy *looks* with complete attention, seems to see past Leavitt or into him. He's not slow, or not exactly; he seems preternaturally alert."[12] Reading further, we clearly see a parallel between the Korean girl and boy and Lark and Termite. At this point in the narrative, Leavitt sees the tunnel as a place of refuge from the strafing, and the Korean girl believes that he has saved their lives.

However, Phillips further develops the life and death motif of the tunnel when, just as Leavitt leads the Korean family to its entrance, he is shot by American troops immediately after telling the girl in Korean, "You'll be safe here":

> When he's hit he falls to his knees like a man in awe, doesn't feel himself take the girl with him, pitching forward to cover her with his body. She throws the child from her as she goes down; Leavitt sees the boy fly from them in slow, pillowed suspension but feels only the disjunct lurching of his own body as the bullets make impact. Flames rip into his legs and hips like staccato blades and explode in one burst. They've shot him from behind, the stupid fools, his own men or the jumpy troops dug in farther back, fanned out in their trenches at two-hundred-yard intervals. Spooked by noise, panicked, reading the ricochet of their own rifle fire off the scarred concrete walls of the tunnels, they've shot the hell out of him. . . .[13]

Like the ricocheting of the bullets, each of the scenes from Leavitt's point of view echoes and reverberates through the rest of the novel. Leavitt falls in and out of consciousness and alternates between two activities. He continually tries to convince the Korean girl that their only chance of survival is for her to drag him to the edge of the tunnel so he can show the military unit outside that they are not the enemy. He also dreams of Lola and their time together, and he envisions her in labor with Termite.

In the final Korean section, Leavitt recognizes that his death is imminent, while sensing, almost supernaturally, that his son has been born. Just before the time of Leavitt's death, the Korean boy has been hiding behind him, allowing Phillips to create another scene that links the Korean and American characters. The U. S. soldiers begin to kill everyone in the tunnel, and Leavitt thinks of his newborn son. "He wants to lift his baby away from this beautiful deadly world. The planes always come, he wants to say, like planets on rotation, a timed bloodletting with different excuses. Part of a long music. Don't look, only listen. His son is born. Leavitt feels him turn in the salt and the blood, squalling and screaming in the close hot wet. Stop screaming, Leavitt tells him. Never scream. They'll find you. Stay still. Listen. You can't come with me now. Breathe, breathe. Take your turn."[14] In this scene, we see how the tunnel motif works. It focuses the reader's attention on the details of the present scene, while at the same time revealing the interconnectedness of the moments that transform lives in different settings. It is a recurring theme in Phillips's works that each generation faces the same tests confronting the previous one, in some ways reliving what has gone on before. Thus, in the Korean tunnel scenes, Phillips includes in her depictions of birth and death the possibility of rebirth.

The scenes in the tunnels in West Virginia, revealed through Termite's reminiscences, focus on two types of experiences: Lark and Solly's sexual encounters and Termite's vision of refugees in the tunnel. In the first flashback, Termite remembers Solly's words to Lark, who continually refuses to have intercourse with Solly (all of Termite's flashbacks in the novel are italicized): "*I'll do what you say. Everything you say. You want to. You want to every day, as much as me . . . . Wear your clothes then. I know what you look like, just not all at once. I'll be still, so still. Here's the train, do it now.*"[15] Interestingly, as the train passes over the tunnel, Termite's mind flashes to a scene that is eerily reminiscent of Leavitt's experiences in the Korean tunnel. "*There's a picture inside the roar, a tunnel inside the tunnel. He's been here before and he looks deeper each time and he sees. There are sleepers everywhere, bodies crowded together. The bodies are always here, so many of them in the tunnel when the train roars across, bodies spilled and still, barely stirring. . . . One shape stands and turns toward him, a man's shape opening his glowing hands as though to be sure he can.*"[16] This scene links Termite with his father, Leavitt, suggesting that the characters live on after death, like the ghosts of war Leavitt imagined when he was in Korea. A similar scene is repeated later in the text that emphasizes the tunnel as a place where life and death, love and sex, and past and present are experienced and contemplated with more clarity than anywhere else.

A second parallel between the Korean and West Virginia scenes involves an older sister taking care of a younger brother with a physical disability but also a sense of second sight that allows him to "see" things that the other characters cannot. Leavitt would never have met the Korean family if the girl had not been trying to protect her brother, a situation that mirrors Lark's caregiving role with Termite. The Korean girl convinces Leavitt to carry her brother to the cave, an ill-fated decision that ends tragically, but at the time one she perceives as positive. After Leavitt is wounded and the girl has to take care of him as well, Leavitt understands why. "She thinks he saved them. It's why she won't leave him."[17] As Leavitt lies dying, he begins to see the boy less and less as a person with a physical disability and more and more as someone toward whom he feels a personal connection. "Gently, [the Korean girl] turns the boy's head so that his gaze falls unseeing on Leavitt's face. The uneven blue of his pupils is impenetrable, depthless, and cloudy, but the blue seems quietly lit. The blue never wavers. What does he see behind it. Shadows. Sounds. Leavitt doesn't ask but the boy inclines his head as though to answer. *Ihae hamnida*, Leavitt says. I understand."[18] Leavitt's recognition of the boy's personal worth and the description of the girl turning the boy's head link this Korean scene with Lola back in the States, giving birth to Termite, another boy with special qualities with an older sister who will care for him. The scenes with Leavitt and the Korean boy allow him, in a sense, to experience what it would be like to know his own son, Termite.

Phillips had earlier explored the theme of a sister feeling responsible for a younger brother in *Machine Dreams*, in the scenes in which Danner Hampson tried to convince Billy to avoid Vietnam. At the end of that novel, Phillips also explored the theme of transcendence, with Billy living on in Danner's memories of their lives together. In *Lark and Termite*, however, the sibling relationship involves everyday dependence on the part of the younger brother. Lark understands Termite's expressions, sounds, and even his silences in a way that transcends language, just as Leavitt understood the Korean boy's head movement. Mature beyond her seventeen years, Lark happily accepts her role as caregiver for Termite. She defends him from any who would try to marginalize or dehumanize him. For example, in one of Lark's narrated sections, she objects when her aunt Nonie says that some of the other children monitored by social services are not as disabled as Termite is:

> "So-called disabled," I say. "I'm not going to talk about him that way."
> "Well now, Lark." She looks at me dead-on. Arches her brows in that way that shows up the star-flared lines around her eyes, the shadows beneath them. She turns back to the dishes. "How do you want to talk about him then?" she asks me.
> "They're not as well off," I say, "not as well off as Termite."[19]

Later in the novel, when Charlie's mother, the mean-spirited Gladdy, says that Lark and Termite might look related, but no one can tell "what he'd look like, if whatever happened to him hadn't happened," Lark again rises to her brother's defense. "Nothing happened to him . . . . He was born just as he is. And he can hear every word you say."[20] Lark's selfless care for her brother earns the reader's admiration precisely because she does not see the responsibility as a burden. And it provides another important parallel with the Korean scenes.

The third parallel between the Korean and American scenes involves two suicides, both with a gun that belongs to Leavitt. As Leavitt falls in and out of consciousness, he overhears at one point the Korean girl's great-aunt talking. "He's a murderer, she says, a demon, he's not alive." Leavitt realizes that old woman "believes he's a murderous spirit wandering among the dead."[21] A few pages later, the old woman kills herself, using Leavitt's gun, an action that foreshadows Lola's suicide with the pistol that once belonged to his mother. "The day before he left Louisville, he gave Lola his mother's little derringer, the pearl-handled pistol she kept out of sight beside the cash register . . . ."[22] He jokingly refers to his mother's gun as "a wedding present."[23] After Leavitt dies in Korea, Lola, left alone in Louisville, decides to take her own life, and leaves Termite with her sister, Nonie. Leavitt's closeness with his mother and the suicides of the Korean woman and Lola suggest the impossibility of protecting anyone from life's harsh realities. The fact that the Korean girl ends up with Leavitt's revolver and Lark finds the derringer among Lola's belongings symbolically underscores that the younger generation must inevitably grapple with the older generation's trials.

These parallel scenes further establish the idea that certain emotional and psychological issues resonate across generations. Leavitt resented his father's treatment of his mother, and then he becomes involved with Lola, eight years his senior. Lola seems to understand Leavitt's issues completely. In one scene, after he plays "My Funny Valentine" on the trumpet for her, he tells her that "it was his mother's song." Lola replies, *"Of course it was and you're the whole world mended,"*[24] revealing how she understands that he is still trying to resolve some of his childhood issues. Leavitt and Lola had planned to move to Florida after the war, and by the end of the novel, Lark plans to flee to Lola's home in Coral Gables with Termite to avoid leaving him at the mercy of social services. Thus, in a fourth parallel, linked to Leavitt through his reminiscences, Lark pursues her parents' dream of living in Florida. She imagines a happy life with Solly helping her raise Termite. These parallels demonstrate what Phillips herself has said. "Children take on their parents' unresolved issues and emotional dramas . . . . Not to resolve them, but to help carry the burden—to keep their parents alive, in a sense."[25] Once again, Phillips interweaves the theme of transcendence through the younger generation engaging with the emotional issues of the previous one.

This theme finds major expression in the novel's depiction of personal relationships as life-affirming. The most important of these is the sibling relationship between Lark and Termite. Accepting the role of caregiver with exemplary grace, Lark, as we have seen, communicates with Termite as no one else can, and she defends him from demeaning criticism. Lark makes a beautiful statement after Termite has seemingly mocked the ever-derisive Gladdy. Lark wonders how Nonie cannot see that Termite knows what is happening around him, thinking, "She doesn't understand. That's the point: he's got a rhyme and reason. We only see the surface, like when you look at a river and all you see is a reflection of the sky."[26] As a result of Lark's ability to see beyond the surface to her brother's true character, Termite is treated by most of the townspeople as if he has no disability.

Another exploration of the theme of transcendence is found in Phillips's presentation of sexuality. In *Lark and Termite*, romantic relationships can transform lives. This marks a departure for the author. In her early fiction, Phillips, while occasionally depicting sexuality as joyous, often presented sexuality as unfulfilling. Characters in her early work either fear sexuality, find it frustrating, or try to minimize its importance through meaningless encounters. Consider the following examples. In "Home," from Phillips's first collection of short fiction, *Black Tickets*, which was published in 1979, the narrator moves from fear of sex as an adolescent to guilt as a young woman over a sexual encounter with a friend in her mother's home, the complications destroying any potential happiness. A similar arc is found with Danner Hampson in Phillips's first novel, *Machine Dreams*. Danner experiences the awkwardness of adolescence—blushing when another girl mocks her French braids at a dance and growing uncomfortable when older boys stare at her when she was in the eighth grade. "They scared Danner; they were like men, big and grown, with shadows on their faces and big hands like her father's hands."[27] She feels too young for a serious relationship at age fifteen when Riley, her older boyfriend, pressures her to become engaged. In college, Danner begins to have affairs but many of her commitment issues remain unresolved.

Similar to the college-age Danner, the narrator in the title story of Phillips's second short story collection, 1987's *Fast Lanes*, has grown to find passion unfulfilling and numbing. She talks about how at one point in her life, she frequently had casual sex, minimizing its importance by comparing it to greeting someone. "It's easy when you do it a lot. You get stoned and you don't even think about it. Easy. Like saying hello."[28] This casual attitude toward sex of some of Phillips's characters masks the fact that they rarely find fulfillment in their relationships. Therefore, for many of the characters in Phillips' early work, sex is not an elevating or celebratory experience.

However, the depictions of sexual frustration in some of her early fiction make the potential for fulfillment through sexuality in *Lark and Termite* so striking in comparison. The power of passion can be seen in the relationships of three couples in the novel: Lola and Leavitt, Nonie and Charlie, and Lark and Solly. In the Korean scenes, Leavitt's memories of his relationship with Lola help him survive the drudgery and destruction of war. His first physical encounter with her demonstrates the life-affirming and life-altering power of his passion:

> The sounds of the club under them throbbed in the walls as she ascended above him through the narrow stairwell, hips and thighs a gauzy oval in her pale sheath skirt. Moving in near darkness like a slow, detached shape, she turned on the stairs as she paused to look down at him. Leavitt sees that shape now in his fragmented sleep or behind his eyes, glowing, asexual, like a flicker of light opening into himself. He can't shake the feeling that seeing her, wanting her, playing behind her in the club, making love to her days and nights in her rooms that became his rooms, were practice for staying alive. Then as now he moved in what he couldn't quite have, get to, reach, until her body gave it up to him like flames he sparked inside a darkness. She was luminous ground he worked and sowed, sweated for and lost. They found each other in blinding, convulsive instants that seared him open.[29]

As with the tunnels, Phillips in this passage uses a nearly archetypal image, climbing a stairway, to underscore the experience's transformative power. In this scene, the transition from detachment to emotional involvement mirrors the presentation of sexuality in the entire novel, with romantic love transforming the main characters' lives.

Another example of this transformative power of love can be found in Nonie and Charlie's relationship. Although they have their share of disagreements and disappointments, they also find much happiness in their love for each other. The challenges are detailed in many of the sections told from Nonie's point of view. Gladdy, Charlie's mother, hates Nonie. After Charlie had an affair with Lola, Nonie decides that she wants to maintain a certain degree of independence from him by buying her own home. She says, "Charlie wanted me to buy in a better part of town and help me with the payments, but I wasn't owning a house with Charlie. This is my place, I told him, not yours."[30] Still, in spite of their differences, he and Nonie become long-time partners in more ways than one. She helps him save the restaurant when business is bad. "I arranged to borrow enough from Billy Onslow to help us turn the business around."[31] And their passion for each other does not wane. "I've been married. It wasn't like this. We still want each other, we're practiced, it all works."[32] Nonie clearly understands the way a romantic relationship can transform a person. She advises Lark about the dangers of sexual relationships, " . . . never let a man inside you unless you want him around forever, because you can't get rid of him after that, no matter how many times he leaves you or you leave him."[33] Lark takes the advice to heart, willing to experiment but refusing to have intercourse with Solly.

In the depiction of Lark's sexual awakening, we again are reminded that no one writes more masterfully about adolescence than Jayne Anne Phillips. She brilliantly captures the awkwardness of puberty, the concerns about body image, the fear of having sex combined with the fear of missing something if one does not, and the uncertainty about the degree to which sexuality can bond two individuals together who may not be entirely compatible. When she is alone, Lark imagines what intercourse might be like, she thinks about different males, and she senses that the experience could transport her to another place:

> There's no controlling who I might think about—Solly and Joey, or Nick Tucci, even Charlie, or other men I barely know. But they don't look at me the way men mostly do. In my thoughts, they're more like women, or they're men who know what women know. They know it all and they look inside me, straight into where I'm getting to. I get to that place and fall through it. Then I open my eyes and I'm here, and tonight the whole of the alley and all the backyards past the frame of the window look sleepy, turned inside out. Gray and pretty, fuzzy with dusk. Not like Winfield at all, not like anywhere.[34]

By the end of the novel, Lark seems ready to find love on her own terms. She confides in Solly about her plans to go to Florida and hopes he will join Termite and her there. She seems well on her way to a fulfilling relationship.

Some reviewers of *Lark and Termite* have understandably commented on the novel's similarities with *The Sound and the Fury*. Such analyses are nothing new, for critics have previously compared Phillips's work to that of Faulkner. For example, Sarah Robertson points to a connection regarding one of Phillips's major themes. "In her treatment of family, Phillips'[s] work brings into focus Faulkner's Jason Compson for whom 'blood is blood and you can't get around it.'"[35] The connection between Phillips and Faulkner comes to mind for three main reasons: the use of multiple points of view, the idea that the past is a continual part of the present, and, in *Lark and Termite*, a clear similarity between Termite and Benjy of *The Sound and the Fury*. Kathryn Harrison has delineated some of the key parallels between the two novels:

> "Lark and Termite" takes a few sentences from "The Sound and the Fury" as one of its three epigraphs: "Because no battle is ever won he said. They are not even fought. The field only reveals to a man his own folly and despair, and victory is an illusion of philosophers and fools." Like Faulkner, Phillips divides her narrative into four parts and uses multiple points of view that diverge and overlap. . . . Termite's perceptions are sometimes rendered in a third-person stream-of-consciousness, reminiscent of Benjy Compson's first-person musings in "The Sound and the Fury."[36]

Harrison adds that Phillips's novel is not as "bleak and despairing" as *The Sound and the Fury*, a point worth exploring in greater detail, for the comparison with Faulkner only takes us so far when trying to understand *Lark and Termite*.

One explanation for why this novel is not as bleak as *The Sound and the Fury* can be attributed to another influence—magical realism, a term most often associated with Latin American writer Gabriel Garcia Marquez, who has said that he developed the style from his grandmother. She "told things that sounded supernatural or fantastic, but she told them with complete naturalness," Garcia Marquez said.[37] Phillips once acknowledged her connection to "what might be called Magical Realism, the term coined for South American writers which also applies to Kafka, Bruno Schultz, and William Burroughs." Phillips said that she admires how these writers "are working at the edge of how reality is apprehended. It's almost that perception itself is a kind of religion, meditation, a journey or a travail. Writers dealing with this material are my sources, or allies."[38] Magical realism relies upon the presentation of extraordinary or supernatural events in a straightforward, almost journalistic style. In *Lark and Termite*, Phillips employs this style of writing in depicting a number of seemingly supernatural occurrences. In addition to the previously discussed scene in which Termite envisions the Korean tunnel scene, late in the novel there are several more such supernatural incidents: the transformation brought about by the flood in Winfield, the appearance of the ghostly Robert Stamble, and the novel's climactic scene as Lark and Termite hop a train for Florida and Termite sees one final vision. These final scenes all reinforce the theme of transcendence.

During the flood, Lark and Termite retreat to the attic, ignoring Solly's advice to flee to the armory. The flood transforms Lark's vision of the town and provides her with a clear sense of direction. From that day on, Lark is not the same. Sitting in the attic with Termite, she serves some food and thinks, "Everything tastes better than it really could, like fairy-tale food."[39] After their meal, she looks out the window and notices how the town looks different. "The river is in the flood now, racing, rushing along over gardens and tipped-up cars and the surprised tops of trees. They're strange trees, new ones, and they trail their leaves in one direction, like they all hear the same music. The houses stand up chopped off, showing their roofs and second-story windows. The blank windows look glazed and shiny. It's a new town in a new world, an empty town for water and wind in the dark."[40] Lark's perception of this alteration in the town also suggests that she herself has been transformed, seeing more clearly than ever her importance as her brother's caregiver. After the flood and Nonie's altercation with Gladdy, Lark understands that she must take full responsibility for Termite, that he will always be a part of her. With this realization, she plans to flee to Florida. She also decides that Solly is the one for her, confiding in him and inviting him to share a life with her and Termite in the Sunshine State. Throughout the novel, Phillips develops a motif of vision, where characters perceive reality, or even the supernatural, with increased clarity, further developing the theme of transcendence.

Other instances of the supernatural involve the social services worker who visits Lark and Termite. Even though the reader initially perceives him as a realistic character, Robert Stamble becomes a supernatural presence in the novel, one of the ghosts of the war. It is later in the novel during the flood when he brings a new wheelchair for Termite that we begin to sense his more fantastic qualities. And when Solly rescues Lark and Termite from their house, Lark sees Stamble in the motorboat, but Solly does not. She calls social services to ask about Stamble, only to find that no one by that name has ever worked there. Reflecting upon certain details regarding Stamble, the reader begins to suspect that he is the ghost of Leavitt. They both share the first name Robert, and Stamble is described as very pale with blond hair, similar to Leavitt's. And one remembers this line from early in the novel: "The soldiers, Leavitt thinks, the invaders and foreign protectors, become the ghosts, flying through time, across oceans, nothing to guide them but intent and need."[41] The idea that Stamble could be a ghost is further established by Termite's perception of him when he first visits the house. "The man steps closer, air that moves in a shape. The glow falls through the door onto Termite's face and shoulders, a cool pale beam that's found him . . . . He's more than himself. Lark doesn't hear, she doesn't see. Termite sees him, a shape glowing through the door that Lark keeps nearly closed. The shape shines like a light."[42] Of course, these details alone would not be enough to suggest that Stamble is a ghost if not for the scenes on the boat during the flood and the phone call Lark makes later. It is during these latter scenes involving Stamble that Phillips presents the supernatural as if it were totally natural, a technique that links the novel to magical realism and emphasizes the link between the supernatural and the theme of transcendence.

The novel's conclusion further explores this theme through Termite's vision on the train. After Solly arrives on his motorcycle, Termite once again envisions a scene that recalls the tunnel in Korea. "The man who stands alone and hears the shape lies still, but a shape stands up in his shape." Gradually, Termite realizes the true identity of the man:

> He looks at Termite. The ribbons all around them are veiled as smoke and move like the river moves, rippling and curling, pulled in the air. No eyes, no ears, the ribbons only move and flow. Thin silvery ribbons, moving in the tunnel. So many of them, more and more, moving toward the opening, to where the light gets big and bright. He sees his father clear against the light and his father turns and walks. His father has a boy like him and a girl like Lark, and he takes them with him, out of the tunnel. He sees his father walking between the ribbons and the ribbons make everything blue.[43]

Termite's recognition of his father brings into focus Phillips' larger themes: the idea that human destiny is more interconnected than we often realize, the extent to which the past lives on in the present, and the way younger generations relive the dramas of the older generations. In these scenes of magical realism, the author further develops the theme of transcendence.

In *Lark and Termite*, Jayne Anne Phillips returns to the subject matter she has explored throughout her career. Drawing on her West Virginia childhood, she vividly depicts small town Appalachia of the mid-twentieth century. She reveals the senseless loss of war, where enemies are hard to recognize and death seems more arbitrary than glorious. She writes beautifully and insightfully about adolescence, with all of its awkwardness and possibility. Perhaps most importantly, she captures the challenges and unbreakable bonds of family politics, where the parents' difficulties almost always affect the children, and where siblings feel responsible for each other's welfare. However, the novel also presents, to a degree not seen in her previous work, the possibility of transcendence and redemption. Phillips depicts characters who discover in themselves the power of connecting the self with something greater and of rising above their situations. And she tells their stories in breathtakingly beautiful prose. Her style is so lyrical, as one reviewer noted, Phillips "can take 'a piece of a dry-cleaner bag a yard long and a few inches wide,' and turn it into a movable piece of the sky."[44] Throughout *Lark and Termite*, Phillips presents the Appalachia of her youth as a magical place. In his review of the novel, Michael Dirda describes the sense of community among the characters in the town of Winfield, West Virginia:

> Despite its many sorrows, the book is something of a fairy tale. All the characters, save one or two, are likable, well-meaning, and admirable. Lark is a particularly wonderful creation, and one can understand why everyone loves her—she is as kind as she is beautiful, but also tough and resourceful and wise. . . . And while the town of Winfield may be run down, it still seems an idyllic paradise, a lost Fifties world where hardworking people help each other through hard times.[45]

This blending of fairy tale elements with unflinching realism suggests a new direction in Jayne Anne Phillips's work. Perhaps *Lark and Termite* is the book she has been working toward all along, one in which the previous generations, "souls in drifting suspension," stay with us in hopes that we can "save something, keep something from fading away."

CHAPTER 8

Pinckney Benedict's
Miracle Boy and Other Stories

In an interview, Pinckney Benedict made the following comment about his most accomplished collection of short stories:

> It's called *Miracle Boy and Other Stories* because that's the title that speaks to all of the book. The entire collection speaks to the supernatural or the strange, and heretofore, my work has been very realist. Recently, I've become more interested in the surreal. My hope for this book is that if it has any effect at all, I'd like it to take the curse off the literary short story. Right now, short stories are only read by writers. When Hemingway was writing short stories, it wasn't just writers and university professors who read them. I don't mean for these stories to be these gravestones of seriousness, as the modern short story is thought to be. I would dislike it if my own work were thought of in that way.[1]

Pinckney Benedict's *Miracle Boy and Other Stories*, published in 2010, challenges the reader's preconceptions of the possibilities of fiction. Benedict created an innovative collection of stories by blurring the lines between literary and genre fiction, between human and animal behavior, between humans and machines, and between reality and dream. He enhances literary realism with the mythic, the horrific, and the fantastic. The collection shifts Appalachian fiction ever so slightly from a focus on the landscape to greater emphasis on the dreamscape, with a cast of characters who might seem ordinary or forgettable if not for their compelling inner lives. Benedict seems at least as interested in their dreams as he does in their everyday behavior. Years ago he addressed the importance of dreams to his work:

Everybody's a really good storyteller, at least when they're asleep. Because your dreams are you, right? You generate your dreams. They come out of things you know. You recognize people in them. You recognize places in them. And you have some kind of control of them, in that, without you, they don't exist. And they're utterly convincing. And they terrify you. Or delight you. You can laugh in your dreams. You can scream. You can cry. You can have sexual adventures. And at the same time, the dream is using the material of your brain in some way to shape itself.[2]

It is through the characters' most secret fears and desires that one can understand their trials and tribulations. Benedict delights in exploring the characters' attempts to rise above their difficulties. By incorporating three types of transcendence—a preternatural connection between two individuals, everyday lives imbued with magical qualities, and the experience of a highly personal spiritual experience that offers at least a fleeting sense of immortality—Benedict makes it possible for his characters to transcend the limitations and challenges of their lives.

Increasingly in his work, Benedict has made his stories what he describes as more apocalyptic. He once wrote about the distinction between a vignette and a story in a way that sheds light on his creative vision:

Here's the difference as I see it: in a vignette, nothing much changes. The world does not shift on its axis. Intriguing, sometimes fascinating, things take place, but without a larger context, there's relatively little resonance. A story, on the other hand, involves apocalypse. I'm pretty specific by what I mean by the use of that word: I mean a revelation (the literal meaning of the word apocalypse; "a lifting of the veil"), and a very specific type of revelation: the destruction of an old order, followed by a time (however brief, even a moment, a flicker) of disorder and chaos, and the replacement of the old order by a new and completely different order (though that new order may in its external details resemble the old).[3]

In *Miracle Boy and Other Stories*, Benedict includes the following apocalyptic narratives: a teenaged boy transforms, at least temporarily, into a fighting cock ("The Butcher Cock"); a space alien inhabits the body of a farmer and then learns to become human ("Zog 19"); a dog takes on human traits, while his owner takes on dog-like characteristics, much to the horror of his wife ("The Beginnings of Sorrow"); and a police officer kills a homicidal drug addict and then undergoes a spiritual experience at an evangelical carnival attraction ("Pig Helmet & the Wall of Life"). These apocalyptic stories involve upheaval in the lives of these characters and the possibility of some kind of transcendence, with Benedict's experimentation potentially taking Appalachian literature in a new and fresh direction. This collection marks a new direction for Benedict, whose early work was frequently compared to that of Breece Pancake.

Like Pancake, Pinckney Benedict published his short fiction at an early age. As noted in Chapter Three, Benedict read Pancake's fiction as an undergraduate and almost instantly fell under its influence. At age twenty-two, Benedict enjoyed his first success as a writer when in 1986 his story "The Sutton Pie Safe" won the Nelson Algren Award and was published in the *Chicago Tribune*. In 1987 Benedict's first collection of stories, *Town Smokes*, was published to rave reviews. Eudora Welty said, "With the appearance of *Town Smokes* we are beyond question in the presence of a strong talent." Joyce Carol Oates added, "*Town Smokes* introduces a young writer of exceptional gifts and promise."[4] Another collection of stories, *The Wrecking Yard*, followed in 1992. In a review in *The New York Times Book Review*, Nancy Willard wrote that Benedict's second book has established him as a highly original writer whose vision of the American frontier is as contemporary as it is compelling. In 1994, Benedict published his first novel, *Dogs of God*, about which Barry Hannah wrote, "Superb narrative drive and full vision—delightful and exciting. Young Benedict joins Jayne Anne Phillips and Breece D'J Pancake as one of the considerable literary forces of what should be a proud West Virginia."[5] All three of these works were named "notable books" by *The New York Times*. Then came a sixteen-year hiatus from book publishing, as he continued to write quality short fiction, placing two stories in each of the following collections: the *O. Henry Awards*, *Pushcart Prize*, and *New Stories from the South*. Oddly, when Benedict published his most recent collection in 2010, it was virtually ignored by reviewers in the mainstream media.

When asked about how he manages to write about down-and-out West Virginians in a way that seems organic and free from condescension, Benedict explained the gap between books:

> The desire is to inhabit the story so fully that it would be impossible to manipulate from outside. That by the writer inhabiting the world of these characters and dwelling with these characters and exploring what their world is like that there is no externality. That there isn't any condescension because there's no place to condescend from. Now that's my theoretical perfection. Believe me,

I don't claim ever to reach it, but that's what I would hope to do as a writer, that it's not me doing anything with the characters. It's part me living with the characters, living in the characters' world, and part me remembering having lived with the characters. I try to live in those worlds sufficiently and I try to imagine those worlds for a sufficient amount of time. I don't write a lot of stories these days because I'm an academic and have this kind of leisure. I often don't begin to write stories until years after I have thought about the worlds in which the stories will take place. So the hope is to write them not as if they are something you are creating but that more like something you are remembering, something that actually happened.[6]

As noted previously, *Miracle Boy and Other Stories* challenges the reader's preconceptions of fiction. At times, it is difficult to discern what is real from what is imagined, as the characters' fears, frustrations, and fantasies fuel the narratives. Is Esau, the boy in "Pony Car," haunted by the ghosts of his Uncle Rowdy and the beautiful Astrid he claims to have won in a poker game, or was Esau killed with Uncle Rowdy years before while joyriding in the Dodge Challenger? A reader could choose either interpretation, but what matters is that Esau feels haunted by the issue of whether Uncle Rowdy could be his real father, whether Uncle Rowdy survived the attempt to outrun a train with his car, and whether Esau can escape all of the fear of his family member's ghosts haunting him. Similarly, in "The Beginnings of Sorrow," Bridie is haunted by Xerxes, her father-in-law who was continually molesting her and who would not stop touching her when she told him no, a monster of a man whose abusive behavior ended only when he suffers a stroke while once again assaulting Bridie. Xerxes's spirit then inhabits the body of a hound dog named Hark, who exhibits increasingly human traits. When Hark starts speaking and telling his master "no," Bridie fears her husband, Vandal, will not stand up to Hark, just like he did not stand up to Xerxes. Of course, a more traditional reader might reject some of the seemingly impossible action, but as the story develops more and more into a horror narrative, the reader sees that Bridie's fears that she will never escape Xerxes's abuse inform our understanding of the story. The characters' deepest fears drive the narrative, not the reliance upon a traditional plot.

Again and again, the characters' motivations and inclinations assume as much significance as their actions. In "The Secret Nature of the Mechanical Rabbit," Buddy Gunn has worked a number of gruesome jobs—"lugging carcasses" to a slaughterhouse, driving dead greyhounds to a mass grave after their racing careers have ended, and collecting unwanted and stray dogs to feed to Moloch, a brutal fighting dog, to keep him thirsty for blood. After collecting two puppies from a young girl that reminds him of his sister and observing the brutish behavior his traveling companion ogling the girl, Buddy reconsiders his livelihood. The story ends with Buddy contemplating poisoning Moloch, so he can end the senseless slaughter of these dogs. As the story concludes, it is likely but not certain that Buddy will actually kill Moloch, but clearly Buddy has become more humanized during the course of the story. The somewhat inconclusive ending leaves the reader focusing less on what will happen next and more on the change in Buddy's attitudes.

The experimental nature of Benedict's fiction does not mean that the author has abandoned the typical Appalachian themes—but, rather, that he has found new ways to explore them. Like the other writers included in this book, Benedict writes about limitations related to class, place and gender, while allowing his main character the possibility of transcendence over these limitations. He portrays a number of characters who live in poverty or who find themselves marginalized from mainstream society. Occasionally, a character is overcome by difficult circumstances. Scurry, in "Bridge of Sighs," faces the prospect of having to see his cattle exterminated during an epizootic and seems overcome by defeat and denial. Other characters—for example, Ivanhoe in "The Butcher Cock" and the title character of "Pig Helmet & the Wall of Life (discussed in detail below)—do not accept defeat, each imagining a better life for himself.

In some stories, this vision of a better life involves a recognition of the limitations of place. A number of stories identify the Seneca Valley as their setting. In the title story of the collection, Lizard climbs a telephone pole to retrieve Miracle Boy's tennis shoes and looks at the landscape from on high. "From his new vantage point, he noted with surprise the state of the roof of the shop shed, the tin scabby and blooming with rust, bowed and beginning to buckle. He had never noticed before what hard shape the place was in."[7] Likewise, the title character in "Joe Messenger Is Dreaming" dreams of achieving glory in flight and knows that his father, the county constable is respected, "but his authority ended at the county line. Past that he was just a good man who lived in a poor little valley in a poor little state in the poorest region of a wealthy nation."[8] In both of these stories, characters recognize the shortcomings of the region, while imagining a better life for themselves.

Gender issues in Benedict's fiction often involve father-and-son relationships. Sometimes, as is the case with Joe Messenger, the son envisions himself becoming superior to his father in some way. When a father is absent, the son feels obliged to take on traditional male roles. For example, Lizard, in "Miracle Boy, has lost his father and puts on his father's tool belt, a symbolic action as he prepares to retrieve the title character's shoes. In other stories, the sons feel unmanly in comparison with their fathers. In "The Beginnings of Sorrow," Vandal knows that his father, Xerxes, would not have tolerated the insubordination of the hunting dog, Hark. Vandal clearly sees himself as less masculine than his father. In "The Angel's Trumpet," Albertus Goins feels physically inferior to his father and his brothers, who work diligently on the dairy farm while Albertus reads books and takes naps. Benedict often employs father-and-son relationships to demonstrate how sons assess their masculinity through comparison with their fathers and thus have a difficult time breaking from traditional gender roles.

One of the most important stories in the collection that involves a father-and-son relationship is "Bridge of Sighs," alluded to earlier. The son is tasked with using his ability to tell a story to try to distract Scurry from the extermination of his cattle during the epizootic. His father puts on a suit called the Exterminator, which makes him seem more like an alien than a man. The father is clearly attempting to instill mental and physical toughness into his son. As Katherine Egerton has written, "The father uses the epizootic, as well as the Exterminator itself, to teach his son the most important lesson '[a]bout the world jumping its tracks, and how you just held on until it came back onto them again. Not to scare the women and the little kids.' Any sacrifice is worth this price, including for the father, perpetual exile on the far side of the Bridge of Sighs, the slaughterhouse ramp that leads to death."[9] Egerton shows how the son learns the hard lesson about performing the tough, but essential tasks. In "Bridge of Sighs," it is important that the son demonstrates to his father than he is tough enough to be of assistance during the challenging time.

In some stories in *Miracle Boy*, Benedict incorporates elements of the horror genre to dramatize a character's gender-related concerns. In "Mudman," a modern-day golem narrative, Tom Snedegar worries about several gender-related concerns. He struggles to keep up with the work load on his dairy farm. He worries that his wife is having an affair with her boss. Benedict demonstrates Snedegar's deficiencies in a number of creative ways. When Snedegar feels a surge of power from grabbing the nose ring of his bull, Great Caesar's Ghost, he feels a surge of energy and momentarily imagines sexually overpowering his wife. Through his use of comparison, Benedict indicates that Snedegar will not act upon his desires. The bull is past his prime as a breeder of cattle. While waiting in vain for his wife to join him upstairs, Snedegar looks at photographs of ancestors in their prime as movers and shakers, not overwhelmed but invigorated by their work. Through these details, Benedict establishes that Snedegar is inferior to these other men.

Benedict then infuses his story with elements of the supernatural. When Snedegar creates a mudman out of mud, wasp larvae, and liquid nitrogen, he writes a sign, urging the mudman to "Kill Vermin." Snedegar awakes to see groundhogs nailed to every fencepost, clearly the work of the mudman, and then finds the mudman sitting on a hill looking at Snedegar's wife through the bedroom window. This horror narrative ends with Snedegar telling the mudman to "leave her alone," to which the mudman laughs. Snedegar realizes that someday "the mudman was going to rise and set about his work."[10] Thematically, Snedegar has tried to create someone to help him on the farm, but has instead created a monster that further underscores his limitations as a man.

The theme of masculinity has always been important to Benedict's work. In Benedict's earlier short fiction, the male characters often attempt to gain or regain self-respect, but most of them end up defeating themselves physically or emotionally. In many of the stories, the protagonist feels slighted, with his self-esteem diminished in some way, and impulsively decides to re-establish his masculinity. In "The Sutton Pie Safe," Jack Albright repeatedly acts upon self-defeating impulses in an attempt to regain his pride after being slighted by his wife. He kills the useful black snake, he opposes selling the pie safe for $300 that would help him repair the barn, and he cuts up the snake instead of using its skin to make a belt (an action that can be seen as symbolically self-emasculating). None of these actions is a matter of life and death, but they make Jack look foolish in the eyes of those he was trying to impress. Indeed, the pattern in "The Sutton Pie Safe" is found in many of Benedict's stories: a male with injured pride acting upon self-defeating impulses. Other examples from Benedict's earlier short fiction of males behaving in self-defeating ways include Curtis Makepeace in "All the Dead," Timmy Lee Purvis in "Hackberry," Brunty in "Pit," and Loftus and Bone in "Getting Over Arnette." While one can find examples of males transcending their limitations in Benedict's early fiction (the narrator of "Town Smokes," for example), there is a greater chance for transcendence in *Miracle Boy and Other Stories*.

This contrast, made possible by Benedict's creation of dreamscapes, marks a sharp departure from Appalachian literature that depict men as defined by their socio-economic class. One of the most accomplished of the stories in the collection, "The Butcher Cock" addresses each of the three themes of class, place, and gender and explores different ways for the main character to rise above his limitations. The story begins with the gritty realism of a trip to a cockfight and ends with a journey up a magical mountain, where the narrative ventures into fantasy literature. Gender is introduced right away in the character of Ivanhoe, a fifteen-year-old boy who is often taunted for his "girl's lips,"[11] and called names like "Sweetboy" and "Hogbody." He suffers from a "pancake heart," which he fears will stop beating as he wrecks the car, driving his father, Snag, to a cockfight. Ivanhoe loses control of the vehicle, demolishing several concrete chickens that line the road, and setting himself up for attacks on his male ego. The theme of socio-economic class is introduced when the local kingpin, Big Billy Shoemaker, gives Ivanhoe and Snag a ride. Ivanhoe finds his masculinity mocked again, as Billy's beautiful date from the exotic Irish Mountain stares at Ivanhoe "like he's something from Mars."[12] She converses with him at the cockfight, and says, "You've never been much of anywhere, have you?" The beautiful woman introduces the theme of place, and her comment provides Ivanhoe with an epiphany. "It's true that he's never been much of anywhere. Never seen anything, really, except for the room where he lives, the thin-walled clapboard house of his old man's, the patch of land in the foothills with its strutting gamecocks, over which Irish Mountain glowers."[13] The conversation ends with the girl saying that she could show Ivanhoe the Eye of God at the top of Irish Mountain. So in the exposition of the story, Benedict has introduced the themes of gender, class, and place, and hinted at the possibility of Ivanhoe overcoming his limitations.

Ivanhoe faces much adversity in this story, and he often dreams of transcending his limiting circumstances. Sometimes he dreams that he is a fighting rooster, destroying his opponents, including his father's favorite, King Tut. However, he rarely remembers his dreams, and his daily life is one of drudgery and squalor. After the humiliation of the car accident, he realizes that he wants to escape. "Suddenly he doesn't want to sit down anymore, he doesn't want to cry. He wants to walk down the road, he wants to disappear into the dark. He wants to forget about the smashed car and the shaken roosters and his worried old man and the line of shattered concrete chickens. He wants to leave them all far behind."[14] Ivanhoe's interaction with the girl allows him to envision a specific possibility for transcendence. "He decides then that he will climb Irish Mountain. There, he can leave behind Ivanhoe of the foothills, he can leave Snag and the beast-men of the pit and the stinking chookhouses and *Hogbody* and *Sweetlips* and his pathetic pancake heart behind. He will leave the waking world behind, he will leap and slash and fly, his heart will pound in his chest without pain, without leaving him breathless and weak. He will be whole."[15]

It is at this point that the story enters the realm of fantasy fiction. Ivanhoe takes his favorite cock with him, the Kelso Yellow-Leg, and starts up the mountain. He falls asleep under a massive hemlock tree and "dreams of the girl."[16] From this point of the story onward, it is sometimes difficult for the reader to distinguish between reality and fantasy. However, it becomes clear that Benedict is blurring the line between the real and the fantastic in order to focus on Ivanhoe's escape, be it literal or figurative.

Benedict relies upon a seemingly supernatural ending to achieve his artistic purpose. Ivanhoe assumes the body of a rooster and encounters the girl in a waterfall, but the force of the water tears away his feathers. Eventually, she leads him to the Eye of God, "the ruined hulk of a three-hundred-foot-wide transit telescope, erected on the mountaintop by scientists from the National Radio Astronomy Observatory."[17] Ivanhoe realizes that above the clouds he cannot see the world that he has known. "Undetectable: the chookyard, the foothills, Pluskat's pit, Snag, and all the rest of Ivanhoe's old life, the entire waking world, drowned beneath the cloud sea." Ivanhoe and the young woman "will enter each other's dreams."[18] The story ends as the Kelso Yellow-Leg stands on the edge of the telescope and "crows his defiance into the face of the rising sun."[19] In "The Butcher Cock," Benedict challenges our conception of the form of the short story. He has blended the realistic and the fantastic to give Ivanhoe's hopes for transcendence in a resolution that is as much dreamscape as it is denouement. In this story, the transcendence is of two types: a preternatural connection between Ivanhoe and the young woman and Ivanhoe's drab everyday life has been imbued with magical qualities.

Another story that treats the theme of transcendence is "Miracle Boy." The title character is given his name because of the amazing surgical reattachment of his feet after they had been severed from his legs in a farming accident. The story begins with three of the Miracle Boy's classmates—Eskimo Pie, Geronimo, and Lizard—tackling him and taking off his shoes in order to examine his feet. "Show us the scars, Miracle Boy, they said."[20] They throw his shoes over a telephone wire and look for the supposed miracle. They are not impressed with what they see. One of the boys, Eskimo Pie, says, "Don't look like any miracle to me," and Miracle Boy replies, "It's miracles around us every day." When pressed to explain by Geronimo, Eskimo Pie's skeptical brother, Miracle Boy says, "Jesus, he made the lame to walk . . . . And Jesus, he made me to walk, too." Geronimo remains unconvinced. "But you wasn't lame before, Geronimo said. Did Jesus take your feet off just so he could put them back on you?"[21] When the two brothers deny the occurrence of a miracle, they diminish Miracle Boy's self-worth, as well as his claim to fame.

The story begins to explore the possibility that miracles actually happen when Lizard starts to feel guilty about what he has done to Miracle Boy. We learn that Lizard's father is no longer around and that as a result the boy feels lost. The father had always given Lizard toys, including the boy's favorite, the Limber Jack. Coupled with the guilt about his treatment of the title character, Lizard's sense of loss leads him to decide that the only way he can make amends is to retrieve Miracle Boy's shoes from the telephone wire. He straps on his father's tool belt and puts his plan into action:

> His plan was this: to drive one of the sixtypenny nails into the utility pole about three feet off the ground. Then to stand one-footed on that nail and drive in another some distance above it. Then he would stand on the second nail and drive a third, and so on, ascending nail by nail until he reached the humming transformer at the top of the pole. Then, clinging to the transformer, he imagined, he would lean out from the pole and, one handed, pluck the shoes from the wire, just like taking fruit off a tree.[22]

After experiencing greater difficulty than he had anticipated, Lizard eventually retrieves the shoes. While he is climbing the utility pole, he begins to see his home as less significant than he had ever noticed before. "Lizard was mildly surprised to realize that the valley in which he lived was such a narrow one. He could easily traverse it on foot in a day."[23] Through details like this, Benedict indicates that Lizard is undergoing a transformation.

The remainder of the story recounts a pilgrimage of penance, as Lizard returns the shoes to Miracle Boy. When he arrives at Miracle Boy's house, Lizard encounters an annoyed father, still angry about the three boys' mistreatment of his son. When Lizard says he is sorry, Miracle Boy's father replies, "It's not me you need to be sorry to."[24] Then, in a beautifully rendered conclusion,

Miracle Boy appears at the screen door and beckons to Lizard to come forward. Suddenly, Lizard hears "his old man's voice, his long-gone old man, singing, accompanied by chattering percussion: the jigging wooden feet of the Limber Jack."[25] For the first time, the reader senses the connection between the two boys: both of them have lost their childhoods, Miracle Boy due to the accident and Lizard because of the death of his father. By forgiving Lizard and accepting the shoes, Miracle Boy gives Lizard a moment of transcendence, the connection with another human being and, as evidenced by the sound of the old man's voice, the momentary return to the happiness and innocence of childhood. In a sense, Lizard experiences a kind of redemption that bears out Miracle Boy's earlier statement that "it's miracles around us every day."

Both "The Butcher Cock" and "Miracle Boy" focus on two types of transcendence: deep, preternatural connection between two people, as well as characters experiencing their everyday lives becoming imbued with magical qualities. However, the story "Pig Helmet & the Wall of Life" adds to those two types of transcendence a third type: the discovery of a sense of immortality. Pig Helmet, the main character of the story, is a police officer who became disfigured when a man he was attempting to take into custody threw acid in his face trying to avoid capture. In describing the disfigurement, Benedict wrote, "The acid missed his eyes but crisped him pretty good otherwise, and the left side of his head is kind of a nightmare. The teeth show through permanently on that side, and the flesh is rippled and brown like old melted candlewax."[26] Pig Helmet is described as "the sort of fellow that, in olden times, you'd have been of the Civilized People, trying like hell, with fire and boiling oil and molten lead and such, to keep him and his kind out . . . ."[27] In addition to the limitations brought on by his disfigurement, Pig Helmet has experienced a crisis that has left him feeling depressed and lost. As Benedict said, "The bad experience that he underwent can briefly be described as follows: OxyContin addict, alcohol, family Monopoly game gone bad, shotgun deployed, multiple homicide."[28] After arriving at the scene of the crime and having had to shoot and kill the OxyContin addict, Pig Helmet has become depressed and keeps thinking about how he believed that death lived in the house at the scene of the crime and that if he had entered the house, his life would have taken a terrible turn. "He knew that, if he had walked into that place alone, he was finished. When backup arrived, he would be gone."[29]

It is at this point in the story, when Pig Helmet has reached the depths of despair, that his life undergoes a supernatural transformation. "And then—

this is his take on it—a miracle happened. A woman called his name. At the time he thought it was his wife. It was definitely a woman's voice. And it wasn't his regular name that she called, it was his secret name, a name no one knew him by. It was a name he himself didn't know he owned, or that owned, or that owned him, until he heard the woman's voice speak it."[30] Pig Helmet then goes to the Wall of Life, operated by an evangelical preacher and his family. It is a carnival attraction in which motorcyclists ride "around the inside of a big wooden cylinder, centrifugal force sticking him perpendicular to the sides," while the crowd looks down on him from above. The evangelist has given the attraction a Christian theme and uses the Wall of Life to attract potential converts. Feeling as if death is clinging to him after he has killed the OxyContin addict, Pig Helmet becomes captivated by the word *Life* on the wall. He watches the motorcyclists zoom near him at the top of the cylinder and notices a beautiful young woman standing with snakes all around her at the bottom of the cylinder. She is speaking, but Pig Helmet cannot discern her words. He realizes that when he looks into the cylinder, it is like he is staring into the muzzle of the OxyContin addict's shotgun.

Then the grim reality of the recent altercation becomes transformed. Instead of staring down into a muzzle of a gun, Pig Helmet feels as if he is staring upward through a telescope. Words are pouring out of him, and he realizes he is repeating the exact words the young woman had been saying to him earlier. Earlier in the story, the narrator had told us about how Pig Helmet, who reads a great deal, was fascinated with how when savage German warriors were converted to Christianity, they would not allow their sword hands to be submerged during their baptism, because that hand still belonged to the god of battle. At the end of the story when the beautiful young woman calls him again by his one true name, Pig Helmet sees her as his chance for salvation. "Pig Helmet thrusts his killing hand, his unbaptized hand, out toward the girl. She is far away and getting further, but she extends her hand toward him as well, and her lips shape his true name. If Pig Helmet is strong enough, if he strains far enough, if the motorcycles spin fast enough, and if he keeps stretching out his unclean hand forever, he will reach her."[31]

In this story, we see three types of transcendence. Pig Helmet has experienced a preternatural connection with the young woman who called him by his true name; he has seen his everyday life inverted from staring down at death, in the form of the muzzle of a gun, into staring at life, gazing upward at the young woman; and he has discovered a possible spiritual solution to his problems. Taking us to the brink of a transformative action by Pig Helmet, Benedict ends the story before the character completes the action. When asked about the ending of the story in an interview, Benedict said, "The thing that was exciting to me was Pig Helmet discovering the way the universe shifted when he moved a particular way. And so any action after that would be anti-climactic. There's no way to complete an action after his discovery that the universe is vaster and weirder than he could possibly have imagined."[32]

In his use of the theme of transcendence and an approach that relies upon appropriation of narrative ideas from horror, science fiction, fantasy, myth, and the Bible, Pinckney Benedict has presented a new possible direction for literary fiction. In an interview, he outlined his artistic vision:

> . . . I think we would benefit significantly as writers if we were to lose our fetishistic interest in "originality." "The thing that hath been, it is that which shall be; and that which is done is that which shall be done: and there is no new thing under the sun." Ecclesiastes says it all, right? If we would simply acknowledge the models from which we work, the paradigms we employ, the influences we feel, then we'd produce better, more honest work, and people could trace those influences all the way back to the Epic of Gilgamesh, and the journey would be fun and educational. Every work of fiction would be this interesting tributary off the great river of Narrative, that leads all the way back to humanity's beginnings and the fountain head of Story. Instead, we pretend, or even imagine, if we can fool ourselves, that we're doing something new and different, and that others in whom we recognize influence are somehow deficient in imagination or creative energy.[33]

Miracle Boy and Other Stories addresses the restrictions that place, class, and gender can place upon individuals by presenting stories that explore exciting new possibilities for transcending the traditional limitations of the region and of Appalachian literature. While twentieth century West Virginia literature chronicles a proud people's struggles through mining wars and the Great Depression, through the turbulence of the sixties to the continual struggles of the working class during the most recent decades, twenty-first century West Virginia literature like *Miracle Boy and Other Stories* moves beyond literary realism into the world of dream and myth and imagines new responses to cultural impediments. Benedict moves from the landscape to the dreamscape, calls into question the reader's assumptions of what fiction can do, and offers Appalachian literature a possible new direction.

AFTERWORD

This book was written to celebrate the accomplishments of West Virginia writers and to demonstrate how their recent work suggests a possible new direction for Appalachian literature. The great champion of West Virginia literature, Irene McKinney, read early drafts and offered encouragement because she believed in the work of her fellow West Virginia writers and lamented that they had not found a wider audience. This is an attempt to reinvigorate the process of championing these writers, and also a means of beginning a dialogue that could lead to a more expansive view of what constitutes Appalachian literature. There is much left unaddressed: the work of other worthy writers, including many emerging talents; depictions of a range of diversity related to race, ethnicity, and sexual orientation; as well as other impressive works by the writers presented here.

Another important purpose of this book is to entice its audience into reading or rereading these texts, with an eye toward developing a greater understanding of what literature can do. Unfortunately, many of these writers have been dismissed as genre writers or regional writers. Such perceptions are reductive and restrictive. If this book has effected in its readers a curiosity about literary works that are unfamiliar but inviting, then it is deemed a success.

NOTES

Introduction

1. Joyce Carol Oates, "From England to Brooklyn to West Virginia," Feb. 23, 1983, *New York Times*, accessed Oct. 8, 2009, http://www.nytimes.com.
2 Pinckney Benedict, *Town Smokes* (New York: Ontario Review Press, 1987).
3. Flannery O'Connor, *Mystery and Manners* (New York: Farrar, Straus, and Giroux, 1961), 847.
4. "County Economic Status, Fiscal Year 2015: Appalachian West Virginia," Appalachian Resource Commission, accessed May 20, 2014, www.arc.gov.
5. "Child Poverty in West Virginia: A Growing and Persistent Problem," West Virginia Center on Budget and Policy, Feb. 2013, www.legis.state.us, pdf document, 13–16.
6. Dan Witters, "North Dakota No. 1 in Well-Being, West Virginia Still Last," Feb. 20, 2014. Gallup. www.gallup.com.
7. James Dao, "T-Shirt Slight Has West Virginia in Arms," Mar. 23, 2004, *New York Times*, accessed May 20, 2014, www.nytimes.com.
8. Ashley Woods, "Zlati Meyer, Detroit Journalist, Enrages Twitter with West Virginia Incest Joke, *Huffington Post*, updated Jan. 25, 2014, www.huffingtonpost.com.
9. Irene McKinney, *Vivid Companion* (Morgantown, WV: Vandalia, 2004), 55–56.
10. Irene McKinney interview by Boyd Creasman, October 29, 2009.
11. Thomas E. Douglass, *A Room Forever: The Life, Work, and Letters of Breece D'J Pancake* (Knoxville: University of Tennessee Press, 1998), 61.
12. Ann Pancake, *Strange as This Weather Has Been* (Emeryville, CA: Shoemaker & Hoard, 2007), 3.
13. Avery F. Gaskins, "Middle-Class Townie: Jayne Anne Phillips and the Appalachian Experience," *Appalachian Journal* 19.3 (1992), 309.
14. Irene McKinney, *Backcountry: Contemporary Writing in West Virginia*. (Morgantown, WV: Vandalia, 2002), 9.
15. McKinney interview by Creasman.
16. Ibid.
17. My discussion of these categories owes much to the chapter on feminist theory in Lois Tyson's *Critical Theory Today* (New York: Garland, 1999). Tyson offers a rich discussion of the concept of patriarchal woman and credits Mary Helen Washington with the term "emergent woman." I developed the concept of deferential woman.
18. Nancy Carol Joyner, "Appalachian Women's Writing and Identity Theories," in *Appalachia Inside Out: Custom and Culture*, Vol. 2, Robert J. Higgs, et al., eds., (Knoxville: University of Tennessee Press, 1995), 715.
19. Davis Grubb, *The Night of the Hunter* (London: Prion, 1999), 205.

Chapter 1

1. "The Night of the Hunter (1955)," Roger Ebert, Roger Ebert.com, November 24, 1996, http://rogerebert.suntimes.com.

2. Gene Baro, "A Terrifying and Impassioned Narrative," review of *The Night of the Hunter* by Davis Grubb, *New York Herald Tribune Book Review,* February, 21, 1954, 5.

3 Thomas E. Douglass, "Before the Appalachian Literary Renaissance, There Was Davis Grubb's *The Voices of Glory." Appalachian Heritage* 33.3 (2005): 83.

4. Jack Welch, *"Davis Grubb: A Vision of Appalachia"* (Ph.D. diss., Carnegie-Mellon University, 1980), 1.

5. Edwin T. Arnold, "Davis Grubb," *American Novelists since World War II,* (Detroit: Gale, 1980), *MLA International Bibliography*, 118, accessed through EBSCO, July 28, 2009, ebscohost.com.

6. Welch, 20.

7. Ibid., 22.

8. Ibid., 57.

9. Douglas Fowler, *Ira Levin* (Mercer Island, WA: Starmont House, 1988), 11.

10. Arnold.

11. Davis Grubb, *The Night of the Hunter*, (London: Prion, 1999), 9.

12. Ibid., 122–23.

13. Jessie Bernard, "The Good Provider Role: Its Rise and Fall." *Men's Lives,* 3rd Ed. Michael S. Kimmel and Michael A. Messner, eds. (Boston: Allyn and Bacon, 1995), 152–53.

14. Grubb, 29.

15. Ibid., 207.

16. Ibid., 13.

17. Ibid., 101.

18. Ibid., 22.

19. Ibid., 24.

20. Ibid., 38.

21. Ibid., 66.

22. Ibid., 37.

23. Ibid., 83.

24. Ibid., 154.

25. Ibid., 86.

26. Ibid., 84

27. Ibid., 154.

28. Ibid., 99.

29. Ibid., 101.

30. Ibid., 103.

31. Ibid., 104.

32. Ibid., 106–7.

33. Ibid., 107.

34. Ibid., 107–8.
35. Ibid., 124.
36. Ibid., 125.
37. Ibid., 143.
38. Ibid., 147.
39. Ibid., 148.
40. Douglass, "Before," 87.
41. Grubb, 73.
42. Ibid., 203.
43. Ibid., 204.
44. Ibid., 220.
45. Ibid., 222.
46. Ibid., 227.
47. Ibid., 238.
48. Ibid., 259.
49. Ibid., 265–66
50. Welch, iv.

Chapter 2

1. George Garrett, *Understanding Mary Lee Settle* (Columbia: University of South Carolina Press, 1988), 10.
2. Brian Rosenberg, *Mary Lee Settle's Beulah Quintet: The Price of Freedom* (Baton Rouge: Louisiana State University Press, 1991), xii.
3. Garrett, 1–2
4. Ibid., 5
5. Matt Schudel, "Novelist Mary Lee Settle." *Washington Post*, September 29, 2005, www.washingtonpost.com.
6. Denise Giardina, "My Literary Mother," *Appalachian Heritage* 34.1 (2006): 10.
7. Valerie J. Nelson, "Mary Lee Settle, 87; Novelist and PEN/Faulkner Award Founder," October 2, 2005, articles.latimes.com.
8. Joyce Dyer, "Introduction." *Bloodroot: Reflections on Place by Appalachian Women* (Lexington: University of Kentucky Press, 1998), 1–45.
9. Rosenberg, 2.
10. Ibid., 8.
11. Ibid., 12.
12. Ibid., 14.
13. Garrett, 39.
14. Rosenberg, 57.
15. Ibid., 164.
16. Mary Lee Settle, *Prisons* (Columbia: University of South Carolina Press, 1996), 48.
17. Ibid., 63.
18. Ibid., 59.

19. Ibid., 65.
20. Ibid., 67.
21. Ibid., 79.
22. Ibid., 80.
23. Ibid., 102.
24. Ibid., 106.
25. Ibid., 125.
26. Ibid., 211.
27. Rosenberg, 165.
28. Jane Gentry Vance, "*O Beulah Land*: The 'Yaller Vision,'" *An American Vein: Critical Readings in Appalachian Literature*, Danny J. Miller, et al., eds (Athens: Ohio University Press, 2005), 113.
29. Mary Lee Settle, *O Beulah Land* (Columbia: University of South Carolina Press, 1996), 48.
30. Ibid., 159.
31. Ibid., 351.
32. Rosenberg, 82.
33. Settle, *O Beulah Land*, 6.
34. Ibid., 325.
35. Ibid., 368.
36. Rosenberg, 85.
37. Mary Lee Settle, *Know Nothing* (Columbia: University of South Carolina Press, 1996), 74.
38. Ibid., 77.
39. Ibid., 78.
40. Ibid., 174.
41. Ibid., 90.
42. Ibid., 92.
43. Ibid., 166.
44. Ibid., 172.
45. Ibid., 218.
46. Ibid., 219.
47. Rosenberg, 164.
48. Ibid., 101.
49. Mary Lee Settle, *The Scapegoat* (Columbia: University of South Carolina Press, 1996), 172.
50. Ibid., 23.
51. Ibid., 274.
52. Ibid., 23.
53. Ibid., 35.
54. Ibid., 38.
55. Ibid., 52.
56. Ibid., 54–55.

57. Ibid., 198.
58. Ibid., 254–55.
59. Ibid., 214–14.
60. Ibid., 192.
61. Ibid., 90.
62. Ibid., 244.
63. Ibid., 189.
64. Ibid., 13.
65. Ibid., 278.
66. Mary Lee Settle, *The Killing Ground* (Columbia: University of South Carolina Press, 1996), 184.
67. Ibid., 206.
68. Ibid., 224.
69. Ibid., 180.
70. Ibid., 165.
71. Ibid., 284.
72. Ibid., 337.
73. Rosenberg, 164.
74. Settle, *The Killing Ground*, 271.
75. Ibid., 274.
76. Ibid., 305.
77. Garrett, 50–51.
78. Settle, *The Killing Ground*, 384.

Chapter 3

1. Albert E. Wilhelm, "Breece D'J. Pancake," *Dictionary of Literary Biography*, Vol. 130 (Detroit: Thompson Gale, 1993), 253.
2. Thomas E. Douglass, *A Room Forever: The Life, Work, and Letters of Breece D'J Pancake* (Knoxville: University of Tennessee Press, 1998), 98.
3. Ibid., 92.
4. Wilhelm, 254.
5. Breece D'J Pancake, *The Stories of Breece D'J. Pancake* (New York: Holt, Rinehart and Winston, 1984), 174.
6. Douglass, 4.
7. Ibid., 7–8.
8. Ibid., 5–6.
9. Jeff Mann, "A Conversation with Irene McKinney." *In Her Words: Diverse Voices in Contemporary Appalachian Women's Poetry*. ed. Felicia Mitchell. (Knoxville: University of Tennessee Press, 2002), 197.
10. Thomas E. Douglass, Interview of Denise Giardina, *Appalachian Journal* 20 (1993): 393.
11. Thomas E. Douglass, Interview of Pinckney Benedict. *Appalachian Journal* 20 (1992): 70–71.

12. Ibid., 71.
13. Breece Pancake, 41.
14. Ibid., 44.
15. Ibid., 45
16. Douglass, 111.
17. Breece Pancake, 46.
18. Wilhelm, 254.
19. Breece Pancake, 83.
20. Ibid., 87.
21. Douglass, 129.
22. Ibid.
23. Breece Pancake, 87.
24. Angela B. Freeman, "The Origins and Fortunes of Negativity: The West Virginia Worlds of Kromer, Pancake, and Benedict," *Appalachian Journal* 25 (1998): 245.
25. Review of *"The Stories of Breece D'J. Pancake,"* *Publishers Weekly*, December 3, 1982: 50.
26. Douglass, 121.
27. Ibid., 94.
28. Flannery O'Connor, *Mysteries and Manners* (New York: Farrar, Straus, and Giroux, 1961), 112.
29. Douglass, 113.
30. Breece Pancake, 101.
31. Ibid., 102.
32. Ibid., 103.
33. Ibid., 101.
34. Ibid., 102.
35. Ibid., 112.
36. Ibid., 109.
37. Ibid., 107.
38. Ibid., 107–8.
39. Ibid., 113.
40. Ibid., 113–14.
41. Ibid., 114.
42. Ibid., 152.
43. Ibid.
44. Ibid., 149.
45. Ibid., 154.
46. Ibid., 149.
47. Douglass, 114.
48. Breece Pancake, 157.
49. Ibid.
50. Douglass, 114.
51. Geoffrey Galt Harpham, "Short Stack: The Stories of Breece D'J. Pancake," *Studies in Short Fiction* 23.3 (1986): 266.

52. Breece Pancake, 21.
53. Harpham, 266.
54. Douglass, 110–11.
55. Breece Pancake, 25.
56. Ibid., 31.
57. Douglass, 112.
58. Breece Pancake, 22.
59. Ibid., 31–32.
60. Ibid., 32.
61. Ibid., 22.
62. Ibid., 32.
63. Ibid., 35.
64. Douglass, 113.
65. Breece Pancake, 36.
66. Ibid., 37.
67. Ibid., 74.
68. Ibid., 67.
69. Ibid., 68.
70. Ibid., 80.
71. Ibid., 81.
72. Ibid.
73. Douglass, 41–42.
74. Ibid., 77.
75. Ibid., 119.
76. Wilhelm, 39.
77. Ibid., 44.

Chapter 4

1. "ASA Awards." *Appalachian Studies Association*. www.appalachianstudies.org.
2. "Denise Giardina." DeniseGiardina.com, http://www.denisegiardina.com.
3. Ibid.
4. "Denise Giardina." Contemporary Authors Online. http://go.galegroup.com
5. Denise Giardina, "Let Us Be Clear: Mountaintop Removal Not About Creating Jobs." *Charleston Gazette* 22 May 2007: 5A.
6. Norman Oder, "Denise Giardina: Mining History in West Virginia and World War II," *Publishers Weekly* February 9, 1998: 69.
7. Denise Giardina, *Storming Heaven* (New York: Ivy, 1987), 6
8. Ibid., 9.
9. Ibid., 12.
10. Ibid., 19.
11. Ibid., 71.
12. Ibid., 93.
13. Ibid., 99.
14. Ibid., 163.

15. Robert Shogan, *The Battle of Blair Mountain: The Story of America's Largest Labor Uprising* (Boulder: Basic Books, 2006), 14.
16. Giardina, *Storming Heaven*, 54.
17. Ibid., 34.
18. Ibid., 61.
19. Cecelia Conway, "Slashing the Homemade Quilt in Denise Giardina's *Storming Heaven*," *NWSA Journal* 11.3 (1999): 138–56.
20. Giardina, *Storming Heaven*, 41.
21. Oder, 70.
22. Giardina, *Storming Heaven*, 73.
23. Ibid., 106.
24. Ibid., 110–11.
25. Ibid., 140.
26. Ibid., 166.
27. Ibid., 200.
28. Ibid.
19. Ibid., 207.
30. Ibid., 146.
31. Ibid., 173.
32. Ibid. 206.
33. Ibid., 243.
34. Ibid., 246.
35. Ibid., 262.
36. Ibid., 111.
37. Ibid., 24–25.
38. Ibid., 39.
39. Ibid., 141.
40. Ibid., 202.
41. Conway, 147.
42. Giardina, *Storming Heaven*, 34.
43. Ibid., 114.
44. Ibid., 130.
45. Conway, 147.
46. Shogan, ix.
47. Tim Boudreau, "Fighting Back: Denise Giardina Talks about *Storming Heaven*," *Now and Then* 5:1 (1988): 9.

Chapter 5

1. Irene McKinney, *Unthinkable: Selected Poems: 1976–2004*, (Los Angeles: Red Hen Press, 2009).
2. Sandra Ballard, "Introduction," *Listen Here: Women Writing in Appalachia*, (Lexington: University of Kentucky Press, 2003), 1.

3. Jeff Mann, "A Conversation with Irene McKinney," In *Her Words: Diverse Voices in Contemporary Appalachian Women's Poetry*, Felicia Mitchell, ed., (Knoxville: University of Tennessee Press, 2002), 203.

4. McKinney interview by Creasman.

5. Irene McKinney, *Vivid Companion*, (Morgantown, West Virginia: Vandalia, 2004), 97.

6. Irene McKinney, *Six O'Clock Mine Report*, (Pittsburgh: University of Pittsburgh Press, 1989), 31.

7. *Vivid Companion*, 61–62.

8. *Vivid Companion*, 55.

9. Ibid.

10. Irene McKinney interviewed by Emily Corio, "McKinney Releases Book of Selected Poems," *West Virginia Public Broadcasting*, March 24, 2009, October 21, 2009, http://www.wvpubcast.org.

11. Ibid., 42.

12. "Interview with Poet Irene McKinney." *wickpoetrycenter.blogspot.com*. 28 Aug. 2009, http://wickpoetrycenter.blogspot.com.

13. *Vivid Companion*, 49.

14. Ibid.

15. Ibid., 50.

16. Ibid., 66.

17. Ibid., 68.

18. Casie Fedukovich, "Dancing Naked," Review of *Vivid Companion*, *American Book Review*, 26.6 (2005): 22.

19. *Vivid Companion*, 46.

20. Ibid.

21. Ibid., 47.

22. Patti Capel Schwartz, "Vivid Companion: Poems," Review of *Vivid Companion*, *Journal of Appalachian Studies*, 12.1 (2006): 137.

23. Fedukovich, "Dancing Naked," 22.

24. *Vivid Companion*, 10.

25. Ibid., 11.

26. Ibid., 97.

27. "Interview with Poet Irene McKinney." *wickpoetrycenter.blogspot.com*. 28 Aug. 2009. http://wickpoetrycenter.blogspot.com.

28. *Vivid Companion*, 24.

29. Ibid., 94.

30. Ibid.

31. Ibid.

32. Ibid., 10.

33. Ibid., 63.

34. Ibid.

35. "Interview with Poet Irene McKinney." *wickpoetrycenter.blogspot.com*. 28 Aug. 2009, http://wickpoetrycenter.blogspot.com.
36. Ibid.
37. *Vivid Companion*, 77.
38. Ibid.
39. Ibid., 78.
40. Ibid. 79.
41. Irene McKinney interview by Boyd Creasman, October 29, 2009.
42. *Vivid Companion*, 86.
43. Ibid.
44. Ibid., 87.
45. Ibid., 93.
46. Ibid.
47. Ibid., 94.
48. Ibid.
49. Ibid., 95.
50. Ibid.
51. "Interview with Poet Irene McKinney." *wickpoetrycenter.blogspot.com*. 28 Aug. 2009, http://wickpoetrycenter.blogspot.com.
52. "In Their Own Country: Irene McKinney." *wvcenterforthebook.org*. 28 Aug. 2009. http://wvcenterforthebook.org.

Chapter 6

1. This quotation appears on the back cover of the novel.
2. "ASA Awards." *Appalachian Studies Association*. www.appalachianstudies.org.
3. Pendarvis, Jack. "Buried Alive." Review of *Strange as This Weather Has Been*. *New York Times* 14 Oct. 2007. http://www.nytimes.com.
4. Pam Houston, "Tell It on the Mountain," Oprah.com www.oprah.com/omagazine.
5. Nicholas Arnold and Michael Baccam. "A Conversation with Ann Pancake." Willow Springs. http://willowsprings.ewu.edu, 4.
6. Pendarvis.
7. Ann Pancake, *Strange as This Weather Has Been*, 3.
8. Ibid., 10.
9. Ibid., 20.
10. Ibid., 79.
11. Ibid., 26.
12. Ibid., 265.
13. Ibid., 74.
14. Ibid., 71.
15. Ibid., 83.
16. Ibid., 51.
17. Ibid., 276.
18. Ibid., 277.

19. Ibid., 26.
20. Ibid., 194.
21. Ibid., 235–36.
22. Ibid., 55.
23. Tyson, 55–56
24. Ann Pancake, 276.
25. Ibid., 131.
26. Ibid., 304.
27. Kai T. Erikson, *Everything in Its Path* (New York: Simon and Schuster, 1976), 26.
28. Ibid., 26–27.
29. Ibid., 29.
30. Ibid., 32.
31. West Virginia Division of Culture and History, "Buffalo Creek," http://www.wvculture.org.
32. Ann Pancake, 224.
33. Ibid., 236.
34. Ibid., 237.
35. Ibid., 238.
36. Ibid., 217.
37. Ibid., 268.
38. Ibid., 275.
39. Ibid., 272.
40. Ibid., 273.
41. Ibid., 308.
42. Ibid.
43. Ibid., 302.
44. Ibid., 305.
45. Ibid., 102.
46. Arnold and Baccam, 12.
47. Ann Pancake, 11.
48. Ibid., 143.
49. Ibid., 183.
50. Ibid., 188.
51. Ibid., 63.
52. Ibid., 251.
53. Ibid., 252.
54. Ibid., 87.
55. Ibid., 183.
56. Ibid., 80.
57. Ibid., 81.
58. Ibid., 133.
59. Arnold and Baccam, 12.
60. Ann Pancake, 356–57.

61. Ibid., 10.
62. Ibid., 168.
63. Ibid., 172–73.
64. Ibid., 174.
65. Ibid., 174–75.
66. Ibid., 176.
67. Ibid., 179.
68. This quotation appears on the back cover of the novel.
69. Ann Pancake, dedication to *Strange as This Weather Has Been*.

Chapter 7

1. Thomas E. Douglass, Interview with Jayne Anne Phillips, *Appalachian Journal* 21.2 (1994): 182–89.
2. "Jayne Anne Phillips: American Writer," Jayne Anne Phillips.com, http://www.jayneannephillips.com.
3. Michael Dirda, "A Family Worth Knowing," *New York Review of Books* April 30, 2009: 47.
4. Jayne Anne Phillips, *Lark and Termite* (New York: Knopf, 2009), 5.
5. Ibid., 5–6.
6. Ibid., 74–75.
7. Michiko Kakutani, "In War and Floods, a Family's Leitmotif of Love, Memories, and Secrets." January 6, 2009. *New York Times,* http://www.nytimes.com.
8. Phillips, *Lark and Termite*, 26.
9. Ibid., 195.
10. Ibid., 27.
11. Ibid.
12. Ibid., 28.
13. Ibid., 66.
14. Ibid., 220.
15. Ibid., 111.
16. Ibid., 111–12.
17. Ibid., 75.
18. Ibid.
19. Ibid., 94.
20. Ibid., 132–33.
21. Ibid., 116.
22. Ibid., 217.
23. Ibid., 218.
24. Ibid., 122.
25. A. M. Homes, "Jayne Anne Phillips." *Bomb* 49 (1994): 46
26. Phillips, *Lark and Termite*, 134.
27. Jayne Anne Phillips, *Machine Dreams* (New York: E.P. Dutton, 1984), 169.
28. Jayne Anne Phillips. *Fast Lanes* (New York: E.P. Dutton, 1987), 48–49.

29. Phillips, *Lark and Termite*, 9–10.
30. Ibid., 150.
31. Ibid.
32. Ibid., 50.
33. Ibid., 90.
34. Ibid., 97.
35. Sarah Robertson, *The Secret Country: Decoding Jayne Anne Phillips' Cryptic Fiction* (Amsterdam: Rodopi, 2007) 3.
36. Kathryn Harrison, "Songs of Innocence," *New York Times* January 16, 2009, http://www.nytimes.com.
37. Douglas Hunt, *The Riverside Anthology of Literature* 2nd ed. (Boston, Houghton Mifflin, 1991), 353.
38. Homes, 49.
39. Phillips, *Lark and Termite*, 193.
41. Ibid., 74–75.
42. Ibid., 105.
43. Ibid., 250.
44. Yvonne Zipp, Review of *Lark and Termite*. 13 Jan. 2009. *Christian Science Monitor* October 21, 2009. http://features.csmonitor.com.
45. Dirda, 47.

Chapter 8

1. Lacey Lyons, "Breaking the Curse of Literary Short Fiction: An Interview with Pinckney Benedict," *Charlotte Viewpoint* July 10, 2010, http://www.charlotteviewpoint.org.
2. "In Their Own Country." West Virginia Center for the Book. http://wvcenterforthebook.org.
3. Pinckney Benedict, "Vignette vs. Story: The Apocalyptic Arc." *RedRoom.com.* http://redroom.com.
4. This quotation appears on the back cover of *Town Smokes* (New York: Ontario Review Press, 1987).
5. This quotation appears on the back cover of *Dogs of God* (New York: Nan A. Talese, 1994).
6. Pinckney Benedict interview by Boyd Creasman, July 16, 2014.
7. Pinckney Benedict, *Miracle Boy and Other Stories* (Winston Salem, NC: Press 53), 7.
8. Ibid., 65.
9. Katherine Egerton, "'When You Were a Man': Pinckney Benedict's Fathers and Sons," *Appalachian Heritage* 38.1 (2010), 44. *Literature Resource Center*.
10. Pinckney Benedict, *Miracle Boy and Other Stories*, 96.
11. Ibid., 24.
12. Ibid., 27.
13. Ibid., 29.

14. Ibid., 26.
15. Ibid., 34.
16. Ibid., 37.
17. Ibid., 43.
18. Ibid., 44.
19. Ibid.
20. Ibid., 1.
21. Ibid., 2–3.
22. Ibid., 7.
23. Ibid., 10.
24. Ibid., 11.
25. Ibid., 12.
26. Ibid., 184.
27. Ibid., 183.
28. Ibid., 184.
29. Ibid., 188.
30. Ibid.
31. Ibid., 194.
32. Benedict interview by Creasman.
33. Derek Alger, "Pinckney Benedict," *Pif Magazine*, October 1, 2012, http://www.pifmagazine.com.

Primary Sources

Benedict, Pinckney. *Miracle Boy and Other Stories*. Winston-Salem: Press 53, 2010.
———. *Town Smokes*. New York: Ontario Review Press, 1987.
———. *The Wrecking Yard*. New York: Plume, 1995.
Giardina, Denise. *Storming Heaven*. New York: Ivy, 1987.
Grubb, Davis. *The Night of the Hunter*. 1953. London: Prion, 1999.
McKinney, Irene. *Six O' Clock Mine Report*. Pittsburgh: University of Pittsburgh Press, 1989.
———. *Unthinkable: Selected Poems: 1976–2004*. Los Angeles: Red Hen Press, 2009.
———. *Vivid Companion*. Morgantown, West Virginia: Vandalia, 2004.
Pancake, Ann. *Strange as This Weather Has Been*, Shoemaker & Hoard/Counter-point. 2007.
Pancake, Breece D'J. *The Stories of Breece D'J. Pancake*. New York: Holt, Rinehart and Winston, 1984.
Phillips, Jayne Anne. *Lark and Termite*. New York: Knopf, 2009.
———. *Fast Lanes*. New York: E.P. Dutton, 1987.
———. *Machine Dreams*. New York: E.P. Dutton, 1984.
Settle, Mary Lee. *Know Nothing*. 1960. Columbia: University of South Carolina Press, 1996.
———. *O Beulah Land*. 1956. Columbia: University of South Carolina Press, 1996.
———. *Prisons*. 1973. Columbia: University of South Carolina Press, 1996.
———. *The Killing Ground*. 1982. Columbia: University of South Carolina Press, 1996.
———. *The Scapegoat*. 1980. Columbia: University of South Carolina Press, 1996.

Secondary Sources

Alger, Derek. "Pinckney Benedict," *Pif Magazine*. October 1, 2012. http://www.pifmagazine.com.
Arnold, Edwin T. "Davis Grubb." *American Novelists since World War II*. 117–22. Detroit: Gale, 1980. *MLA International Bibliography*. EBSCO. 28 Jul. 2009. www.ebscohost.com.
Arnold, Nicholas and Michael Baccam. "A Conversation with Ann Pancake." *Willow Springs* 20 Jan. 2010 http://willowsprings.ewu.edu.
"ASA Awards." *Appalachian Studies Association*. 21 Dec. 2009. www.appalachianstudies.org.
Ballard, Sandra L. and Patricia L. Hudson. "Introduction." *Listen Here: Women Writing in Appalachia*. Lexington: University Press of Kentucky, 2003. 1–5.
Baro, Gene. "A Terrifying and Impassioned Narrative." Review of *The Night of the Hunter*. *New York Herald Tribune Book Review* 21 Feb. 1954: 5.
Benedict, Pinckney. Interview by Boyd Creasman. July 16, 2014.

———. "Vignette vs. Story: The Apocalyptic Arc." RedRoom.com. http://redroom. com.

Bernard, Jessie. "The Good Provider Role: Its Rise and Fall." Men's Lives. 3rd Ed. Kimmel, Michael S. and Michael A. Messner, eds. Boston: Allyn and Bacon, 1995. 149–63.

Boudreau, Tim. "Fighting Back: Denise Giardina Talks about *Storming Heaven*." *Now and Then*. 5.1 (1988): 9–10. http://www.wvculture.org.

"Child Poverty in West Virginia: A Growing and Persistent Problem," West Virginia Center on Budget and Policy, Feb. 2013, www.legis.state.us.

Conway, Cecelia. "Slashing the Homemade Quilt in Denise Giardina's Storming *Heaven*." NWSA Journal 11.3 (1999): 138–56.

Corio, Emily. "McKinney Releases Book of Selected Poems." *West Virginia Public Broadcasting*. 24 Mar. 2009. 21 Oct. 2009. http://www.wvpubcast.org.

"County Economic Status, Fiscal Year 2015: Appalachian West Virginia," Appalachian Resource Commission, accessed May 20, 2014, www.arc.gov.

Dao, James. "T-Shirt Slight Has West Virginia in Arms." *New York Times* March 23, 2004. www.nytimes.com.

"Denise Giardina." *Contemporary Authors Online*. 15 Jan. 2010. www.go.galegroup.com

"Denise Giardina." *DeniseGiardina.com*. 15 Jan 2010. http://www.denisegiardina. com.

Dirda, Michael. "A Family Worth Knowing." Review of *Lark and Termite*. *New York Review of Books* 30 Apr. 2009: 45–47.

Douglass, Thomas E. *A Room Forever: The Life, Work, and Letters of Breece D'J Pancake*. Knoxville: University of Tennessee Press, 1998.

———. "Before the Appalachian Literary Renaissance, There Was Davis Grubb's *The Voices of Glory*." *Appalachian Heritage* 33.3 (2005): 83–91.

———. Interview of Denise Giardina. *Appalachian Journal* 20 (1993): 384–93.

———. Interview of Pinckney Benedict. *Appalachian Journal* 20 (1992): 68–74.

Dyer, Joyce. "Introduction." *Bloodroot: Reflections on Place by Appalachian Women*. Lexington: University of Kentucky Press, 1998. 1–14.

Ebert, Roger. "The Night of the Hunter (1955)." 24 Nov. 1996. *RogerEbert.com* http://rogerebert.suntimes.com.

Egerton, Katherine. "'When You Were a Man': Pinckney Benedict's Fathers and Sons" *Appalachian Heritage* 38.1 (2010), 44. *Literature Resource Center*.

Erikson, Kai T. *Everything in Its Path*. New York: Simon and Schuster, 1976.

Fedukovich, Casie. "Dancing Naked." Review of *Vivid Companion*. *American Book Review* 26.6 (2005): 22.

Fowler, Douglas. *Ira Levin*. Mercer Island, WA: Starmont House, 1988.

Freeman, Angela B. "The Origins and Fortunes of Negativity: The West Virginia Worlds of Kromer, Pancake, and Benedict." *Appalachian Journal* 25 (1998): 244–69.

Gardiner, Judith Kegan. "Introduction." *Masculinity Studies and Feminist Theory: New Directions*. New York: Columbia University Press, 2002. 1–29.

Garrett, George. *Understanding Mary Lee Settle*. Columbia: University of South Carolina Press, 1988.

Gates, Anita. "Mary Lee Settle, 87, Author of 'Beulah' Novels Is Dead." *New York Times* 29 Sep. 2005: 9.

Giardina, Denise. "Let Us Be Clear: Mountaintop Removal Not About Creating Jobs." *Charleston Gazette* 22 May 2007: 5A.

———. "My Literary Mother." *Appalachian Heritage* 34.1 (2006): 10.

Harpham, Geoffrey Galt. "Short Stack: The Stories of Breece D' J. Pancake." *Studies in Short Fiction* 23. 3 (1986): 265–74.

Harrison, Kathryn. "Songs of Innocence." Review of *Lark and Termite*. 16 Jan. 2009. *New York Times* 3 June 2009. www.nytimes.com.

Homes, A.M. "Jayne Anne Phillips." *Bomb* 49 (1994): 46–51.

Houston, Pam. "Tell It on the Mountain." Review of *Strange as This Weather Has Been*. *Oprah.com*. 1 Feb. 2010. http://www.oprah.com.

Hunt, Douglas. *The Riverside Anthology of Literature* 2nd ed. Boston, Houghton Mifflin, 1991.

"In Their Own Country: Irene McKinney." West Virginia Center for the Book. www.wvcenterforthebook.org.

"In Their Own Country: Pinckney Benedict." West Virginia Center for the Book. www.wvcenterforthebook.org.

"Interview with Poet Irene McKinney." *wickpoetrycenter.blogspot.com*. 28 Aug. 2009 http://wickpoetrycenter.blogspot.com.

"Jayne Anne Phillips: American Writer." *jayneannephillips.com*. 18 May 2009. http://www.jayneannephillips.com.

Joyner, Nancy Carol. "Appalachian Women's Writing and Identity Theories." *Appalachia Inside Out: Culture and Custom*. Vol 2. eds. Higgs, Robert J., Ambrose N. Manning, and Jim Wayne Miller. Knoxville: University of Tennessee Press, 1995. 713–19.

Kakutani, Michiko. "In War and Floods, a Family's Leitmotif of Love, Memories, and Secrets." Review of *Lark and Termite*. 5 Jan. 2009. *New York Times* 19 May www.nytimes.com.

Lyons, Lacey. "Breaking the Curse of Literary Short Fiction: An Interview with Pinckney Benedict," *Charlotte Viewpoint* July 10, 2010, www.charlotteviewpoint.org.

Mann, Jeff. "A Conversation with Irene McKinney." *In Her Words: Diverse Voices in Contemporary Appalachian Women's Poetry*. ed. Felicia Mitchell. Knoxville: University of Tennessee Press, 2002. 194–205.

McKinney, Irene. *Backcountry: Contemporary Writing in West Virginia*. Morgantown, West Virginia: Vandalia, 2002.

———. Interview by Boyd Creasman. October 29, 2009.

———. "Marginalia: Windows and Bones." *Memoir (and)* 2.2 (2009): 103–6.

Miller, Danny L. *Wingless Flights: Appalachian Women in Fiction*. Bowling Green, OH: Bowling Green State University Popular Press, 1996.

Nelson, Valerie J. "Mary Lee Settle, 87; Novelist and PEN/Faulkner Award Founder," October 2, 2005, http://articles.latimes.com.

Oates, Joyce Carol. "From England to Brooklyn to West Virginia." 23 Feb. 1983. *New York Times* 8 Oct. 2009. http://nytimes.com.

———, ed. *The Oxford Book of American Short Stories*. Oxford: Oxford University Press, 1992.

O'Connor, Flannery. *Mystery and Manners*. New York: Farrar, Straus, and Giroux, 1961.

———. "The Regional Writer." *Collected Works*. New York: Library of America, 1988. 843–48.

Oder, Norman. "Denise Giardina: Mining History in West Virginia and World War II." *Publishers Weekly* 9 Feb. 1998: 69–70.

Pendarvis, Jack. "Buried Alive." Review of Strange as *This Weather Has Been*. *New York Times* 14 Oct. 2007. http://nytimes.com

"Poverty Rates in Appalachia, 2000." *Appalachian Resource Commission*. 11 Aug. 2008. http://www.arc.gov.

Review of *The Stories of Breece D'J. Pancake*. *Publisher's Weekly* 3 Dec. 1982: 50.

Robertson, Sarah. *The Secret Country: Decoding Jayne Anne Phillips's Cryptic Fiction*. Amsterdam: Rodopi, 2007.

Rosenberg, Brian. *Mary Lee Settle's Beulah Quintet: The Price of Freedom*. Baton Rouge: Louisiana State University Press, 1991.

Schudel, Matt. "Novelist Mary Lee Settle." *Washington Post* 29 Sep. 2005. http://washingtonpost.com

Shogan, Robert. *The Battle of Blair Mountain: The Story of America's Largest Labor Uprising*. New York: Basic Books: 2004.

Swartz, Patti Capel. "Vivid Companion: Poems." Review of *Vivid Companion*. *Journal of Appalachian Studies* 12.1 (2006): 137–38.

Tyson, Lois. *Critical Theory Today*. New York: Garland, 1999.

Vance, Jane Gentry. *"O Beulah Land*: The 'Yaller Vision.'" *An American Vein: Critical Readings in Appalachian Literature*. eds. Danny J. Miller, Sharon Hatfield, and Gurney Norman. Athens: Ohio UP, 2005. 104–14.

Welch, Jack. *Davis Grubb: A Vision of Appalachia*. Dissertation. Carnegie-Mellon University, 1980.

West Virginia Division of Culture and History. "Buffalo Creek." http://www.wvculture.org.

Wilhelm, Albert E. "Breece D'J. Pancake." *Dictionary of Literary Biography*. Vol. 130. Detroit: Thompson Gale, 1993. 253–59.

Willis, Meredith Sue. "Seduced into Consciousness: The Art of Jayne Anne Phillips." *Appalachian Heritage* 37.1 (2009): 22–28.

Witters, Dan. "North Dakota No. 1 in Well-Being, West Virginia Still Last," Feb. 20, 2014. Gallup, http://gallup.com.

Woods, Ashley. "Zlati Meyer, Detroit Journalist, Enrages Twitter with West Virginia Incest Joke, *Huffington Post*, updated Jan. 25, 2014, www.huffingtonpost.com.

Zipp, Yvonne. Review of *Lark and Termite*. 13 Jan. 2009. *Christian Science Monitor* 21 Oct. 2009. http://features.csmonitor.com.

Beulah Quintet (Settle): *(cont'd)*
Ground, 12, 31–32, 34; and *Know
Nothing*, 31, 41; and liberty in 17th
century England, 11, 31; and Lily Lacey
in *The Scapegoat*, 12, 32, 45, 47–49,
51; and metafiction, 49; and *O Beulah
Land*, 31, 38–41; and political, spiritual
and philosophical issues, 32; publishing
of, 34; and pursuit of liberty, 38–39,
51–52; and sacrifice, 11–12; and *The
Scapegoat*, 12, 31, 34; and slavery, 11,
34, 41–42, 51; and socio-economic class,
12, 31, 39–41, 52; and tensions between
powerful and powerless, 11, 31, 34–35,
51–52; and "the price of freedom," 52;
and tragedy, 51; and transcendence, 51;
and writing career of Hannah McKarkle
in *The Killing Ground*, 49, 51. See also
Killing Ground, The (Settle); *Know
Nothing* (Settle); *O Beulah Land* (Settle);
Prisons (Settle); *Scapegoat, The* (Settle)
Blood Tie (Settle), 32
Buffalo Creek disaster, 14, 85, 105, 106,
108, 111–12

Charleston, WV, 108; as birthplace of Mary
Lee Settle, 32; and Canona, West Virginia
of Mary Lee Settle, 12, 49, 50; as largest
city in WV, 3
coal industry: and coal companies, 1, 13,
14, 45–46, 72, 73; and coal strikes,
31, 45–47, 77; and corporate control
of mining, 46, 112; corruption of,
14, 72, 74; and creation of a wealthy,
industrial class, 11, 12; and damages
due to mining, 112–13, 119–20; and
environmental issues, 106, 107–9,
111–13, 119–20; and *Everything in Its
Path* (Erikson), 111–12; and greed, 114;
and "Hollow," 56; and intimidation of
private police force, 72, 76, 77; and
Jimmy Make's search for a job, 109; and
living conditions for workers, 72, 75, 84;
and Miles as a coal company executive
in *Storming Heaven*, 84; mine guard
system of, 85; and miners' deaths from
black lung, 112, 119–20; and mining

deaths and injuries, 112, 119–20; and
mountaintop removal of coal, 14, 73, 85,
105, 107–9, 113–14; and Pittston coal
company, 111–12; and shootings of labor
supporters, 76, 85; and taking of land,
72, 73, 74, 85; and treatment of workers,
72, 74–75, 84–85, 108; and unions, 13,
46–47, 75–76, 85, 109; and *The Unquiet
Earth* (Giardina), 72, 85–86; and U.S.
government's use of force against miners,
72, 86; and West Virginians' fight against
coal companies, 113–14; and WV, 59, 71,
113–14. *See also* Buffalo Creek disaster;
Storming Heaven (Giardina); *Strange as
This Weather Has Been* (Pancake, Ann)
Cromwell, Oliver, 35, 36–37

democracy: dynamics of, 35, 38; and
promise of freedom, 52
Dillard, Annie, 71, 72

Faulkner, William: and fiction, 14; and
human heart, 54; and *The Sound and the
Fury*, 132
female characters: Bant in *Strange as This
Weather Has Been*, 106, 107–9, 117,
120; in *Beulah Quintet* , 12, 39–52;
Bo's mother in "Fox Hunters," 68–69;
Bridie in "The Beginnings of Sorrow,"
140; Cally in "The Scrapper," 61–62;
Carrie Bishop in *Storming Heaven*, 1, 8,
13, 73, 75, 76, 77–78; and challenges
faced by Appalachian women, 8–9;
Cousin Annie in *Know Nothing*, 43, 44;
and deferential female characters, 8;
and emergent female characters, 8, 14;
Ginny in "Trilobites," 65–66; Gladdy in
Lark and Termite, 128, 131, 133; Hannah
Catlett in *O Beulah Land*, 40, 41, 42, 51;
Hannah McKarkle in *The Killing Ground*,
12, 49, 50–51, 52; Icey Spoon in *The
Night of the Hunter*, 8, 22–23, 25; and
independent female characters, 7, 8, 11,
12, 14, 17, 51, 52; Lace See in *Strange
as This Weather Has Been*, 14, 106–11,
113–15, 120; Lark in *Lark and Termite*,
122–29, 133–34, 135; Lily Lacey in *The*

Scapegoat, 12, 32, 45, 47–49, 50, 51, 52; Lola in *Lark and Termite,* 122, 123, 124, 125–26, 127, 128; Loretta Hughes in *Strange as This Weather Has Been,* 113, 114, 120; Lucy in "Fox Hunters," 69; Lydia Catlett in *Know Nothing,* 43; Melinda Lacey in *Know Nothing,* 43–44, 51; Mother Jones in *The Scapegoat,* 45–47, 48; Nell in *Prisons,* 36; Nonie in *Lark and Termite,* 122, 127, 128, 129, 131, 133; and patriarchal female characters, 8, 17, 22–23; Pearl in *The Night of the Hunter,* 26, 27–28; Rachel Cooper in *The Night of the Hunter,* 1, 8, 10, 11, 21, 26–29; Rachel Honaker in *The Unquiet Earth,* 85, 86; Ruby in *The Night of the Hunter,* 27–28; Sally Brandon Neill McKarkle in *The Killing Ground,* 49, 50, 51; Sally in "Hollow," 56–57; Sally Lacey in *Know Nothing,* 42–43; Sally Lacey in *O Beulah Land,* 39–41, 43; Sara Lacey in *Know Nothing,* 43; Sara Lacey in *O Beulah Land,* 39–40, 41, 42; and sexuality, 23–25, 28, 69–70; Sheila Gerlock in "In the Dry," 63–64, 65, 70; and traditional female roles, 49, 50, 51; Trudy in "The Scrapper," 60; Willa Harper in *The Night of the Hunter,* 11, 21, 22–26, 29

"Fox Hunters" (Pancake, Breece): and Bo, 68–70; and Bo's boss Enoch, 69; and Bo's fabrication of a sexual conquest, 8, 69; and Bo's mother, 68–69; and Bo's rejection of immorality, 69–70; and dignity, 69; and fox hunting scene, 69; and friendship with Lucy, 69; and theme of leaving WV, 2, 55, 69; and theme of sexual assault, 13, 69–70

Garcia Marquez, Gabriel, 14
Giardina, Denise, 1, 14, 15, 33; and gender construction, 83–84; impact of Breece Pancake on writing of, 55; on mountaintop removal of coal, 73; novels of, 72, 73; as one of WV's finest writers, 11; and portrayals of regions, 59, 73; and positive portrayals of West Virginians, 73–74; religious and political activities

of, 73; and social justice, 72–73; upbringing and education of, 72–73. See also *Unquiet Earth, The* (Giardina)
Grubb, Davis, 1, 11, 15; and ability to create suspense, 30; and birthplace of Moundsville, 18; and childhood experiences of shaping material for *The Night of the Hunter,* 18, 19–20; and Clarksburg, 18; and father's heart attack, 18; later work of, 19; and life during the Depression era, 18; and New York City, 18; and Ohio River culture, 18; parents of, 18; and social criticism, 17, 26, 30; and society's treatment of children and the poor, 26, 27; Stephen King on work of, 17; and writing of *The Night of the Hunter,* 18–19

Hemingway, Ernest, 1, 137
"Hollow" (Pancake, Breece): and Buddy, 56–58, 65, 70; and Fuller, 56; and masculinity, 56, 70; and poverty, 56, 57; and pressure on men to be providers, 7–8; and Sally, 56–57; and self-defeating behavior of male characters, 12, 57; and socio-economic class, 55–58; and use of violence, 12, 56–58, 70
"Honored Dead, The" (Pancake, Breece), 55

independent female characters: and breaking from traditional female roles, 7, 12, 27, 49–51, 77–78; Carrie Bishop in *Storming Heaven,* 77–80, 86; and challenges faced by Appalachian women, 9; and Hannah McKarkle in *The Killing Ground,* 12, 49–51, 52; and Lace See in *Strange as This Weather Has Been,* 14, 116–17; and lack of dependence on men, 8, 27; and Lily Lacey in *The Scapegoat,* 12; and Rachel Cooper, 11, 17, 26–27, 29; and self-sustainability, 27; Tommie Justice in *The Unquiet Earth,* 86
"In the Dry" (Pancake, Breece): and Bus, 64, 65; and description of landscape, 64; and dignity, 65; and Mr. Gerlock, 63–65; and need for redemption, 64–65; and Ottie, 63–65, 70; and Ottie's decision to

"In the Dry" (Pancake, Breece): (cont'd)
leave the Gerlocks, 64, 65; and Ottie's
feelings of lovelessness and rejection,
65; and Ottie's moment of grace, 63, 65;
and Ottie's tragic accident, 63–64; and
Ottie's visit to foster home, 63–65; and
relationship between Bus and Ottie, 64,
65; and Sheila Gerlock, 63–64, 65

Kanawha valley, 31, 38
Killing Ground, The (Settle): and Canona,
WV, 49, 50; and death of Johnny
McKarkle, 49, 50; and death of the father,
49; and family obligations, 49, 50;
and gender roles, 2–3, 12, 49, 50; and
Hannah and Johnny's attitudes towards
sexuality, 50; and Hannah McKarkle, 49–
51, 52; and Hannah McKarkle's desire to
leave WV, 2–3, 50; and issue of marriage,
50; and Johnny McKarkle, 8, 49–50, 51;
and mother Sally Brandon Neill McKarkle,
49, 50, 51; and motives of Johnny
McKarkle's killer, Jake Catlett, 50–51;
and murder of Johnny McKarkle, 49; and
Sally McKarkle's romanticized image of
her father, 49–50; and search of main
character for heritage, 32; and sexuality
as fulfilling a basic human need, 8; and
socio-economic class, 31, 49–51, 52; and
"the price of freedom," 50; and women
characters' fight for independence,
49, 50; and writing career of Hannah
McKarkle, 49, 50
Know Nothing (Settle): and Battle of
Philippi, 41; and Book One, 41; and Book
Three, 41; and Book Two, 41, 42–43;
and Brandon and Sally Lacey's visit to
the Catletts, 42; and capitalism, 43;
and Crawford Kregg, 43, 44; and Egeria
Springs, 41, 42–43, 44; and Englishman
Wellington Smythe, 42–43, 44; and
family estate of Catletts, 12, 41; and fear
of slave uprising, 42; and Johnny Catlett,
11–12, 41, 44; and Johnny Catlett
in Confederate army, 41; and Johnny
Catlett's tragic choices, 51; and Lewis
Catlett, 41, 43, 44; and Lydia Catlett,

43; and Melinda Lacey's engagement
to Crawford Kregg, 44, 51; and Melinda
Lacey's relationship with the Catletts, 43,
44; and perpetuation of slavery, 9, 12,
41–42, 44, 51; and pre-Civil War years,
31, 41; and romantic love, 43–44, 51;
and Sally Lacey, 42–43; and Sally Lacey's
attempts to find a husband for her
daughter Sara, 43; and Sara Lacey, 43;
and slave-owning family at Beulah, 41;
and slavery, 41–42; and socio-economic
class, 9, 12, 42–44; and "the price of
freedom," 44–45; and title of novel, 41–
42; and tragedy, 9, 44; xenophobia in, 42

Lark and Termite (Phillips): and Appalachia,
15, 135; and birth, death and rebirth,
125–26; and Charlie's affair with Lola,
131; and Charlie's mother Gladdy, 128,
131, 133; and coming of age, 121, 131;
and comparisons with The Sound and
the Fury (Faulkner), 132; and Corporal
Robert Leavitt, 121–28, 130, 134; and
desire, 121, 130, 131; and Florida as
destination for Lark and Termite, 124,
128–29, 131, 133; and gender, 122; and
ghostly Robert Stamble's appearance,
133–34; and ghosts of war, 123, 133–34;
and heightened awareness, 123, 126–27,
133; and immortality, 123, 126; and
interconnectedness with other human
beings, 1, 10, 15, 122–23, 127, 134;
and Korean woman's suicide, 124, 128;
and Lark, 122–29, 134, 135; and Lark as
caregiver for developmentally challenged
brother, 10, 15, 122, 123, 126–29, 133;
and Lark's sexual encounter with Solly,
124, 126, 131; and Leavitt in friendly
fire incident, 122, 125; and Leavitt's
bonds with Lark and Termite, 124; and
Leavitt's dying at tunell's entrance, 124,
125, 127, 128; and Leavitt's gun, 128;
and Leavitt's interaction with blind boy,
125, 127; and life-affirming nature of
personal relationships, 129; and Lola,
122, 123, 124, 128; and Lola giving
birth to Termite, 124, 125–26, 127; and

Lola's fascination with leaving for FL, 124; and Lola's suicide, 128; and love's transformative power, 130–31; and magical realism, 123, 124, 132–33, 134; and male characters' businesses, 122, 131; and male characters' relationships with their mothers, 122, 128; and mortality, 121; and multiple points of view in narration, 132; and Nonie, 122, 127, 128, 129, 131, 133; and past as a continual part of present, 132, 134; and Phillips's treatment of family, 132; and place, 122; praise for, 121; and recurring theme of tests for each generation, 122, 126, 128–29, 134, 135; and redemption, 121, 123, 135; and relationship between Lark and Solly, 130, 131, 133; and relationship between Lola and Leavitt, 128, 130; and relationship between Nonie and Charlie, 130–31; and rites of passage in tunnels, 124–26; and scenes in Winfield, WV, 121–24, 131, 133; and self-discovery, 15, 121, 122, 131, 135; and sense of community in fictional Winfield, WV, 135; and sexuality as connection, 122, 126, 129–30, 131; and similarity between Termite and Benjy of *The Sound and the Fury*, 132; and socio-economic class, 122; and South Korean scenes, 121–24, 126–27, 130; and suicide theme, 124, 128; and supernatural events, 122–23, 132–34; and supernatural interconnectedness with family members, 1, 10, 122–23, 125–26; and Termite, 122, 124–26, 127, 129, 132; and Termite's seeing bodies in the tunnel, 124, 126; and Termite's vision of his father, 134; and theme of older sister taking care of a younger, disabled brother, 122, 123, 126–29, 133, 135; and themes of *Machine Dreams*, 121, 122, 127; train motif in, 123, 134; and transcendence, 14–15, 121, 122–23, 127, 129, 133, 134; and transcendence and redemption, 135; and transformation from flood, 122, 133; tunnel motif in, 123, 124–26, 130, 133, 134; and war,

121, 122, 123, 126, 130, 135; and women breaking with traditional gender roles, 122

Laughton, Charles, 17, 19

Love Eaters, The (Settle), 32, 33

Machine Dreams (Phillips), 121, 122, 127, 129

male characters: Albion Freeman in *Storming Heaven*, 73, 75–76, 78, 80–81, 85; Avery Taylor in *Strange as This Weather Has Been*, 106–7, 110, 111–13, 118; Ben Harper in *The Night of the Hunter*, 11, 20–21, 28, 29; Beverly Lacey in *The Scapegoat*, 45, 46, 47; Bo in "Fox Hunters," 8, 65, 68–70; Buddy Gunn in "The Secret Nature of the Mechanical Rabbit," 140–41; Buddy in "Hollow," 12, 56–58, 60, 65, 70; Bund in "The Scrapper," 60, 61, 63; Bus in "In the Dry," 64; Carlo Michele in *The Scapegoat*, 47, 52; Charlie Blizzard in *Strange as This Weather Has Been*, 113, 114, 120; Charlie in *Lark and Termite*, 122, 130–31; C.J. Marcum in *Storming Heaven*, 73, 74, 75, 77, 82, 85; Colly in "Trilobites," 12, 65–68; Corey in *Strange as This Weather Has Been*, 106, 108, 110, 115–16; Corporal Robert Leavitt in *Lark and Termite*, 122–28, 130, 134; Crawford Kregg in *Know Nothing*, 43, 44; Dane in *Strange as This Weather Has Been*, 106, 108, 116; Dan Neill in *The Scapegoat*, 47, 49; and desperate acts of Appalachian men, 70; Doc Booker in *Storming Heaven*, 76, 77, 79, 80; Eduardo Pagano in *The Scapegoat*, 45, 48, 52; Enoch in "Fox Hunters," 69, 70; Esau in "Pony Car," 140; Ezekiel Catlett in *O Beulah Land*, 39–40, 41; Fuller in "Hollow," 56; General Braddock in *O Beulah Land*, 39; and inadequacies due to economic difficulties, 7–8, 11, 12–14, 26, 70; Isom Justice in *Storming Heaven*, 76, 77, 82, 85; Ivanhoe in "The Butcher Cock," 141, 144–45; Jack Albright in "The Sutton Pie Safe," 143; Jake Catlett in *The Killing Ground*, 50–51;

male characters: (cont'd)

Jake Catlett in *The Scapegoat*, 46–47; Jeremiah Catlett in *O Beulah Land*, 40, 41, 42; Jim Gibson in "The Scrapper," 61–63; Jimmy Make Turrell in *Strange as This Weather Has Been*, 7, 9, 14, 107, 111, 113–15; Joe Messenger in "Joe Messenger is Dreaming," 141–42; John (son of Willa Harper) in *The Night of the Hunter*, 25–30; John Lilburne in *Prisons*, 35; Johnny Catlett in *Know Nothing*, 11–12, 41, 43, 44, 51, 52; Johnny Church in *Prisons*, 11–12, 31, 35–38, 50, 51, 52; Johnny McKarkle in *The Killing Ground*, 49–50, 51; Jonathan Lacey in *O Beulah Land*, 38–40, 41, 51; Lewis Catlett in *Know Nothing*, 41, 43; Lizard in "Miracle Boy," 141, 142; and masculinity, 7–8, 12–13, 39, 55–58, 60–62, 65–66; Miles Bishop in *Storming Heaven*, 75, 77–78, 84, 85; Miracle Boy in "Miracle Boy," 141, 145–47; Mogey in *Strange as This Weather Has Been*, 106–7, 118–19; Mr. Gerlock in "In the Dry," 63–65; Oliver Cromwell in *Prisons*, 35, 36–37; Ottie in "In the Dry," 63–65, 70; Peregrine Lacey in *O Beulah Land*, 40; Pig Helmet in "Pig Helmet & the Wall of Life," 141, 147–49; Preacher in *The Night of the Hunter*, 11, 17, 18, 20, 21–29; Rondal Lloyd in *Storming Heaven*, 13, 73, 74–77, 78, 80–83, 85; Scurry in "Bridge of Sighs," 141, 142; and sexuality, 7–8, 21–22, 28, 61–62; Sir Valentine in *Prisons*, 36; Skeevy in "The Scrapper," 12–13, 60–63, 68; Termite in *Lark and Termite*, 122, 125–27, 129, 132; Thankful Perkins in *Prisons*, 37, 52; Tom Corey in "The Scrapper," 61; Uncle Birdie in *The Night of the Hunter*, 26; and violence, 56–63; Walt Spoon in *The Night of the Hunter*, 21, 22, 23; Wellington Smythe in *Know Nothing*, 42–43, 44

McKinney, Irene: and advocacy for other poets, 90–91; and *Backcountry: Contemporary Writing in West Virginia*, 6, 89; on Breece Pancake, 5, 53, 55, 90–91; and career at West Virginia Wesleyan College, 90; and connection to the land, 93, 103; and early life in WV, 90, 93; and *The Girl with the Stone in Her Lap*, 90; at Hamilton College, 98; and hardships of poverty, 6–7, 90; influences of, 90; and label of regional writer, 6; and Maureen Seaton's *Furious Cooking*, 90; and nature, 13, 91, 92, 97–98, 100; as one of WV's finest writers, 11, 15, 89; and perceptions of WV, 91–93; and poem "At 24," 8; and poem "Home," 92; and poem "Monkey Heart," 4–5, 92–93; as Poet Laureate of West Virginia, 89–90; poetry books of, 89, 90; poetry of, 1, 5, 8, 13–14; and rejection of traditional gender roles, 104; and role of poetry, 89–90, 104; and sexuality, 96–98; and struggle with cancer, 14, 91, 103–4; and theme of leaving WV, 55; and women's struggles to define themselves, 13–14, 91, 95–98. See also *Vivid Companion* (McKinney)

Miracle Boy and Other Stories (Benedict): and "Bridge of Sighs," 141, 142; and Bridie in "The Beginnings of Sorrow," 140; and Buddy Gunn in "The Secret Nature of the Mechanical Rabbit," 140–41; and challenges to readers' preconceptions of fiction, 137, 140; and characters' fears, frustrations and fantasies as fuel for narratives, 140; and characters imagining better lives for themselves, 141; and elements of myth, horror, science fiction and fantasy literature, 137, 140, 142–43, 144, 145; and Esau in "Pony Car," 140; and father-and-son relationships, 141–42; and gender, 141–43, 144, 149; and immortality, 147; and Irish Mountain, 144, 145; and Ivanhoe in "The Butcher Cock," 141, 144–45; and Jack Albright in "The Sutton Pie Safe," 143; and Joe Messenger, 141–42; and "Joe Messenger is Dreaming," 141–42; and limitations of place, 141; and Lizard, 141, 142; and magical qualities of everyday life, 145, 147; and masculinity, 142–43, 144; and

"Miracle Boy," 141, 142, 145–47; and
Miracle Boy, 145–47; and "Miracle Boy,"
145–47; and "Mudman," 142–43; and Pig
Helmet, 141, 147–49; and "Pig Helmet &
the Wall of Life," 15, 138–39, 141, 147–
49; and "Pony Car," 140; and possibility
of miracles, 146; and preternatural
interconnectedness with other human
beings, 145, 147; and Scurry in "Bridge
of Sighs," 141, 142; and Seneca Valley
as location for stories, 141; and shift
in focus from landscape to dreamscape,
137, 149; and socio-economic class,
144, 149; and the supernatural, 137,
143, 145; and "The Angel's Trumpet,"
142; and "The Beginnings of Sorrow,"
138, 140, 142; and "The Butcher Cock,"
138, 141, 144–45, 147; and theme of
place, 144, 149; and "The Secret Nature
of the Mechanical Rabbit," 140–41; and
"The Sutton Pie Safe," 139, 143; and
Tom Snedegar in "Mudman," 142–43;
and traditional male roles, 142; and
transcendence, 139, 141, 143, 145, 147;
and upheaval in characters' lives, 139;
and "Zog 19," 138
Mitchum, Robert, 11, 17
Mother Jones (Mary Harris Jones), 45–48

New York City: and Davis Grubb, 18;
as destination for Lily Lacey in *The
Scapegoat*, 48; and women's equality, 48;
and writing, 3, 6; and writing career of
Hannah McKarkle, 50
Night of the Hunter, The (Grubb): and Ben
and Willa Harper, 9, 20, 23, 24, 25, 26;
and Ben Harper, 7, 11, 20; as a critique
of the capitalist ideology, 17; and the
Depression, 19, 21, 29; and effects used
to create suspense, 19; evil in, 19, 21,
25–26; and fairy tales, magic stories,
mythology, 19; and features of a terror
narrative, 19; film adaptation of, 11,
17; and gender, 11, 17, 19, 27, 29, 30;
and greed, 20, 21; Grubb's childhood
experiences shaping material for, 18,
19–20; Grubb's writing of, 18–19; and

handling of plot and suspense, 17, 30;
and Harry Powell, 18; and independent
female characters, 8, 11, 17, 21, 26–27,
29; inspiration for, 18; and John and
Pearl, 26, 27–28, 29; and marriage
between Willa and Preacher, 24–25, 26;
and murder of Willa Harper, 25–26; and
patriarchal female characters, 8, 17, 23;
and Preacher, 17, 20–29; and Preacher's
love and hate tattoos, 1, 11, 17, 18; and
Preacher's murders of widows, 21–22; and
pressure on men to be providers, 11, 20–
21, 29; and Rachel Cooper, 2, 8, 10, 11,
26–29; and Rachel Cooper's adoption and
care for children, 21, 26, 27; and Rachel
Cooper's saving John and Pearl, 28–29;
and sexuality, 11, 17, 21–25, 28; and
society's treatment of children and the
poor, 26, 29; and socio-economic class,
11, 17, 19–21, 29, 30; and tragedy,
18, 25–26, 29; and transcendence, 18,
29; and Uncle Birdie's relationship with
John, 26

Oates, Joyce Carol, 1, 59, 139
O Beulah Land (Settle): and 18th century
America, 31, 38; and American dream,
38; and Battle of Monongahela, 38, 39;
and Beulah county, 31, 38, 39, 40, 41;
and Beulah settlement willed to Sara,
40; and Captain Orme, 39; and Ezekiel
Catlett, 39–40, 41; and French and
Indian War, 39; and General Braddock's
defeat, 39; and Hannah Catlett's struggle
for survival, 40, 51; and Jeremiah
and Hannah Catlett's origins, 42; and
Jeremiah Catlett, 40; and Jonathan Lacey
in British army, 38; and Jonathan Lacey's
defiance of the British government, 39;
and Jonathan Lacey's election to the
House of Burgesses, 38, 39, 40; and
Jonathan Lacey's rise in VA society,
38; and Jonathan Lacey's settlement
of Beulah, 38, 39, 51; and Jonathan
Lacey's trading land to Catletts for a red
stone and riding crop, 40; and Jonathan
Lacey's wife Sally, 39–41; and King

O Beulah Land (Settle): (*cont'd*)
George III's restrictions on settlements
in western VA, 38, 39; and origins of
affluent families of WV, 39; and Peregrine
Lacey, 40; and personal qualities of
Jonathan Lacey, 38–39, 40; and pre-
revolutionary America, 38–39; and
pursuit of American liberty, 39, 51; and
Sally Lacey, 39, 40, 43; and Sally Lacey's
class-consciousness, 41; and Sara Catlett,
39–40, 41; and socio-economic class,
39–41; and strength of colonists against
British, 39

O'Connor, Flannery: comic tone of, 60; and
moments of grace for characters, 60, 63;
and regional American fiction, 2; and
satire of poor rural characters, 59–60;
and use of violence, 60

Pancake, Ann: and childhood in West
Virginia, 105–6; and coal industry, 106,
109, 119–20; and collection of stories
Given Ground, 106; and documentary
Black Diamonds, 106; education of, 106;
and gender in *Strange as This Weather
Has Been*, 118, 119; and mountaintop
removal of coal, 1, 14, 105; as one of
West Virginia's finest writers, 11, 15;
and relation to Breece Pancake, 105;
and spirituality's link with nature, 14,
118–19; and the supernatural, 10; and
West Virginian literature, 91; and West
Virginians' connection to the land, 107,
120

Pancake, Breece D'J: and characters' inner
conflict about leaving their region, 55,
65–67; and cultures of VA and WV, 90–
91; dignity in characters of, 56, 59–60,
63, 65, 69; and Flannery O'Connor's
work, 59–60; and influence on Pinckney
Benedict, 15, 55, 139; and influence
on West Virginia's writers, 55, 70, 139;
lack of opportunity for characters of,
12, 70; and masculinity, 7–8, 12–13,
55–56, 66, 70; and mentor John Casey,
54; and Milton, WV, 53; as one of West
Virginia's finest writers, 11, 139; and

portrayal of poor West Virginians, 59; and
poverty, 12, 55, 70; prose style of, 54,
55; and redemption, 64–65, 70; and self-
defeating behavior of male characters,
56, 70; and *The Stories of Breece D'J.
Pancake*, 54–55; and studies at UVA,
5, 53–54; suicide of, 54; and theme of
leaving WV, 55; and theme of place, 55,
70; Thomas Douglass's biography of, 5,
16, 70; and transcendence, 56, 70; and
"Trilobites," 54, 55, 66, 67; and use of
violence, 60, 70; work of, 12–13, 53, 55,
59, 69–70

patriarchal female characters: and accepting
male-dominated culture, 8, 22–23; and
Icey Spoon, 17, 22–23; and patriarchy as
God's will, 22

Phillips, Jayne Anne: and Appalachian
literature, 55, 71, 89, 105, 135; and
awkwardness of adolescence, 131, 135;
and Breece Pancake, 53; and Clarksburg
incident as basis for *Quiet Dell*, 18; and
collection of short fiction *Black Tickets*,
129; international recognition of, 121;
and label of regional writer, 6; and
Machine Dreams, 121, 122, 127, 129;
and magical realism, 132–33, 134; and
novel *Lark and Termite*, 1, 14–15, 121,
123, 125, 129, 130; as one of WV's finest
writers, 11, 15, 121, 139; and redemptive
quality of fiction, 121, 135; study on, 16;
and the supernatural, 9, 10, 132–34; and
theme of family responsibilities, 135; and
theme of leaving WV, 55; and treatment
of sexuality, 129–30; and West Virginian
literature, 91. See also *Lark and Termite*
(Phillips)

poverty: in Appalachia, 3, 30, 70, 105;
and Ben Harper's reason for committing
crime, 20, 21; and characters in *Miracle
Boy and Other Stories*, 141; children
living in, 29, 110; and effects on self-
esteem, 110; and Hannah Catlett in *O
Beulah Land*, 51; and Irene McKinney,
13, 90; and masculinity, 12, 56, 57, 70;
and Melinda Lacey in *Know Nothing*, 51;
and Miles's efforts to escape in *Storming*

sexuality: and asserting masculinity,
7–8; and Ben and Willa Harper in *The
Night of the Hunter*, 11, 23, 24, 25;
in Breece Pancake's stories, 7–8, 68,
69–70; and Carrie's relationship with
Rondal, 79, 80–81; and casual sex, 130;
and collection of short fiction *Black
Tickets* , 129; and complex marriage of
members of the Oneida Community, 98;
in *Fast Lanes* (Phillips), 130; in "Fox
Hunters" (Pancake, Breece), 8, 69–70;
and Hannah and Johnny's attitudes in
The Killing Ground, 50; and intimacy
issues of Rondal, 82–83; in *Lark and
Termite*, 122, 124, 126, 130–31; and
love's transformative power, 130; and
Machine Dreams (Phillips), 129; and
marriage between Carrie and Albion, 79;
and marriage of Jimmy Make and Lace,
115; and moral aspect of sex, 70; in *The
Night of the Hunter*, 11, 21–25, 28, 30;
and Oneida community, 91; and poem
"Clitoral," 97–98; and poem "Covering
Up" (McKinney), 96–97; Preacher's
loathing of, 21–22, 28, 30; and
prostitution in Annadel, WV, 76–77, 82;
and repressed sexual attitudes, 11, 23–
25; and Rondal Lloyd's opinion of desire,
78, 80–81; and sex as physical expression
in "The Scrapper," 61; and sex to fulfill
human need, 8, 80, 82; and sexual
encounter of Johnny with Nell in *Prisons*,
36; and sexual orientation, 3; and Sheila
Gerlock in "In the Dry," 65; and Tommie
Justice in *The Unquiet Earth*, 86
Stories of Breece D'J. Pancake, The (Breece
Pancake): and "Fox Hunters," 55, 68–70;
and "Hollow," 56–58, 65, 70; and
importance of internal experience, 54,
70; influence of, 53, 54–55, 70; and "In
the Dry," 55, 63–65; as Pancake's legacy,
54; and poverty, 53, 54, 70; and self-
worth of main characters, 54, 61–62;
and "The Honored Dead," 55; and theme
of place, 54–55; and "The Salvation of
Me," 2, 55; and "The Scrapper," 60–63,
68; and "Time and Again," 58–59;

and "Trilobites," 55, 65–68; and WV's
economy, 54
Storming Heaven (Giardina): and Albion's
battle with consumption, 83; and
Albion's murder, 76, 85; and American
dream, 84, 85; and Baldwin guards or
detectives, 77, 80, 83, 85; and Battle
of Blair Mountain, 1, 13, 71, 76, 80,
85; and Carrie Bishop, 13, 73, 77–80,
83, 87; and Carrie Bishop's job as a
nurse, 75, 76, 78, 79, 80; and Carrie's
relationship with Rondal, 75, 78–79,
83; and Carrie's union participation,
80; changing of names and places
in, 76; and C.J. Marcum, 73, 74, 75,
77, 85; and Clabe Lloyd, 7; and coal
companies' treatment of land, workers
and protesters, 72, 74–75, 84, 85; as
critique of capitalist ideology, 84–85, 86;
and danger in role of union organizer,
81, 82; and Doc Booker, 76, 77, 79, 80,
81; and Ed Chambers and Sid Hatfield,
76; and gender issues, 13, 77–78, 80–84,
107; as historical fiction, 71–72, 76;
and independent female characters, 8,
78, 79–80, 87; and individual liberty
and human rights, 85; and intimacy
issues of Rondal, 78–83; and Isom as
Chief of Police of Annadel, 77; and
labor movement, 13, 72, 76, 77, 78, 80,
86; loss of life and injury in, 85; and
marriage between Carrie and Albion, 76,
79; and masculinity, 13, 80, 81, 83–84,
87; and Matewan Massacre, 71, 76;
and Miles's lack of principles as a coal
executive, 75, 84; and mining experience
of Rondal Lloyd, 73, 75, 82, 84; and
multiple points of view in narration, 106;
and murder of C.J. Marcum's grandfather,
73, 74; and murder of Isom Justice, 76,
85; and political activities of Marcum
and Booker, 77; praise for, 71; and
racially integrated town of Annadel,
76–77, 85; and refusal to give up land
by C.J.'s grandfather, 74; and religious
motivations of Albion Freeman, 73, 75,
76, 81, 83; and reversal of gender roles

of Carrie and Miles, 77–78, 83–84; and
Rondal Lloyd, 8, 13, 74, 80–81; and
Rondal's decision to become a union
organizer, 75; and Rondal's fate at Blair
Mountain, 83; and Rondal's relationship
with his father, 82; and shootings of
labor supporters, 85; and socio-economic
class, 13, 73, 84; and taking of land
by coal companies, 74, 76; and U.S.
government's use of force against miners,
72, 86; and West Virginians' fight against
coal companies, 13, 14, 71, 72, 85–87

Strange as This Weather Has Been (Pancake,
Ann): and Avery Taylor, 106–7, 110, 111–
13; and Bant, 106, 107–9, 117, 120; and
Buffalo Creek disaster, 14, 105, 106, 108;
and characters' connections with the
land, 14, 107, 118–19; and characters'
relating local histories, 106–7; and
characters who refuse to leave land, 120;
and coal industry, 14, 105, 106, 108–9,
111, 113–14; and Corey, 106, 108, 110,
115–16; and Dane, 106, 108, 116; and
dangers to environmentalists, 111, 114;
and *Everything in Its Path* (Erikson),
111–12; and gender, 107, 114–15; and
incorporation of historical fact, 111–12;
and Jimmy Make's back injury, 109, 115,
120; and Jimmy Make Turrell, 7, 9, 14,
107, 109–11, 113; and Lace See, 14,
106–11, 116–18, 120; and Lace See's
children, 106, 107, 108; and Lace See's
employment, 107, 114–15; and lack of
job opportunities, 14, 107, 108, 109,
114–15; and marriage of Jimmy Make
and Lace, 2, 14, 107, 111, 115, 116–17;
and masculinity, 115–18; and mining
company's treatment of out-of-state
workers, 108; and Mogey, 106–7, 118–
19; and Mogey's connection with nature,
2, 118–19; and mountaintop removal
of coal, 1, 2, 14, 105, 107–8, 118; and
multiple points of view in narration, 106;
and negative stereotypes of people of
WV, 5–6; and North Carolina, 109, 110,
117; and novels with political messages,
106; and poverty's effects on self-

esteem, 110–11; praise for, 105, 120;
and socio-economic class, 14, 107, 110,
114–15, 118–20; and theme of leaving
WV, 2, 107, 112, 120; and Tommy, 108;
and transcendence, 118–19; and West
Virginians' fight against coal companies,
14, 111, 113–14, 118, 120

"Time and Again" (Breece Pancake): and
question of redemption, 58–59; and
violence, 58, 70

tragedy: and Ben and Willa Harper, 29;
and Buffalo Creek disaster, 111–12; and
greed, 9; and Irene McKinney's poetry,
93; and lack of self-knowledge, 9; and
Lark and Termite, 121; and *The Night
of the Hunter* , 29; and pride, 9; and
shootings of labor supporters in *Storming
Heaven*, 85; and *Storming Heaven*
(Giardina), 73, 85. See also *Storming
Heaven* (Giardina)

transcendence: and American dream, 85;
and Appalachian literature, 16, 73, 87;
and Christian faith of Rachel Cooper,
10, 11; and gender issues, 77, 141;
and immortality, 9, 10, 15, 147; and
interconnectedness with other human
beings, 9, 10, 15, 122–23, 127; and labor
movement in WV, 80, 85; in *Lark and
Termite*, 10, 133, 134; and limitations
of traditional religion, 14; and magical
qualities of everyday life, 9, 10, 15, 138,
145, 147; in mid-to-late 20th and 21st
century WV literature, 10, 85; and *Miracle
Boy and Other Stories*, 138, 139, 141,
143, 145, 147; and Mogey's connection
with nature, 118–19; and moments of
grace, 70; and natural beauty, 9; and
The Night of the Hunter , 18, 29; and
Pig Helmet's transformation, 148–49;
and poetry of Irene McKinney, 14, 104;
and preternatural interconnectedness
with other human beings, 145, 147; of
Rachel Cooper, 29; and redemption, 135;
and socio-economic class, 141; and the
supernatural, 9, 132–34, 138; and theme
of place, 141

"Trilobites" (Pancake, Breece): and barren land, 66; and Colly's connection with the land, 2, 12, 66, 67; and Colly's father's life as incentive to leave region, 66–67; and Colly's feelings of failure, 65–66; and Colly's interest in trilobites, 66; and Colly's mother, 65, 67, 68; and Colly's problems on the family farm, 65, 66, 67; and Colly's relationship with his girlfriend, 12, 65–66, 67–68; and death of Colly's father, 65, 66, 67; and Florida, 65, 66; and ghosts of ancestors, 67; and Ginny, 65–68; and leaving the region for hopes of better economic opportunities, 65–67; and masculinity, 65, 66; and Ohio, 65, 67; publishing of, 54; and theme of leaving WV, 2, 12, 55; and uncertainty of future, 68

Turkey, 32, 33

Unquiet Earth, The (Giardina): and coal companies' exploitation of workers and land, 85; and Dillon Lloyd, 85–86; gender issues in, 86; and independent female characters, 86; and Rachel Honaker, 85; and Rachel Honaker's choice of husband, 86; and Rachel's daughter Jackie, 86; as sequel to *Storming Heaven*, 85; and taking of land, 85; and West Virginians' fight against coal companies, 85–86

Virginia: and Richmond, 41; and the University of VA, 5, 33, 53, 54, 90; and western VA, 39, 40, 41

Vivid Companion (McKinney): and aging, 97–98, 101–2; and artistic women, 91, 98–101; and the body as subject of poetry, 91, 95–96, 99, 100; and breakdown in verbal communication, 94; and class issues as they relate to place, 91–93; and coming of age, 91; and "Covering Up," 14; and development of voice in poems, 96–97; and "Face," 14; and femininity, 95–98; and gender, 14, 93, 98–99, 102; and independence from patriarchy, 99; and marginalization of women, 96, 99–100; and masculinity, 93,

94–95; and McKinney's loss of her father, 91, 93–94; and McKinney's struggle with cancer, 14, 91, 103–4; and mortality, 91, 93–94; and motherhood, 98–99; and natural world, 100, 102–3; and Oneida poems, 98; and poem "At 24," 14, 98–99; and poem "Clitoral," 97–98, 99; and poem "Constant Companion," 97, 99; and poem "Covering Up," 96–97; and poem "Face," 101–2; and poem "Full Moon: Sitting Up Late At My Father's Bedside," 94; and poem "Homage to Baroness Elsa von Freytag Loringhoven," 91, 100–101; and poem "Ready," 101, 103–4; and poems about Oneida community, 91; and poem "Stained," 99–100; and poem "Three Three Three," 93–94; and poem "Viridian Days," 101, 102–3; and poem "Woods Burning," 93, 94–95; and public and private selves, 96; and solitary nature of a writer's life, 99–101, 102; and stroke of McKinney's father, 93–94; and use of Thomas Hardy's ideas, 97; and WV, 102–3; and women's struggles to define themselves, 95–96, 100–101, 102

West Virginia: Appalachian counties of, 3; and Battle of Blair Mountain, 86–87; and Buffalo Creek disaster, 112; and classism, 92–93; and the Depression, 10, 11, 29; destruction of natural beauty of, 1, 107–9; employment in, 2, 3, 12, 109; and freedom and self-reliance in the works of Settle, 52; and governor Bob Wise, 4; history of, 1, 11, 31–32, 34, 51, 86–87; and incest jokes, 4–5, 93; and "In the Dry," 65; in *Lark and Termite*, 121, 122, 123–4; as location in Settle's writing, 33; and miners' deaths from black lung, 112; and mountaintop removal of coal, 14, 73, 85, 105, 107–9; negative stereotypes of, 3–7, 73, 91–92; and origins of affluent families in, 39; outsiders' perceptions of, 1, 2, 13, 59; and poverty, 3–4, 6–7, 30, 53, 72, 110–11; romanticized views of, 6–7, 91–92, 93; and social and economic marginalization, 1, 73; U.S. government

using military against citizens of, 72,
86; and water crisis of 2014, 4; and
western VA, 39–41; and West Virginians'
fight against coal companies, 13, 14, 71,
72–74, 85–87; writers of, 1–2, 11, 15,
53, 55, 90, 104. *See also* Buffalo Creek
disaster; coal industry

West Virginia literature: and Ann Pancake,
91, 120; and *Backcountry: Contemporary
Writing in West Virginia*, 6, 89; and
characters' connections with the land,
1, 2, 12, 14, 15, 66–67, 107; and
connection to family and traditions,
3, 107, 132; and fiction and poetry, 1,
13–14, 89–91; and gender, 2–3, 7–9,
10, 11–15; and the Great Depression,
19, 21, 29, 149; and independent female
characters, 1, 7, 8, 11, 12, 14; and Irene
McKinney, 89, 90–91, 104; and male
characters' inadequacies due to economic
difficulties, 7–8, 12–13, 70, 114–15;
and mining wars, 149; and *Miracle Boy
and Other Stories*, 149; and negative
stereotypes of WV, 5–6; and poverty,
55, 70; and regional writing, 2, 6; and
residents' and outsiders' perceptions of
WV, 2, 59; and sexuality, 7–8, 11, 23–25,
129; and socio-economic class, 2, 3,
7, 9, 10, 11–15, 149; and spirituality,
9–10, 15; and *The Stories of Breece D'J.
Pancake*, 53–55; and theme of leaving
WV, 2–3, 50, 55, 124, 133; and theme
of place, 2–3, 6, 9, 10, 55, 122; and
traditional female roles, 7, 8, 49, 50; and
tragedy, 9, 51; and transcendence, 2, 9,
15, 51; and types of female characters,
8; and violence against women, 59;
writers of, 15–16, 59. *See also* coal
industry; poverty; sexuality

West Virginia Wesleyan College, 73, 90

www.ingramcontent.com/pod-product-compliance
Lightning Source LLC
Chambersburg PA
CBHW031938090426
42811CB00002B/231